Posthuman Life

We imagine posthumans as humans made superhumanly intelligent or resilient by future advances in nanotechnology, biotechnology, information technology and cognitive science. Many argue that these enhanced people might live better lives; others fear that tinkering with our nature will undermine our sense of our own humanity. Whoever is right, it is assumed that our technological successor will be an upgraded or degraded version of us: Human 2.0.

Posthuman Life argues that the enhancement debate projects a human face onto an empty screen. We do not know what will happen and, not being posthuman, cannot anticipate how posthumans will assess the world. If a posthuman future will not necessarily be informed by our kind of subjectivity or morality, the limits of our current knowledge must inform any ethical or political assessment of that future. *Posthuman Life* develops a critical metaphysics of posthuman succession and argues that only a truly speculative posthumanism can support an ethics that meets the challenge of the transformative potential of technology.

David Roden is Lecturer in Philosophy at The Open University, UK. His published work has addressed the relationship between deconstruction and analytic philosophy, philosophical naturalism, the metaphysics of sound, and posthumanism.

D1610417

Posthuman Life

Philosophy at the Edge of the Human

David Roden

Routledge
Taylor & Francis Group

LONDON AND NEW YORK

First published 2015
by Routledge
2 Park Square, Milton Park, Abingdon, Oxon OX14 4RN

and by Routledge
711 Third Avenue, New York, NY 10017

Routledge is an imprint of the Taylor & Francis Group, an informa business

© 2015 David Roden

British Library Cataloguing-in-Publication Data
A catalogue record for this book is available from the British Library

Library of Congress Cataloging in Publication Data
A catalog record for this book has been requested

ISBN: 978-1-84465-805-3 (hbk)
ISBN: 978-1-84465-806-0 (pbk)

Typeset in Garamond
by Taylor & Francis Books

To Marika Zeimbekis, life partner and friend.

Contents

Acknowledgements

Many people have helped directly or indirectly to make this book possible. Special thanks must go to Iain Hamilton Grant for rousing me from my post-analytic stupor over a garrulous dinner back in the 1990s; Christopher Norris for gently nudging me back into philosophy during the same period; and Darian Meacham and R. Scott Bakker, whose recent intellectual support helped get me through the final year. Kudos also to Pete Wolfendale, Levi Bryant and others on the accelerationist and "speculative realist" fringe for illuminating my work with their own critical star shells. Special thanks are due to Clive Cazeaux for kindly reading and commenting on some draft chapters.

In much the same vein I must thank Stefan Sorgner, Jelena Juga, Jaime del Val, Milivoje Misha Pantovic, Francesca Ferrando, and all at the Beyond Humanism Network for mixing the exploration of posthumanity with warmth, friendship and fun; current or erstwhile colleagues at the Open University, Cristina Chimisso, Keith Frankish, Alex Barber, Nigel Warburton and Tim Chappell for their consistent interest and encouragement. I also owe a considerable debt to Tristan Palmer at Acumen whose friendly and engaged editorship made the completion of this project possible. Finally, and above all, I must thank Marika Zeimbekis for her scrupulous reading of the early, inchoate drafts, for challenging me to explain, and for encouraging me to think lives other than my own.

Introduction

Churchland's centipede

> Mankind's a dead issue now, cousin. There are no more souls. Only states of mind.
>
> (Sterling 1996: 59)

In his autobiography, Bertrand Russell describes witnessing the philosopher Alfred Whitehead's wife, Evelyn, undergoing great physical pain: "She seemed cut off from everyone and everything by walls of agony, and the sense of the solitude of each human soul suddenly overwhelmed me." Russell portrays this event as akin to a religious conversion. It convinced him that the immense gulf between human beings could only be bridged by selfless love. Having been an imperialist, he was now persuaded that war was wrong and "that a public school education is abominable" (Russell 2009: 137).

Maybe not all of us are as profoundly affected by others' suffering. But Russell's evocation of our loneliness rings true. Surely the expression "I feel your pain" is a self-serving euphemism. Whatever consolation we offer, it seems, the other's pain is theirs alone.

This melancholy insight is supported by an abstract claim about the privacy of conscious experience that most philosophers and lay people seem to accept (Hirstein 2012: 6–7). Even if my empathy is at the Russellian end of the scale, I cannot feel your pain because each experience is unique to the one who has it. Where experiences are qualitatively similar, they are distinct tokens of the same type. I cannot have your experience of hearing Nirvana's "Smells Like Teen Spirit" on your blue MP3 player, though I might have qualitatively identical sensations listening to a cloned MP3 on my pink player.

Things change. We can imagine humans acquiring new technological powers, like the ability to hear dog whistles or withstand the cold vacuum of space. But can we imagine how one could experience the pleasures, pains or thoughts of another? Nothing, it seems, can alter the essential human solitude Russell expresses so eloquently.

Well, maybe not quite nothing.

In *Consciousness Explained*, Daniel Dennett defines "Philosophers' Syndrome" as: "mistaking a failure of imagination for an insight into necessity" (Dennett 1991: 401). Perhaps we cannot imagine what it would be like to experience the pleasures and pains of another. But I cannot imagine how it feels to be an octopus either, though there is presumably something this feels like. So perhaps Russell's "insight" into the essential privacy of consciousness is just an artefact of philosophers' syndrome rather than a necessary truth.

Here's a quick and dirty refutation of the privacy thesis adapted from William Hirstein's book *Mindmelding* (Hirstein 2012: 3). Its first premise is a relatively weak version of materialism, which states that all mental states are identical to physical states:

1) All mental states are identical to physical states, as materialists claim.
2) *No physical state is private.*
Conclusion: no mental state is private.
(QED)

Clearly, this is much too fast! Some modern dualists claim that physical states have irreducibly subjective properties, so Premise 2) is ambiguous. Others might object that the privacy thesis is so secure that if materialism implies its falsity, then materialism has to go.

But denying the privacy of mental states in this context only means denying that they are *necessarily* private. It may be a contingent fact about humans that they cannot experience the mental states of others. Perhaps the solitude that Russell describes could be dissolved, not by universal love this time, but by a technology that allows brains to share experiences with other brains.

In a seminal article published in 1981, six years after Russell's autobiography, the philosopher Paul Churchland notes that some human beings are born without a *corpus callosum* – the thick trunk of nerve fibres that allows the cerebral hemispheres of most humans to exchange information. This genetic condition – known as callosal agenesis – is remarkable because its sufferers do not experience significant deficits. Callosal agenesis only shows up in brain scans or surgical procedures. There is no conventional treatment because there does not need to be. Somehow, Churchland reasons, the two hemispheres have learned to share information without this major artery of interhemispheric communication. But if two parts of a human brain can learn to communicate, he asks, might not the same be possible for two or more spatially distributed brains? He proceeds to outline what such an artificial "neural commissure" would be like:

> [Let] us suppose that we can fashion a workable transducer for implantation at some site in the brain the research reveals to be suitable, a transducer to

convert a symphony of neural activity into (say) microwaves radiated from an aerial in the forehead, and to perform the reverse function of converting received microwaves back into neural activation. Connecting it up need not be an insuperable problem. We simply trick the normal processes of dendretic arborization into growing their own myriad connections with the active microsurface of the transducer.

Once the channel is opened between two or more people, they can learn (learn) to exchange information with the same intimacy and virtuosity displayed by your own cerebral hemispheres. Think what this might do for hockey teams, and ballet companies, and research teams! If the entire population were thus fitted out, spoken language of any kind might well disappear completely, a victim of the "why crawl when you can fly?" principle.

(Churchland 1981: 88)

Evidence from the effects of lobotomies and opiates suggests that areas of the frontal cortex are involved in feeling the unpleasantness of pain, whereas discriminations of the nature and location of pain depend on activity elsewhere in the somatosensory cortex (Hardcastle 2001). Suppose that a Churchland commissure has been fitted between the pain discrimination centres in person A's head and the pain evaluation centres in person B's head. Following a "tuning period", the commissure now emulates the patterns of stimulation that would normally occur between Person B's pain evaluation centres and her own pain discrimination centres (Hirstein 2012: 157–8). If all this is in place and B kicks A in the shin, she (or her frontal cortex) should feel the affective backwash of A's pain. Both cry out in response! If such affective tuning became obligatory in Churchland's neuroculture, not only would libraries and spoken language become things of the past, but violence too. A world in which human brains are suffused in microwaved harmony might be kinder than ours: a Neurotopia with particular excellences in team sports and performing arts.

Perhaps the solitude that Russell saw as definitive of the human condition can be overcome by Brain–Machine–Brain Interfaces (BMBIs) that duplicate the functions of our home-grown commissures (*ibid.*: 161–2).

There is evidence that such technologies may soon be with us. For example, a recent scientific report details an experiment in which brain activity in a rat trained for a simple lever-pressing task was encoded and passed down the internet to an untrained "encoder rat" via a Brain–Machine Interface (BMI) – significantly improving the untrained rat's score on the same task (Pais-Vieira *et al.* 2013; see also §1.3). Of course, we do not know that these technologies will fulfil Churchland's happy dreams or others' nightmares. But current work on neuroprostheses at least holds out this prospect. Perhaps the much-vaunted privacy of human consciousness is as technology-dependent as our now dated inability to fly from Paris to New York.

But here's a different perspective on Neurotopia.

Perhaps mental privacy *is* an invariant of human beings. The citizens of Churchland's neuroculture lack this (technology-dependent) property of mind, and thus no longer qualify as human. Neurotopia is an alien civilization whose members are only outwardly similar to human beings. For example, suppose that they share not just perceptual states, such as toothaches, but agency. In this case, evaluations and decisions would be networked between the frontal areas of A's head and B's head, and perhaps between many others. So the inhabitants of Neurotopia would be corporate "human centipedes" whose agency and consciousness is distributed between modified human bodies. With centipedal thinkers, the agency and subjectivity we associate with discrete bodies bleeds into multiply embodied superorganisms.

As Hirstein remarks, there might be analogies between sharing pains using a neural commissure and our empathic responses to witnessing others' pains (Hirstein 2012: 161).

However, while we might imagine feeling the pain and pleasure of another, it is not clear that you or I can imagine our agency distributed over many bodies. There is a sense in which humans *are their bodies*. We experience the world from a single embodied perspective. We die when our bodies die. In contrast, human bodies would be dispensable segments of centipedes. For a centipede, the death of a body would mean the loss of a processing-effector node. This might be traumatic (for reasons that might be best appreciated from its multi-bodied perspective) but not terminal. The centipede's long-term memory and overall goals would need to be available to different bodies just as sensory information is shared between our cerebral hemispheres by the *corpus callosum*. For humans, bodily death is inevitable. For centipedes, the death of the multiple could be deferred so long as the supply of appropriately tooled bodies keeps up.

If we adopt the second perspective on Churchland's neuroculture, we must infer that the centipedes are descendants of humans *that are no longer human as a consequence of technological alteration*.

In contemporary culture, the most common term for such technologically wrought nonhumans is "posthuman". Science fiction writers like Philip K. Dick, Cordwainer Smith, Bruce Sterling and William Gibson have trafficked in posthumans of various sizes and shapes for nearly a century (Sterling's 1996 novel *Schismatrix* is the first fiction in which the word is employed self-consciously). However, Gibson and Sterling have proved to be in the conceptual avant-garde, with commentators from other disciplines running to catch up. Since the mid-1990s, serious discussion of posthumans has migrated from science fiction to contemporary discourse in bioethics, critical theory, and even to mass media discussions of the long-run implications of advanced technology.

The last point is key to understanding the aims of the present work, I think. In 1818 Mary Shelley could imagine Victor Frankenstein giving life to his creature by obscure, semi-magical means (Graham 2002: 73–7). Now, technologies with the potential to engender posthuman successors to humans may be in the alpha phase. The creation of cybernetic hook-ups between organisms or between organisms and machines is just one example of a possible posthuman-maker. Research in artificial intelligence has produced systems that exhibit a certain independence from human decisions, though not yet in systems whose flexibility and fluidity approaches that of higher animals. Elsewhere, developments in biological sciences may lead to some descendants of humans acquiring physical capacities far beyond the human norm, such as effective resistance to ageing. Some even propose that the long-run future of intelligent beings will be as immortal "uploaded" minds running on vastly powerful computer systems (see my discussion of "soul engines" in §1.3).

Moreover, a number of well supported positions in cognitive science, biological theory and general metaphysics imply that a posthuman succession is possible in principle, even if the technological means for achieving it remain speculative. This is because they converge on the view that modest materialism is basically right: capacities for self-consciousness, language and information processing that distinguish us from nonhumans depend on physical facts about our bodily organization and environment such as the absence of inter-cranial commissures (§2.1). When it becomes possible to technologically intervene in that organization, the higher-level subjective and social properties that depend on it may become fundamentally altered.

For many philosophers and ethicists, the combination of these incipient technological trajectories with the modest claim that subjectivity depends on alterable arrangements of matter suggests that posthuman succession is not merely imaginable but may be possible in the near or medium future (Agar 2010; Fukuyama 2003).

Throughout this work I refer to the philosophical claim that such successors are possible as "speculative posthumanism" (SP) and distinguish it from positions which are commonly conflated with SP, like transhumanism (§1.2). SP claims that *there could be posthumans*. It does not imply that posthumans would be better than humans or even that their lives would be compared from a single moral perspective.

The formulation of SP is problematic, however, and not just because it refers to hypothetical technologies whose precursors may never exist. For example, my argument for the posthumanity of the centipedes presupposed that mental privacy was an essential property of humans: a property that something could not lack and be human.

But the assertion that there is a human essence is one that many philosophers – including most avowed "posthumanists", I suspect – have good reason to reject. Becoming posthuman in the sense that I have articulated it presupposes that there is some matter of fact about being human in the first place. But what kind of fact is it? Is being human really just a matter of satisfying a checklist of essential properties? Thus any philosophical theory of posthumanism owes us an account of what it means to be human such that it is conceivable that there could be nonhuman successors to humans.

The notion of succession is also problematic. Posthumans, such as Churchland's centipedes, might not be human, but my account assumes that they would be "descendants" of current humans in some sense. This historical-succession relation requires urgent clarification, given that the processes of descent relevant to SP may be unknown to current biology.

Understanding how the relation human–posthuman should be conceptualized is key for understanding SP's epistemic scope. Are there ways in which we can predict or constrain posthuman possibility based on current knowledge? Some philosophers claim that there are features of human moral life and human subjectivity that are not just local to certain gregarious primates but are necessary conditions of agency and subjectivity everywhere. This "transcendental approach" to philosophy does not imply that posthumans are impossible but that – contrary to expectations – they might not be all that different from us. Thus a theory of posthumanity should consider both empirical and transcendental constraints on posthuman possibility.

What if it turns out that these constraints are relatively weak?

In that case, the possibility of posthumans implies that the future of life and mind might not only be stranger than we imagine, but stranger than we can currently conceive.

This possibility is consistent with a minimal realism for which things need not conform to our ideas about them. But its ethical implications are vertiginous. Weakly constrained SP suggests that our current technical practice could precipitate a nonhuman world that we cannot yet understand, in which "our" values may have no place.

Thus while SP is not an ethical claim, it raises philosophical problems that are both conceptual and ethical-political.

Conceptually, it requires us to justify our use of a term "posthuman", whose circumstances of application are unknown to us. Does this mean that talk of "posthumans" is self-vitiating nonsense? Does speaking of "weird" worlds or values commit one to a conceptual relativism that is incompatible with the commitment to realism?

If posthuman talk is not self-vitiating nonsense, the ethical problems it raises are very challenging indeed. If our current technological trajectories might result in the world turning posthuman, how should we view this prospect and respond to it? Should we apply a conservative, precautionary approach to technology that favours "human" values over any possible posthuman ones? Can conservatism be justified under weakly constrained SP and, if not, then what kind of ethical or political alternatives are justifiable?

The goal of *Posthuman Life* is to define these questions as clearly as possible and to propose some philosophical solutions to them. Although it would be hubristic for a writer on this topic to claim the last word, my formulations do, I hope, provide a firm conceptual basis for philosophical and interdisciplinary work in this area.

I attempt to achieve this by exploiting contributions of divergent philosophical traditions. As I mentioned, an appreciation of the scope of SP requires that we consider empirically informed speculations about posthumans and also engage with the tradition of transcendental thought that derives from the work of Kant, Hegel, Husserl and Heidegger. It requires a discussion of the implications of intellectual tendencies that oppose transcendental thinking such as philosophical naturalism and certain varieties of poststructuralism, anti-humanism and deconstruction. This ecumenism is justified because none of these traditions are suited to tackling the full range of problems that arise from SP on their own. For example, philosophers working in the Anglo-American tradition such as Dennett and Churchland make claims about time and the contingency of subjectivity that are interpreted at higher levels of conceptual abstraction in work of poststructuralists such as Derrida and Deleuze. At certain points, SP needs to frame its assumptions at this level of generality (see Chapters 4, 6 and 7).

This continental-analytic approach imposes expository obligations on those of us who work within it. We cannot presume that all our readers will be equally familiar with terms like *différance*, "supervenience", "deterritorialization", *Dasein* or "radical interpretation". So I apply the rule that all key concepts should be explained in terms accessible to a reader unfamiliar with the relevant traditions or discourses. The result is doubtless longer than it might have been, but hopefully more through-argued and accessible to cross-disciplinary audiences than it could otherwise have been.

Here is the plan of the book in summary. *Posthuman Life* begins by explaining some key concepts in debates over posthumanism and the ethics of technological enhancement – "humanism", "anthropocentrism", "posthumanism" and "transhumanism" – in Chapter 1.

Chapter 2 is also partly clarificatory. It considers whether the anti-humanist arguments propounded by so-called "critical posthumanists" undermine futurist accounts of the posthuman like SP. It argues that they do not and, in so doing, clarifies the metaphysical commitments of both SP and critical posthumanism.

Chapters 3 and 4 focus on the transcendental critique of SP. Chapter 3 sets up the critique by co-opting the work of Immanuel Kant, Edmund Husserl, Martin Heidegger, Donald Davidson and Hilary Putnam. Chapter 4 criticizes the transcendentally constrained version of SP from a position that is simultaneously naturalistic and deconstructive.

Chapter 5 addresses the conceptual problems of posthumanism described above by articulating a theory of human–posthuman difference in terms of the "disconnection thesis".

The disconnection thesis is the theoretical core of *Posthuman Life*. It provides a usable but epistemically modest definition of posthumanity. It highlights our ignorance of the circumstances that might attend a human–posthuman divergence. All the ethical ramifications of speculative posthumanism come from this insight; for it implies that the posthuman can only be understood by making or becoming posthumans.

The final four chapters of the book develop the metaphysical and political implications of the disconnection thesis.

Chapter 6 develops a psychology-free account of agency that allows us to conceptualize posthuman agency without pre-empting the nature of posthuman minds. This is ethically significant in highlighting the disruptive implications of human–posthuman disconnection. Here and elsewhere I employ the resources of the assemblage metaphysics developed in the work of Gilles Deleuze, Felix Guattari and Manuel DeLanda to formulate minimal conditions for posthuman agency and posthuman becoming.

Chapter 7 develops a theory of technology – "new substantivism" – which disarms humanist conceptions of technology as an instrument of human reason. It implies that agency in technological systems is a problematic negotiation with circumstances liable to be unchosen or unanticipated. This account of technological systems frames the concluding discussion of Chapter 8, in which I argue that there is no humanist or "anthropocentric" argument that weighs decisively against making or becoming a posthuman. The place of posthuman ethics, I argue, is not to hand down moral rules to technologists, scientists and politicians but to develop systems which aid us in the intelligent and skilful carving of futures.

1 Humanism, transhumanism and posthumanism

Introduction

The terms "humanism", "transhumanism" and "posthumanism" are widely used among philosophers, critical theorists and professional futurists, but often in ways that are insufficiently nuanced.

For example, Neil Badmington and Katherine Hayles have criticized the "apparently posthumanist aim" of downloading consciousness onto computers, arguing that it is symptomatic of a kind of hyper-humanism which replicates the dualist fiction of an immaterial and autonomous human subject described in Descartes' metaphysics (Badmington 2001: 5–6). Badmington proposes a different – *critical* – posthumanism as a philosophical corrective to humanism. Rather than dreaming of the uploaded minds or intelligent robots to come, critical posthumanism attempts to understand and deconstruct humanism from within, tracing its internal tensions and conceptual discrepancies.

As we shall see over the next two chapters, the main problem with this analysis is not that the deconstructive project pursued by Badmington, Hayles and others is intellectually fruitless but that it conflates two very different kinds of futurist speculation. The first belongs to a *transhumanist* itinerary for the perfection of human nature and the cultivation of human personal autonomy by technological means. Transhumanism is thus an ethical claim to the effect that technological *enhancement* of human capacities is a desirable aim (all other things being equal). The second kind of futurism – *speculative posthumanism* (SP) – is not a normative claim about how the world *ought to be* but a metaphysical claim about *what it could contain*. For speculative posthumanists, posthumans are technologically engendered beings that are no longer human. SP makes no commitments regarding ethical value of posthuman lives. It does not, for example, define the posthuman as an improvement or apotheosis of the human as transhumanist philosopher Nick Bostrom does in "Why I Want to be a Posthuman When I Grow Up" (2008).

The suppression of genuine *post-human* possibilities in both critical posthumanist and transhumanist is an important philosophical failure and not simply a semantic oversight. If SP is true, there could be posthumans. This possibility is arguably a matter of concern to current and future humans, whose technological activities might bring them into being (see Chapters 5 and 8).

To understand the ramifications of SP, then, we need to get clear about the distinction between transhumanism and the various critiques of humanism grouped under the portmanteau term "posthumanism" (see §1.4). In addition to speculative posthumanism and critical posthumanism, I will identify two other positions – speculative realism and naturalism – whose critiques of anthropocentric assumptions are equally important to the debates that inform this book.

As we shall see over the next three chapters, humanism itself has been poorly analysed by many who see it as part of their academic job description to "critique" and seek out alternatives to it. All forms of posthumanism criticize human-centred (anthropocentric) ways of understanding life and reality. However, not all forms of humanism are equally anthropocentric or are anthropocentric in the same way. Many self-styled posthumanists regard Descartes' dualist distinction between a self-transparent human mind and a world governed by strict mechanical laws as the touchstone of modern humanism. Yet, Cartesian dualism imposes fewer anthropological constraints on the nature of things than the transcendental philosophies of subjectivity promulgated by Kant and his successors. *Transcendental humanism* does not only privilege the human ethically (as humanists like Aristotle and Pico della Mirandola are wont to do) but treats certain abstract features of human life and subjectivity as unsurpassable sources of order in the world.

For now, let us set about our distinction-mongering.

1.1 Humanism and anthropocentrism

The word "humanist" has many uses and meanings. For example, it sometimes refers to those who advocate the dignity of all human beings bestowed by their shared moral nature, or to those who eschew religious morality in favour of a morality grounded in human affections and activities.

While such ideas will figure in our discussion of posthumanism and (most importantly) the nature of posthumans, they will be less central than philosophical conceptions of the difference between humans and nonhumans. So rather than appealing to common usage, I will simply stipulate the generic senses in which the terms "humanism" and "anthropocentrism" will be used throughout the book.

A philosopher is a *humanist* if she believes that humans are importantly
distinct from non-humans and supports this distinctiveness claim with

a *philosophical anthropology*: an account of the central features of human existence and their relations to similarly general aspects of *nonhuman* existence.

A humanist philosophy is *anthropocentric* if it accords humans a superlative status that all or most nonhumans lack.

These definitions are not intended to be subtle or historically nuanced. They are intended to highlight what all humanisms must have in common. If a philosophy lacks a philosophical anthropology, it cannot be humanist. If it does not allocate special status to humans, it is not anthropocentric. Crudeness is a philosophical virtue where it helps pinpoint important similarities and differences.

As used here, "humanism" applies to theists who believe in gods or a God and to anti-theists who reject or have no interest in them. In *Existentialism and Humanism*, Jean-Paul Sartre argues that human existence precedes its essence. This means that humans are radically free and self-defining agents whose existence is prior to any concept of what they ought to be (Sartre 1948: 2–3). Sartre's account of radical human freedom draws on his atheism. Since there is no God, he reasons, humans are unlike paper knives or hammers in having no fixed function or purpose. Humans are thus whatever they make of themselves through their actions.

However, in his *Oration on the Dignity of Man*, the Renaissance philosopher Pico della Mirandola grounds a very similar human capacity for self-fashioning in an essential "lack" granted by God at the moment of creation:

> I have placed you at the very centre of the world, so that from that vantage point you may with greater ease glance round about you on all that the world contains. We have made you a creature neither of heaven nor of earth, neither mortal nor immortal, in order that you may, as the free and proud shaper of your own being, fashion yourself in the form you may prefer.
>
> (della Mirandola 1948: 5)

My definition of "anthropocentrism" is similarly general.

Not all human–nonhuman distinctions are anthropocentric. It is not anthropocentric to claim that humans are the only animals that drive cars or the only hairless primates. These claims provide individuating descriptions of humans but they do not award us special honours in the world order.

Moreover, not all humanisms are anthropocentric in the same way or to the same degree. Aristotelian ethics provides a good example of moderate anthropocentricism. In his *Nicomachean Ethics* Aristotle claims that, among living things, only humans are responsive to reason (*NE* 1098a). Rationality allows humans to bypass or suppress emotions and desires and to cultivate socially endorsed dispositions such as courage, generosity and friendship. The fact that I can distinguish between principles like equality and freedom, for example, allows me to see these as alternative principles of conduct.

Aristotle privileges humans by attributing reason exclusively to human animals. This means that there are goods – such as friendship or the contemplation of metaphysical truths – that only humans can aspire to. He also suggests in the *Politics* that there is a hierarchy of beings ordered in terms of their degree of rationality such that the less rational serve the needs of those further up the hierarchy of rationality (*Pol* 1.81256b16-22; Lee 2003: 8).

Nonetheless, Aristotle allows that nonhuman living beings have goods corresponding to their nature. Animals seek pleasures, but neither animals nor gods can exhibit human moral virtues (*NE* 1153b, 1145a). As Keekok Lee argues, this anthropocentrism is less aggressive than those expressed in modern philosophical positions that assert that human subjects are the only source of value and meaning in the world (Lee 2003: 9).

The vision of a "disenchanted" world lacking an intrinsic or human-independent moral order is commonly laid at the door of seventeenth-century scientist-philosophers such as Descartes and Galileo who argued that the world is governed only by mathematically expressible laws and not, as the Aristotelians held, by purposes or "final cases" (Sandel 1998: 175). However, the proponent of radical anthropocentrism whose influence is most enduring is the eighteenth-century philosopher Immanuel Kant. Kant inaugurated a philosophical perspective that I will refer to throughout this book as "transcendental humanism". Transcendental humanists claim that humans do not merely represent the world but actively organize it, endowing it with value, form or meaning (§3.3).

Kant also claims that nothing in nature is intrinsically good. Only beings that are rational and capable of autonomous agency can be regarded as "ends-in-themselves". Lacking reason, animals can only be means to human ends:

> The beings whose existence rests not on our will but on nature nevertheless have, if they are beings without reason, only a relative worth as means, and are called *things*; rational beings, by contrast, are called *persons*, because their nature already marks them out as ends in themselves, i.e., as something that may not be used merely as means, hence to that extent limits all arbitrary choice (and is an object of respect).
>
> (Kant 2002: 46)

Later, we will consider Kantian transcendental humanism and some of its diverse modern variants in some detail (see Chapters 3 and 4). For the moment, it is sufficient to note that my generic characterization of humanism can apply to very different conceptions of the human–nonhuman divide.

1.2 Transhumanist ethics

Most philosophical humanists hold some conception of what gives human life a distinctive value and dignity, whether or not they accord other forms of natural or supernatural life a similar status. Humanists have also developed precepts and methods for protecting and cultivating these valuable attributes. At the risk of oversimplification, the only reliable techniques for achieving these aims, to date, have been *politics* and *education*. For example, Aristotle claimed that moral virtues like courage or generosity are habits. Whether good or bad, habits do not develop naturally but have to be instilled through education and legislation, so that children and adult citizens learn to act and be affected in the right ways. The formal study of ethics is only intelligible against this politically constituted background (*NE* 1095b).

Republican humanists like Machiavelli, Rousseau and Charles Taylor follow Aristotle in seeing the political as the setting in which humans become fully human (Berlin 2000: 47; Taylor 1985). Kant likewise argued that humans needed to be disciplined and educated to become fully autonomous beings "who can and do act from duty" (Moran 2009: 477). His prescriptions include an assortment of child-rearing tips (e.g. Locke's suggestion that children's shoes should be designed to let in water to prevent them becoming too attached to comfort) but also nostrums for cultivating moral understanding (*ibid.*: 477–8).

Transhumanists also sign up to this ethical view of humans as uniquely autonomous or self-fashioning animals. Like their humanist forebears, transhumanists think that human-distinctive capacities like rationality, compassion and aesthetic appreciation are intrinsically valuable and should be cultivated and protected (Bostrom 2008). However, they believe that the traditional methods that humanists have used to foster them have been limited until recently by the material constraints of human biology and of nature more generally (Sorgner 2013; Habermas 2005: 28).

Transhumanists hope to add the fruits of advanced technologies to the limited toolkit of traditional humanism, believing that prospective developments in the so-called "NBIC" suite of technologies will soon allow humans unprecedented control over their own nature and morphology. NBIC stands for "Nanotechnology, Biotechnology, Information Technology, and Cognitive Science". Nanotechnology consists of techniques of very fast and precise atom-scale manufacturing. Biotechnology consists of tools for manipulating life and living systems at the genetic/ sub-cellular level. Information Technology involves computing and cybernetic technologies such as Artificial Intelligence (AI) and Brain– Machine Interfaces (BMI). Finally, "Cognitive Science" is an umbrella term for disciplines such as neuroscience, artificial intelligence and phi- losophy of mind that are gradually revealing the workings of human and nonhuman minds (§§1.3, 2.1).

The 1998 Transhumanist Declaration – signed by many important and active members of the world transhumanist movement including Anders Sandberg, Nick Bostrom, David Pearce, Max More and Natasha Vita-More – is particularly explicit on both these points. Articles one and two state:

> (1) Humanity will be radically changed by technology in the future. We foresee the feasibility of redesigning the human condition, including such parameters as the inevitability of aging, limitations on human and artificial intellects, unchosen psychology, suffering, and our confinement to the planet earth.
> (2) Systematic research should be put into understanding these coming developments and their long-term consequences.
>
> (World Transhumanist Association 1998)

Self-fashioning through culture and education is to be supplemented by technology. For this reason, transhumanists believe that we should add *morphological freedom* – the freedom of physical and mental form – to the traditional liberal rights of freedom of movement and freedom of expression (Bostrom 2005a, 2005b; Sorgner 2009). We should be free to discover new forms of embodiment in order to improve on the results of traditional humanism.

> (4) Transhumanists advocate the moral right for those who so wish to use technology to extend their mental and physical (including reproductive) capacities and to improve their control over their own lives. We seek personal growth beyond our current biological limitations.
>
> *(Ibid.)*

According to many transhumanists, the single most important application of NBIC technology will be to amplify and enhance human cognitive powers. As we become smarter, we become better at realizing personal and social goals. Some of these goals may be morally admirable: for example, eliminating starvation or scarcity with new agricultural and manufacturing techniques, finding cures for diseases or becoming better at deliberating about social policy (Sandberg & Bostrom 2006: 201).

The exercise of rationality requires many cognitive aptitudes: perception, working and long-term memory, general intelligence and the capacity to acquire cultural tools such as languages and reasoning methods. There appear to have been significant increases in the level of general intelligence in industrialized countries during the twentieth century – particularly at the lower end of the scale. These may be explained by modern social initiatives such as the removal of organic lead from paints and petrol, improved nutrition and free public education (Sandberg & Bostrom 2006: 210).

However, there appears to be a limit to the effect of environmental factors upon cognition because the efficiency of our brains is constrained by the speed, interconnectedness, noisiness and density of the neurons packed into our skulls. The best scientists, philosophers or artists currently alive are no more intelligent or creative than Aristotle, Descartes, Leibniz or Newton.

For transhumanists like Bostrom and Kurzweil, really significant improvements of intelligence will require technologies that somehow augment or amplify the powers of our bare brains. Some of these may involve cognition-enhancing genetic interventions or drugs. Ingmar Persson and Julian Savulescu cite the creation of "Doogie" mice, genetically modified to increase production of the neuro-receptor NR2B. Doogie mice "demonstrated improved memory performance, both in terms of acquisition and retention" (Persson & Savulescu 2008).[1] There is also some evidence that the use of pulsed magnetic fields to stimulate neural activity (Transcranial Magnetic Stimulation) can enhance initial encoding of memories or their consolidation in long-term memory (Kirov *et al.* 2009).

Other intelligence amplification technologies may require humans to patch neural wetware into computational hardware. Many early twenty-first-century humans offload tedious tasks like memorizing phone numbers, or searching for the local 24-hour dry cleaner, to portable computing devices. Most transhumanists claim that the process of outsourcing biologically based cognition onto non-biological platforms is liable to accelerate as our artificially intelligent devices get more intelligent and as we devise better ways of patching computing hardware into our neuro-computational wetware.[2] Brain–Computer Interfaces like the BrainGate BCI show that it is possible to directly interface computer-operated systems with neural tissue, allowing tetraplegic patients to control devices such as robotic arms with their thoughts (Hochberg *et al.* 2006). Work is also in hand on Brain–Machine–Brain Interfaces (BMBIs) that provide prosthetic communication links to replace damaged connections between brain areas. For example, Guggenmos *et al.* (2013) showed that using a BMBI to replace neural links between the front and back motor and sensory regions of a rat's brain could dramatically restore food grasping ability lost due to the lesion.

These developments support the principle that biological components that underpin human mental life can be replaced by functionally equivalent devices or by systems that are faster than biological computers by several orders of magnitude. For example, Kurzweil thinks that nanodevices might one day be used to non-invasively stimulate or probe the brain's native neural networks, extending our slow organic minds into more efficient and architecturally varied cognitive systems (Kurzweil 2005: 317).[3]

As neuroprostheses develop over the course of this century, it is conceivable that future humans or transhumans will be increasingly indistinguishable from their technology. Humans will become "cyborgs" or cybernetic organisms like the Borg in the TV series *Star Trek* with many of the functions associated with thinking, perception and even consciousness offloaded onto increasingly fast and subtle computing devices. As *Trek* fans will be aware, the Borg are not an attractive ideal for the humanist who values individual autonomy and reason. They are technological swarm intelligence – like an ant or termite colony – whose individual members are enslaved to the emergent goals of a super-organism (see §2.1, note 2).

However, many argue that those who see cyborgs as colonized and invaded flesh fail to understand that humans have always extended themselves through devices. The philosopher Andy Clark has argued that the integration of technology into biology has defined humans since the development of flint tools. We are, he claims, "Natural Born Cyborgs" whose mental life has always extruded into culturally constructed niches such as languages and archives (Clark 2003; Haraway 1991; see §2.2).

Perhaps, then, the transhuman future that I am sketching here will still be inhabited by beings whose aspirations, values and achievements would be recognizable to ancient and modern humanists. These transhuman descendants might still value autonomy, sociability and artistic expression. They will just be *much better* at being rational, sensitive and expressive – better at being human. Perhaps, also, these skills will repose in bodies that are technologically modified by advanced biotechnologies to be healthier and more resistant to ageing or damage than ours. But the capacities that define that humanist tradition here are not obviously dependent on a particular kind of physical form.

Transhumanists are also interested in the prospect of what computer scientist Ben Goertzel has dubbed Artificial General Intelligence (AGI) for the same reasons that they are concerned with cognitive enhancement more generally. An AGI would be a robot or computer system whose reasoning approximates or exceeds the range and flexibility of human reasoning.

There is plenty of bare bones, "narrow" AI (without the G) around but it consists of software that has been designed for fast and efficient operation in particular task domains (Goertzel 2006). Any system counts as intelligent if it is "optimizing" – able to find good solutions to problems in variably complex environments (p. 1). For example, finding the nearest potential food source or avoiding predators. On this measure, a good internet search engine or the routing software that telecommunication networks use to find the quickest path through a network are intelligent. But their capacities are *domain specific* – unlike a human, they cannot turn themselves to other tasks, such as finding a table in a crowded restaurant, understanding a text message from a friend or considering alternative careers (Ekbia 2008).

A real AGI – like the fictive Commander Data from *Star Trek: The Next Generation* – would be able to apply its intellect flexibly to a vast range of problems, just as humans do.

But fictive representations of AGIs such as Data may reflect our cosy anthropocentric assumptions about what an artificial intelligence could be like. Shane Legg and Marcus Hutter have argued that the abstract definition of intelligence provided here – the ability to optimize in a range of complex environments – implies a mathematical ordering of possible intelligences. Current biological humans exist somewhere on this scale since our ability to realize our goals in complex environments is significant but bounded (Legg & Hutter 2007: 405). But there are conceivable occupants of this space whose cognitive flexibility exceeds the current model of human.

The prospect of AGI is regarded by many transhumanists as having "ambivalent potential" for both good and evil (Bostrom & Cirkovic 2011: 17). Increasing the quantity of intelligence on the planet might allow us to solve many social and technological problems that currently seem intractable. Yet writers like Bostrom are alive to the problems that attend the creation of genuine super-intelligence. For example, the advent of artificial super-intelligence might render the intellectual efforts of biological thinkers irrelevant in the face of dizzying acceleration in machinic intelligence. As the computer scientist and cryptographer Irving Good wrote:

> Since the design of machines is one of these intellectual activities, an ultra-intelligent machine could design even better machines; there would then unquestionably be an "intelligence explosion," and the intelligence of man would be left far behind. Thus the first ultraintelligent machine is the last invention that man need ever make, provided that the machine is docile enough to tell us how to keep it under control.
>
> (Good 1965: 33–4)

This caveat is significant. The best-case scenario here might be one in which humans are made redundant by machinic creations that outpace them with accelerating rapidity (see §1.4).

Cognitive enhancement and developments elsewhere in the NBIC suite might, then, help us to cultivate traditional humanist values such as autonomy and the capacity for individual self-fashioning. However, our brief discussion of AGI prospects suggests one way in which cognitive enhancement could also frustrate these humanist goals.

Persson and Savulescu suggest that other developments in NBIC technologies could also significantly threaten human existence on this planet – for example, making it easier for garage fanatics and psychopaths to weaponize diseases or release deadly nanomachines into the environment. They claim that traditional tools for moral development like anti-racism education have failed to rid us of evolved dispositions – such as an inability to empathize outside immediate peer groups – that are ill-suited to this technologically volatile world (Persson & Savulescu 2008: 166–8). Thus, they argue, using drugs or genetic enhancement to make people more altruistic, cooperative and conscientious could be justified if the net effect is to mitigate these risks (p. 172).

The use of moral enhancement to achieve broad social goals is an ethically fraught area. It implies, at the very least, a repudiation of the Kantian assumption that personal autonomy is a paramount good. Its usefulness is also predicated on disputable assumptions about the evolutionary basis of morality that we lack the space to consider here. However, Persson and Savulescu's proposal illustrates why transhumanists hope to use NBIC technologies to debug ruinous moral dispositions that politics and education have failed to control.

1.3 Soul engines: transhumanism and metaphysics

Just *how* unrestricted and capable transhuman minds and bodies can become is contested since the scope for enhancement depends equally upon hypothetical technologies and upon some hotly contested claims in metaphysics and cognitive science.

For example, many transhumanists hope that developments in the NBIC areas will make it possible to scan the patterns of neural connectivity that allow human brains to generate human minds and selves and replicate these onto fast and powerful computer systems, just as one currently uploads the contents of a Word file onto an email attachment. Uploaded humans would, so the story goes, have the same experiences, beliefs and desires as biologically embodied ones, but they would be running on potentially immortal soul engines rather than messy and all-too-temporary associations of biological cells (Hauskeller 2012). Mind uploading could allow humans to escape death altogether as long they took care to leave enough "backup copies" around (Sandberg & Armstrong 2012; see §3.2).

We do not know whether mind uploading is possible. Its possibility depends on a family of metaphysical positions that hold that minds, mental states (e.g. beliefs and experiences) and mental capacities (such as rationality and intelligence) are substrate-independent. Mind and intelligence would be substrate-independent if they could be exhibited by arrangements of matter very different from human bodies. In particular, it would have to be possible for artificial systems, such as computers, to have mental states and experiences; not merely biological, non-manufactured systems like humans and nonhuman animals.

The best known and most influential of these metaphysical theories, by far, is functionalism. The intuition that underlies functionalism is that mental states are defined by what they do – their roles – rather than by their intrinsic properties. For example, pain could be functionally characterized as a state that is caused by bodily damage and which produces aversive responses to the causes of that damage. Here damage is the input to the functional state while the aversive responses are its outputs. Functional states, then, are defined relationally in terms of their inputs and outputs. Inputs can be environmental stimuli or other mental states. Likewise, outputs can be other mental states or their behavioural effects (avoiding the source of a pain, for example).

If mental states are defined by causal roles (input–output relations) alone, any mental state could be *multiply realized* on any substrate in which there are fillers for those roles: for example, non-biological as well as biological ones. By analogy, many different kinds of system could count as being in the functional state *White Wash* if inputting dirty whites at some earlier time resulted in it outputting clean whites at some later time.[4]

So if functionalism is true, a mental state like experiencing the taste of ice cream could be experienced by you, but also by a functional copy of you that replicated your neural organization to a sufficiently fine grain (see Chalmers 1995). Given multiple realization, not just humans or cats or octopuses, but Martians, interstellar dust clouds, ghosts or robots could be candidates for mindedness given the right kind of functional organization.

As Gualtiero Piccinini observes, there is more than one way of expressing the functionalist thesis. I have introduced it as a claim about what it is for a system to realize a particular mental state such as a belief or a desire. However, at its most abstract, it is the claim that "the mind is the 'functional organization' of the brain, or any other system that is functionally equivalent to the brain" (2010: 270). The more general formulation is key for transhumanist aspirations for uploaded immortality because it is conceivable that the functional structure by virtue of which brains exhibit mentality is at a much lower level than that of individual mental states: for example, at the level of individual neurons and the various chemical messaging systems that modulate their firing behaviour (Philippou 2013).

Thus given a sufficiently global functionalism, a computer simulation of an embodied nervous system that had fillers for every functional role in an individual human mind would also be an emulation *of that mind* lacking none of the preconditions for intentionality (representation) or conscious experience (Bostrom & Sandberg 2008).[5]

This would obviously support the metaphysical possibility of "mind uploading" since it would allow that minds could run on vastly durable and flexible soul-engines and not fragile biological systems. Advances in computation and neuroscience like Kurzweil's speculative neuroprostheses could result in human minds migrating onto non-biological platforms inconceivably faster and far more robust than evolved biological bodies (Kurzweil 2005: 198–202).

As I noted earlier, functionalist claims for the substrate independence of mind and mental attributes have been contested. Ned Block famously argued that a sufficiently abstract version of functionalism entails that a human population – the population of China, say – could be organized so as to realize a human mind for an hour if a sufficient number agreed to be connected by radio so that they could pass signals to one another in a way that realizes precisely the input–output behaviour of neurons in a human brain (Block 1978).

Such a being would implement the functional diagram of a human – albeit on a much slower time scale – but it seems prima facie objectionable (to some) to claim that this corporate entity would have a mind. Some functionalists bite this particular bullet by arguing that humans, like nations, are corporate entities made of neurons and other functional components (Clark 1994). Others may hope to qualify functionalism in a way that precludes China Brains and their ilk.

Block's objection is salutary because it suggests that there is a genuine metaphysical issue concerning the *degree* of substrate independence exhibited by mental properties. It might, after all, be possible for minds to run on platforms that are very different to human bodies; but they might differ in important ways to human minds (§§1.4, 3.1, 3.2). This possibility raises very different issues for transhumanists – who genuinely hope to realize human-type minds differently – and speculative posthumanists, who advocate the possibility of technologically engendered nonhumans.

1.4 Posthumanism

Like humanism, posthumanism – or the philosophical critique of anthropocentrism – comes in different flavours. All are opposed to some form of human-centred worldview. However, they apply to different domains and often use antithetic methods of argument and analysis:

- Speculative posthumanism (SP) – the primary concern of this book – opposes human-centric thinking about the long-run implications of modern technology.
- Critical posthumanism is a broadly based attack on the supposed anthropocentrism of modern philosophy and intellectual life (§1.1).
- Speculative realism opposes the philosophical privileging of the human–world relationship in Kantian and post-Kantian transcendental philosophy.
- Philosophical naturalism is also opposed to the claim that philosophical truth claims can be arbitrated from a transcendental point of view but uses scientific theory as a constraint on philosophical truth claims. By contrast, while speculative realists are equally hostile to transcendentalism, many also oppose naturalism on the grounds that science is just another way of translating a mind-independent reality into forms that humans can understand.

Despite the doctrinal and stylistic differences between these posthumanisms, their concerns are overlapping. SP proposes that there could be technologically engendered nonhumans who may experience and understand the world very differently to humans. Thus, like speculative realism, it cannot view reality as a human mental or social construction and, like critical posthumanism, it is sensitive to any privileging of human standpoints. I will also argue that philosophical naturalism provides a powerful weapon against transcendental humanism (see Chapters 3 and 4). It is arguable, though, that SP need not be committed to philosophical naturalism.

Let us sample each posthumanism in turn.

Speculative posthumanism

The radical augmentation scenarios discussed in the previous two sections indicate to some that a future convergence of NBIC technologies could lead to a new "posthuman" form of existence: the emergence of intelligent and very powerful nonhumans. In particular, we noted that the development of artificial general intelligence might lead, in Good's words, to an "intelligence explosion" that would leave humans cognitively redundant, or worse. Following an influential paper by the computer scientist Virnor Vinge, this hypothetical event is often referred to as "the technological singularity" (Vinge 1993).

Like Good, Vinge claims that were a superintelligence created, it could produce still more intelligent entities, resulting in a growth in mentation to intellectual plateaus far above our current capacities. The precise form of this technology is unimportant for Vinge's argument. It could be a powerful cognitive enhancement technique, a revolution in machine intelligence or synthetic life, or some as yet unenvisaged process. As David Chalmers points out, the technology needs to be "extendible" in as much that improving it yields correlative increases in the intelligence produced. Our only current means of producing human-equivalent intelligence is non-extendible: "If we have better sex, it does not follow that our babies will be geniuses" (Chalmers 2010: 18).

This recursively improvable technology for intelligence amplification would, according to Vinge, constitute a point beyond which biological constraints on human and nonhuman life on this planet would cease to apply. The "posthuman" minds it would produce would be so vast that we have no models for their transformative potential. They would consequently occupy a distant region within Legg and Hutter's ordering of intelligences (see §1.3). The best we can do to grasp the significance of the technological singularity, he claims, is to draw analogies with an earlier revolution in intelligence:

> And what happens a month or two (or a day or two) after that? I have only analogies to point to: The rise of humankind. We will be in the Post-Human era. And for all my rampant technological optimism, sometimes I think I'd be more comfortable if I were regarding these transcendental events from one thousand years remove ... instead of twenty.
>
> (Vinge 1993: np)

Current humans, it seems, may be no more capable of understanding a post-singularity dispensation than a rat or nonhuman primate can understand public transportation or distributive justice.[6]

The claim that a singularity is possible nicely exemplifies the philosophical position of speculative posthumanists – though, as I will argue in later chapters, *it does not exhaust it* (Chapter 5). Posthumans in this sense are hypothetical wide "descendants" of current humans that are *no longer human* in consequence of some history of technological alteration.

I've coined the term "wide descent" because exclusive consideration of biological descendants of humanity as candidates for posthumanity would be excessively restrictive. Future extensions of NBIC technologies may involve discrete biotechnical modifications of the reproductive process such as human cloning, the introduction of transgenic or artificial genetic material or seemingly exotic processes like mind uploading. Thus entities warranting our concern with the posthuman could emerge via modified biological descent, recursive extension of AI technologies (involving human and/or nonhuman designers), quasi-biological descent from synthetic organisms, a convergence of the above, or via some technogenetic process yet to be envisaged![7]

As I will emphasize in my discussion of critical posthumanism, it is vital to appreciate that the metaphysics of SP is independent of the ethics of transhumanism. One can espouse transhumanist ethics for which enhancing human capacities is a moral priority or a political right, while discounting claims that wide descendants of current humans could become posthuman. Similarly, speculative posthumanism is consistent with the rejection of the ethics of transhumanism or any technological itinerary with posthuman potential. One can hold that a posthuman divergence from humanity is a significant metaphysical possibility but far from a desirable one (Roden 2012a; Chapter 5). This is not to say, of course, that SP lacks ethical and political implications of its own but these will only become apparent once we appreciate the conceptual scope of a posthuman divergence.

Critical posthumanism

Critical posthumanists argue that Western Humanism is based on a dualist conception of a rational, self-governing subject whose nature is transparent to itself and, as Veronika Hollinger puts it, "unmarked by its interactions with the object-world" (Hollinger 2009: 273). It is unsurprising, then, that many take René Descartes to be the arch-humanist since he makes an uncompromisingly sharp distinction between the human capacity for transparent self-knowledge and an altogether shakier access to a physical nature "outside" the self.

Descartes' claim for epistemic self-transparency is supported by the famous "evil demon" thought experiment applied at the end of the first of his *Meditations* to filter out beliefs that are not resistant to maximal doubt. The demon (*malin génie*) is a being every bit as powerful as God (God's Evil Twin, so to speak) who is supposed to have simulated the whole of material reality in our minds:

> I will suppose, then, not that Deity, who is sovereignly good and the fountain of truth, but that some malignant demon, who is at once exceedingly potent and deceitful has employed all his artifice to deceive me; I will suppose that the sky, the air, the earth, colours, figures, sounds and all external things, are nothing better than the illusions of dreams, by means of which this being has laid snares for my credulity; I will consider myself as without hands, eyes, flesh, blood, or any of the senses, and as falsely believing that I am possessed of these.
>
> (Descartes 1986: 84)

In order for this deception to occur, the mind's contents must be *world-independent*. Suppose it is only possible for me to have beliefs about material objects if material objects exist. Then it would not be possible for me to be radically mistaken about their existence if the material world is a simulation. Descartes' epistemology thus presupposes a doctrine now known as "internalism". Internalists claim that the meanings of our thoughts and intentions are fixed independently of the possible realities to which they refer by the autonomous powers of the thinking subject.[8] Descartes also requires that these contents are transparent or directly evident to the subject. This allows existence and content of mental states to be inspected directly even in cases where the objects to which they refer do not exist. Thus the interior realm of the mind affords a bulwark against the skeptical doubts raised by the evil demon thought experiment.

This idea of human subjectivity as a self-determining "interior realm that can resist skeptical doubt" is successively criticized and reformulated by later philosophers in the idealist and empiricist traditions such as Kant (Farrell 1996: 11; see §3.3). It also motivates Descartes' famous and widely contested metaphysics of substance dualism, for which minds and material bodies are distinct entities with utterly different attributes.

According to Hayles and Badmington, the term "posthuman" is appropriately applied to a late stage of modernity which the legitimating role of the self-authenticating, self-governing human subject handed down from Descartes to his philosophical successors has eroded. This erosion is, in part, technoscientific in origin. Descartes' dualisms between inner and outer, mind and mechanism have become harder to maintain since the computational revolution showed that rational operations can be implemented by appropriately structured mechanical processes, a point lucidly conveyed by Donna Haraway in her "Manifesto for Cyborgs":

> Late twentieth-century machines have made thoroughly ambiguous the difference between natural and artificial, mind and body, self-developing and externally designed, and many other distinctions that used to apply to organisms and machines. Our machines are disturbingly lively, and we ourselves frighteningly inert.
>
> (Haraway 1991: 152)

Critical posthumanism is a response to this displacement of human–nonhuman dualisms within the most advanced academic humanities – a complex re-conception of a human subject *presumed* autonomous and self-present "with a view to the deconstruction of anthropocentric thought" (Badmington 2003: 15). This "deconstruction" consists of a demonstration of the myriad ways in which texts that depict or imagine human transcendence and separateness from a machinic or material nature fail to insulate the human from these – often threatening – inhuman "others".

For Hayles, there is nothing less "posthuman" than futurist scenarios about uploaded immortality or cybernetically extended consciousness detailed above. Rather than questioning anthropocentrism, these recapitulate it as a kind of space operatic saga in which humanity gets to draw its face in the stars. She thinks this "hyper-humanism" is best exemplified in the proposal that minds could transcend bodies by uploading to soul-engines:

> I was reading Hans Moravec's *Mind Children: The Future of Robot and Human Intelligence*, enjoying the ingenious variety of his robots, when I happened upon the passage where he argues it will soon be possible to download human consciousness into a computer. To illustrate, he invents a fantasy scenario in which a robot surgeon purees the human brain in a kind of cranial liposuction, reading the information in each molecular layer as it is stripped away and transferring the information into a computer. At the end of the operation, the cranial cavity is empty, and the patient, now inhabiting the metallic body of the computer, wakens to find his consciousness exactly the same as it was before.
>
> How, I asked myself, was it possible for someone of Moravec's obvious intelligence to believe that mind could be separated from body? Even assuming such a separation was possible, how could anyone think that consciousness in an entirely different medium would remain unchanged, as if it had no connection with embodiment? Shocked into awareness, I began to notice he was far from alone.
>
> (Hayles 1999: 1)

Likewise, Elaine Graham also assumes that a posthuman successor species should be conceived as the apotheosis of the rational self, free to subjugate a bodily nature conceived as abject and threatening (Graham 2002: 9; Braidotti 2013: 2).

Hayles, Graham and Badmington may be right to slam transhumanists for being insufficiently vigilant about conceptions of agency and subjectivity but accusations of philosophical naivety can cut many ways. Their analysis confuses *metaphysical* claims about nonhuman succession and *ethical* aspirations to transcend our death-prone biology. As our brief foray into the metaphysics of mind uploading shows – and Hayles seems to recognize here – non-biologically instanced minds would *only* resemble ours if a very liberal substrate neutrality applies. Thus, while castigating transhumanism for its penchant for anthropocentrism, they overlook the possibility that posthuman succession might result in *posthumans* rather than another iteration of *us*: "Humanity 2.0". We will consider (critical) posthumanist objections to (speculative) posthumanism in greater detail in the next chapter.

As my allusions to "deconstruction" imply, the critical posthumanist project is heavily influenced by the work of deconstruction's primary philosophical exponent, Jacques Derrida. Hayles goes so far as to claim that "deconstruction is the child of the information age", crediting Derrida with the insight that speech is a cyborg act, never simply present or absent but dependent on operations and contexts that exceed the consciousness or understanding of the speaking subject (Hayles 1999: 44).

It is worth emphasizing that Hayles is using "deconstruction" to refer to a set of philosophical claims about subjectivity, language and textuality that Derrida reiterates throughout his very large corpus. Rather like the proponents of cognitive science and artificial intelligence, Derrida argues that the organizing activity some philosophers attribute to a subject or to language depends on opaque and very rudimentary operations that can be thought of as a kind of "generalized writing" – a metaphor drawing on writing's ambiguous status as an external technical medium that emancipates meaning from its source in speakers, thinkers and originating contexts of utterance. This passage from an important early essay, "Freud and the Scene of Writing", sums up Derrida's attempt to complicate and diffuse the traditional view of the human subject as the monarch of its meanings:

> The "subject" of writing does not exist if we mean by that some sovereign solitude of the author. The subject of writing is a system of relations between strata, the psyche, society, the world. Within that scene, on that stage, the punctual simplicity of the classical subject is not to be found.
>
> (Derrida 1978: 226–7)

However, as well as being a philosophy, deconstruction is also a reading strategy for exhibiting discrepant and contradictory elements within a text. The major works in which Derrida articulates his account of generalized writing argue that philosophical texts which formulate an ideal of epistemic transparency are bound to compromise that ideal, thus implying its dependence on something foreign to presence; a "supplement" for a past present or a present to come: memory, representation and writing (Derrida 1998).

On the basis of these readings, Derrida argues that the rational subjectivity proclaimed by some humanists depends on a generative system woven of minimal units of textual difference and repetition (see §2.1 for further discussion of Derrida's argumentation). Rodolphe Gasché likens this textual "infrastructure" of thought to the "tain of the mirror": the dull laminate under a mirror that makes philosophical reflection possible while remaining invisible to the mirrored gaze (Gasché 1986).

In "Theorizing Posthumanism", Badmington applies this strategy to a passage in the fifth part of Descartes' *Discourse on Method* which seems an exemplary act of the kind of "ontological hygiene" that the posthuman era is now overturning. Here the philosopher supports his substance dualism by arguing that no machine (no material body) could exhibit the fluid general intelligence of ordinary humans because this would entail a mechanism of infinite complexity. The human mind and its machines are consequently partitioned into absolutely distinct ontological domains.

Descartes allows that a complex automaton of the kind that would have been familiar to his seventeenth-century readers could imitate the motions and sounds of human language and particular human responses to sensory input, "for example, if touched in a particular place it may demand what we wish to say to it; if in another it may cry out that it is hurt, and such like" (Descartes 1986: 44). However, to ape rationality, a mechanical system would need to integrate special purpose mechanisms suited to every occasion (in computational terms, a "look up table" – see Wheeler 2005: 32–4). Since these occasions could vary infinitely yet still elicit a sensible response from a rational human adult, a mechanical system that could generate rational responses for all occasions would require an infinite number of parts. Since reason is a "universal instrument that is alike available on every occasion" and infinite complexity is impossible, the rational mind must be a non-spatial, immaterial substance distinct from the body (Descartes 1986: 45).

Badmington argues that this separation of mind and machine is less hygienic than it might appear, for it implies that a material system with the complexity to generate flexible performances would be functionally rational. "Reason," Badmington writes, no longer capable of "distinguish[ing] us from the beasts, would meet its match, its fatal and flawless double" (Badmington 2003: 18). He then springs his *coup de théâtre*:

> On closer inspection, in other words, there lies within Descartes' ontological hygiene a real sense in which, to take a line from one of Philip K. Dick's novels, "*[l]iving and unliving things are exchanging properties*". Quite against his will, quite against all odds, Descartes has begun to resemble Deckard, the troubled protagonist of *Do Androids Dream of Electric Sheep?* and *Blade Runner* (dir. Ridley Scott, 1982), who utterly fails to police the boundary between the real and the fake.
>
> (Badmington 2003: 12)

So if humanity is a functional category – not one that applies in virtue of some intrinsic difference like the presence or absence of an immortal soul – the difference between the android that simulates humanity and the human, in itself, is no difference at all. This strange reciprocation comes to a head in the culmination of the TV series *Battlestar Galactica*.

Here a fugitive group of humans and the humanoid versions of the Cylons – androids that, like the replicants in *Blade Runner*, were created by humans but rebelled and eventually destroyed the human home worlds in a nuclear attack – form a commonwealth of human and machine in which the former antagonists co-operate to achieve common political aims, fall in love and raise hybrid Cylon–Human children.

Significantly, this social union becomes possible only after a group of Cylons elect to destroy the mind-uploading technology that formerly made them immortal (see §1.3). Prior to this, Cylons were functionally immortal revenants, able to upload their mind to a cloned body after death. This technological capacity made them too different to be accommodated within the humans' recognizably liberal, North American-style republic. The destruction of their posthuman infrastructure ironically lays the foundation for a shared state in which both groups have equal interests (see Roden 2008).

Yet, the slippage from human–posthuman difference to a cyborg–social union implies, once more, that humans and machines are functionally differentiated by the historical and technological relationships in which they enter, *not* by having a biological as opposed to a machinic lineage (see Chapter 5). *Both* are, in Haraway's terms, "cyborgs" – ambiguous assemblages of the natural and the artificial that destabilize oppositions between entrenched political identities (Haraway 1991).

This spirit of ethical and political complication is a goal of Haraway's posthumanist ontology as it is of more recent posthumanist theorists like Rosi Braidotti (see Chapter 8). As Haraway puts it:

> The cyborg would not recognise the Garden of Eden, it is not made of mud and cannot dream of returning to dust. Perhaps that is why I want to see if cyborgs can subvert the apocalypse of returning to nuclear dust in the manic compulsion to name the enemy.
>
> (Haraway 1991: 151)

Cyborgs do not mourn lost origins or halcyon pasts; cyborg politics likewise disclaims universal history, eschewing dreams of reconciliation in favour of experimental alliances like the human–machine couplings of *Galactica*. Braidotti claims that the levelling of the difference between minds, machines and living organisms which opens up the space for this experimentation with subjectivity is also expressed in a global bio-politics in which living beings are meshed into restrictive systems of surveillance and exploitation (Braidotti 2013; see §8.2). Along with Claire Colebrook, she also claims that a liberal politics oriented towards the rights and welfare of humans is incapable of addressing issues such as climate change or ecological depletion in the so-called "anthropocene" epoch, in which humans "have become a geological force capable of affecting all life on this planet" (Braidotti 2013: 66; Colebrook 2012b: 188).[9]

In the later parts of this book, I will suggest ways in which this ethico-political conception of the posthuman can illuminate some of the deep ethical problems raised by SP. However, this will require that we pass through a more sustained analysis of posthuman possibility than is afforded in the majority of critical posthumanist writings.

Badmington's deconstructive reading of Descartes exemplifies some of the philosophical limitations of critical posthumanism. In part, they derive from a textualist obsession with nuances of conceptual expression rather than with the articulation of concepts or the things that concepts are about. For example, Badmington fails to note that Descartes' argument against machine intelligence in *The Discourse* is not an argument for human–machine difference but an argument *from* human–machine difference *to* substance dualism. The purported difference between human and machine is not the conclusion of the argument but its premise. It presupposes that there are manifest *functional differences* between humans and machines, humans and brutes. The hygienic cordon between the human and its other is not in doubt: the point, for Descartes, is to explain it.

This lack of theoretical rigour seeps into critical posthumanist analyses of humanism. Most fail to figure the difference between anthropocentrism and humanism noted above. Moreover, few are attentive to the varieties of humanism and anthropocentrism. For example, Cary Wolfe begins his book *What is Posthumanism?* by citing a Wikipedia entry on "humanism" that identifies it with the cosmopolitan ideal of the dignity and moral autonomy of human persons that we identified with one kind of humanism in §1.1 (Wolfe 2010: xi). On the next page he cites the resonant close of *The Order of Things* where Foucault famously declares "man is an invention of recent date. And one perhaps nearing its end", comparing its erasure with that of a human profile "drawn in sand at the edge of the sea" (Foucault 1970: 387).

Wolfe suggests that the roots of contemporary posthumanism in the academic humanities can be traced back to Foucault's anatomization of the human. However, like Hollinger and Hayles, he identifies his posthumanism with the embrace of materiality (opposing it to transhumanism which, like Hayles and Badmington, he regards as the "intensification of humanism" by technological means – Wolfe 2010: xv).

This genealogy may be accurate, for all I know. If so, it is the history of some confusion. As Béatrice Han-Pile emphasizes, Foucault's "humanism" is not the ethical humanism associated with cosmopolitanism or with Renaissance ideals of individual self-fashioning (Han-Pile 2010). To which we should add that it is not the humanism associated with the separation of mind, body and animality (see Chapter 2). It is, rather, due to Kant's turn *away* from Cartesian epistemology (in which a self-transparent subject represents a mind-independent nature) towards the transcendental subjectivity that actively organizes nature (§§1.1, 3.3). To be sure, Kant supports cosmopolitanism from within his transcendental philosophy. But as humanists as diverse as Mill, Chomsky, Strawson, Rawls and Taylor show, there are many different ways of supporting the claim that most humans have distinctive moral powers. Not all forms of cosmopolitanism presuppose the transcendental humanism that Foucault has in his sights.

In a further conflation of disparate humans and humanisms, Wolfe claims that Daniel Dennett, an inveterate opponent of dualism, succumbs to Cartesianism when claiming that humans have a unique, cultural capacity to represent representation – to believe they believe, etc. (Wolfe 2010: 38). But, if anything, Dennett is expressing a Kantian understanding of the link between the capacity to acquire culture and sapience – the awareness of being a thinker answerable to reasons. As Lee Braver and others have noted, Kant's transcendental philosophy identifies this capacity to think that one is thinking in functional terms, not in terms of the intrinsic attributes of the thinker – which, for Kant, are unknowable in any case (Braver 2007: 54–5; §3.3).[10]

As we will see in Chapter 3, transcendental forms of humanism are very much alive in phenomenological and pragmatist theories of the human subject. All of these reject both substance dualism and Descartes' claim that human mental life is self-transparent.

This functional characterization of a rational subject also involves a kind of dualism; not *substance* dualism but a dualism of languages or descriptions. A "dualist" of this stamp accepts that there are only physical things and events and that all token (individual) mental events are identical to physical events. However, she denies that rational or normative relations between mental events can be described physically (Davidson 2001a: 207–25). Astonishingly, the explanations of bodily processes such as the biochemistry of nerve cells contribute nothing to psychology in this account. At best they support our materialistic worldview by showing us how token psychological facts are "realized" or "instanced" by physical states. But this contributes to metaphysics, not to psychology. According to this "explanatory dualism" – as Mike Wheeler refers to it – "flexible, intelligent action remains conceptually and theoretically independent of the scientific understanding of the agent's physical embodiment" (Wheeler 2005: 51).

To be fair, posthumanist and feminist thinkers such as Hayles, Braidotti and Elizabeth Wilson, as well as proponents of "embodied" approaches to cognition like Wheeler, argue for the incarnate, embodied character of subjectivity and presumably oppose explanatory dualism (see §2.1).[11] But conflating dualisms only undermines the project of putting body and self back together.

Speculative realism

Speculative realists are impatient with textual deconstructions of subjectivity of the kind undertaken in the work of Badmington and Wolfe. They argue that to undo anthropocentrism and human exceptionalism we must shift philosophical concern away from subjectivity (or the deconstruction of the same) towards the cosmic throng of nonhuman things ("the great outdoors"). Most speculative realists repudiate transcendental humanism in some form – that is, Kantian and post-Kantian attempts to understand things in terms of their relationship to human subjectivity and conceptual thinking. In the most exemplary work of speculative realism to date, *After Finitude: An Essay on the Necessity of Contingency*, Quentin Meillassoux refers to any philosophy that holds that thought can only think the relation between thought and its object; never the object as an absolute without relation to cognition as "correlationist" (Meillassoux 2010). Harman, Grant and Meillassoux have argued, against the correlationist, that any reality worth the name must be thought of as absolute, independent of human subjectivity and thus as deeply nonhuman and "weird". Harman sums up the program with brio:

> Inspired ultimately by Immanuel Kant, correlationists are devoted to the human-world correlate as the sole topic of philosophy. This has become the unspoken central dogma of all continental and much analytic philosophy. Speculative realist thinkers oppose this credo (though not always for the same reasons) and defend a realist stance toward the world. But instead of endorsing a commonsensical, middle-aged realism of boring hands and billiard balls existing outside the mind, speculative realist philosophies are perplexed by the strangeness of the real: a strangeness undetectable by the instruments of common sense.
>
> (Harman 2011: vii–viii)

Speculative realists compose a somewhat marginal, fissiparous cell among philosophers influenced by post-Kantian European thought, birthing passionate internet flame wars between the rationalist wings exemplified by Brassier and Meillassoux – who, like Descartes, boldly deduce a theory of the real from an account of the internal demands of thought – and a more swinging camp consisting of philosophers like Harman or Levi Bryant who insist on the priority of ontology to epistemology. As its name might suggest, *speculative posthumanism* seeks to inject some realist attitude into philosophical discussion of posthuman futures by acknowledging and formalizing the independence of posthumans from our current conceptions of them.

Philosophical naturalism

Philosophical naturalism is perhaps the dominant current of post-war Anglo-American philosophy. Most philosophical naturalists – I suspect – would be indifferent to their inclusion among the ranks of posthumanists, but insofar as naturalists offer some of the most trenchant, well-argued challenges to humanist – particularly *transcendental* humanist – thinking, it is important to discuss them alongside their more self-conscious and excitable colleagues.

Naturalist philosophy looks to the truth-generating practices of science rather than to philosophical anthropology to warrant claims about the world's metaphysical structure. Naturalists think that human knowledge is the product of fallible primates whose biology does not equip them to reliably track the deep structure of the world. Philosophical naturalists regard earlier attempts, such as Kant's, to carve out foundational truth claims secure from revision by the findings of science, history and observation as conspicuous failures, for they misinterpret anthropological facts about how we are disposed to think as facts about how the world must be. As James Ladyman and Don Ross remark, "Naturalism is, among other things, the metaphysical hypothesis that the objective world is not constrained by any reasons or standards of reasonableness" (Ladyman & Ross 2007: 288).

Functionalism (§1.3) is an example of naturalism on-the-job in philosophy of mind because its analysis of mental state types as causal roles suggests one way in which mental phenomena can be understood within the ontological framework of contemporary natural science. I will argue in Chapter 4 that a naturalistic account of subjectivity is an effective foil for transcendental philosophies that argue for anthropocentric limits on posthuman possibility.

We will look, then, to naturalism to legitimate a theory of the *posthuman weird*.

Looking forward

We have analysed some of the philosophical positions whose contrasts and affinities will resonate through this book: humanism, transhumanism and posthumanism. Although critical posthumanism is probably the most visible form of anti-anthropocentric thinking within the academic humanities, we have identified some lacunae in the analysis of humanism offered by its leading proponents – including its failure to distinguish the normative claims of transhumanism from speculative metaphysical claims about nonhuman descendants of humans. In Chapter 2 I will argue that the assumption, on the part of many critical posthumanists, that posthuman futurism is really just an exaggerated humanism is not just a conceptual oversight but a betrayal of the project of anti-anthropocentrism, since the prospect of genuine posthumans poses a far greater challenge to the prescriptions of humanist philosophy than deconstruction or allied assaults on the integrity of the human subject.

Notes

1 Though evidence for significant enhancement effects appears to be equivocal to date.
2 Current estimates of the brain's raw processing power run to about 100 teraflops (100 trillion floating point calculations per second). The world's fastest supercomputers currently exceed this this by a factor of ten. The fastest neurons in our heads have a maximum spike frequency of about 200 Hz. The fastest transistors in the world currently operate ten million times faster at about 2 GHz. Moreover, since the 1950s, the increase in the processing power of computer components – integrated circuits – has obeyed Moore's law: approximately doubling every two years. If this trend continues over the next couple of decades, then the artificial processing power on this planet is likely to significantly outpace biological systems.
3 For a rather less sanguine commentary on the state of the art in non-invasive scanning, see Jones (2009).
4 Some systems might *realize* this relationship in the way that a modern washing machine does – running automatically through a wash cycle. Other systems might be kiosks containing human laundry workers who accept the dirty linen at the input hole, rinse and apply detergent, then rinse again, before outputting the clean clothes at a second slot. Finally, in Harry Potter's universe, washing machines may use industrious pixies and dirt-effacing pixie dust to the same effect. The *implementation details* of the state *White Wash* are thus *multiply realizable* in different systems that variably *implement* the same abstract relation.
5 Some philosophers are happy to allow that different types of mental states (beliefs, desires and itches) are a matter of their functional role within an organism but reject functionalism with regard to their representational content (Fodor & Lepore 1992). Others are functionalists about content, but not about the properties that distinguish conscious states like having toothache or seeing pink. Putting some mechanism in the same functional state my gustatory cortex is in when I taste ice cream would not necessarily replicate an experience of taste in the mechanism. If this is correct, replicating or approximating human mental software on an artificial platform like a robot might result in a cognitively sophisticated "zombie" rather than a being with full dress phenomenology. However, if we accept the functionalist accounts of consciousness provided by philosophers like Daniel Dennett and Michael Tye, the prospects for artificial consciousness appear somewhat brighter (Dennett 1991; Tye 2002; Cohen & Dennett 2011).
6 One might be tempted to compare a post-singularity world to the Kantian thing-in-itself which, lacking a mode of presentation in the experiential world of space and time, must remain forever unknowable to us (see Chapter 3). In Roden (2010a, 2012b), however, I consider and reject the applicability of this conception of transcendence to the singularity or the posthuman more generally.
7 The wider significance of Wide Descent will become clearer when I provide a fuller exposition of SP in Chapter 5 (§5.3).
8 Internalism is rejected by so-called "active" or "process" externalists who view mind as embodied activity and by semantic externalists, like Donald Davidson, who argue that the content of our thoughts is established by our interactions with our environments (§§2.1, 5.7).

9 On the surface, this last claim appears difficult to justify. If current environmental problems are a consequence of human mismanagement, their solution will require changes in human institutions and practices.

10 While the existence of a rational, self-aware machine like a Cylon or a Replicant might challenge Cartesian dualism, it would not challenge the Kantian equation of rationality and sapience.

11 See in particular Wilson's excellent discussion of the way in which a Derridean conception of generalized writing can help us understand the phenomenon on "dermographism" (writing on the body) in Wilson (1999).

2 A defence of pre-critical posthumanism

Introduction

As we have seen, critical posthumanists think speculations about such technically engendered posthuman successors as digitally emulated minds, synthetic life forms or robots evince a clumsy naivety. They argue that futurists who worry about roboapocalypses or who dream of becoming an immortal soul engine fail to understand that their fantasies of transcendence or annihilation replicate humanist assumptions about the universal nature of human reason, the dispensability of bodies or the stability of the human essence (§§1.3, 1.4). They fail to grasp that the "human" to which such hypothetical beings are "post" is already a historically variable cultural and technological construction. There can be no posthuman successor species because, as the title of Hayles's *How We Became Posthuman* implies, we have already entered a posthuman dispensation in which the very value and status of the human is put in question by developments in science, political theory and philosophy. If this view is correct, then critical posthumanism is antithetic to SP, and perhaps the only posthumanism worth fighting for.

However, in this chapter I will argue that critiques advanced by theorists like Wolfe and Hayles misdiagnose futurist posthumanism as a technologically intensified version of humanism. This derives, in part, from the basic conflation of SP and transhumanism trailed in the previous chapter. While critical posthumanists make palpable hits on certain technological fantasies of transcendence, SP is not committed to these. It claims that a nonhuman successor to humans could arise in consequence of our technological activity. But it is not committed to the claim that such beings will realize our humanist dreams or apocalyptic nightmares.

Analysing why these arguments fail has the dual benefit of preventing us from being distracted by the anti-humanist hyperbole accruing to theoretical frameworks employed in critical posthumanism – such as deconstruction and cognitive science – but, more importantly, contributes to the development of the rigorous, philosophically self-aware speculative posthumanism that I hope to develop in this book. For example, it will bring into view the extent to which SP is committed to a minimal, non-transcendental and nonanthropocentric humanism and will help up put bones on its realist commitments (see Chapter 5).

This chapter will consider four "dismissals" of SP that occur within the extant literature of critical posthumanists:

- The anti-humanist argument
- The technogenesis argument
- The materiality argument
- The anti-essentialist argument.

All four, I hope to show, are unsound.

2.1 The anti-humanist argument

Critical posthumanists with a deconstructive orientation often accuse speculative futurists of misconceiving the posthuman as a radical break with, or transformation of, the human condition. On the contrary, Hayles and Haraway argue: we are *already posthuman*, living on after our deeply machinic, inhuman nature has been exposed by theories like deconstruction and cognitive science, and by the practical enmeshing of the human body-subject within ramifying NBIC technologies such as biomedicine and cybernetics:

> When the self is envisioned as grounded in presence, identified with originary guarantees and teleological trajectories, associated with solid foundations and logical coherence, the posthuman is likely to be seen as antihuman because it envisions the conscious mind as a small subsystem running its program of self-construction and self-assurance while remaining ignorant of the actual dynamics of complex systems. But the posthuman does not really mean the end of humanity. It signals instead the end of a certain conception of the human, a conception that may have applied, at best, to that fraction of humanity who had the wealth, power and leisure to conceptualize themselves as autonomous beings exercising their will through individual agency and choice.
>
> (Hayles 1999: 286)

SP depicts humanity as determinably different from its others – such that the posthuman would constitute a radical break with it. If we are already not the humans that we thought we were, the possibility of rupture through the emergence of posthumans is foreclosed.

Apocalypse postponed?

This is too quick. There are, as we have noted, many ways in which humans might be distinguished from nonhumans: for example, as a transcendental subject or as a member of a distinctive biological species. The "human being" at issue in this passage from Hayles's *How We Became Posthuman* is not the transcendental subject of Kant or Husserl or *Homo sapiens* but the autonomous moral subject that can reason about its commitments and its plans for life.

So is Hayles at least right to claim that our conception of autonomy has been complicated to the point at which we should reject the distinction between autonomous human persons and "heteronomous" things, machines, animals? This would be a hit against one important component of SP: the claim that posthumans might be significantly *weird*. Vinge suggests, for example, that posthuman life might be more akin to Lovecraft's amorphous "elder gods" than the merely uncanny Cylons or Replicants (Lovecraft 1999; §4.3). If we are already alienated from the subjects we thought we were, then Vinge and Lovecraft's radical aliens might not be as weird as all that.

I have christened this "the anti-humanist objection to posthumanism" because it draws heavily on arguments by prominent French anti-humanists like Derrida and Deleuze. Derrida – as we have seen – argues that what we take to be a unified subject is a complex field of relations: a generalized writing machine whose thought is articulated by events and structures that it cannot control.

In the posthumanist critiques of Hayles and Haraway this deconstructive picture is beefed up with models and theories drawn from cognitive science, complexity theory and cybernetics.

Let us consider cognitive science first.

Classical and embodied cognition

Hayles's account of the posthuman subject is influenced by "embodied" approaches to cognition that emphasize the dependence of thought on its embodiment and material relationships.

Embodied cognition belongs to a number of revisionary responses to so-called "Classical" cognitive science. Classicism in cognitive science draws heavily on Descartes' internalist picture of minds as abstract representational systems for which the body and its environment are mere input devices. All the interesting mental stuff goes on after the body's interaction with its world has caused ideas or concepts to appear in the mind (Wheeler 2005; Samuels 2010; Fodor 1980).

Classicism pictures brains as akin to stored program computers containing discrete symbolic representations of their environments. Mental processes consist in the transformation of these elements according to computational rules or "algorithms". The mental symbols are defined purely by their characteristic shape or structure (their *syntax*) and not by their *semantic properties* (their meaning or content). Formal principles of reasoning are analogous to the rules of game that determine how one position in the game can be succeeded by a later position. They determine how one sentence in the calculus can be derived from another by virtue of its syntactic structure *irrespective of what the symbols mean*.

As an example of how such structure-sensitive rules might yield something like cognition, suppose we have a program with a branching 'If ... Else' rule such as:

If p = "horns", then add x to list [Goats],
Else add x to list [Sheep]

Intuitively, this is a *very* simple categorization rule. It specifies a file location represented by the variable letter "p" and it instructs the computer to add the information contained in another file location "x" to one of two lists [Goats] and [Sheep], depending on whether the data in p corresponds to the character string "horns". The choice of branch comes down to the "shape" of the data stored in particular physical locations on a system that implements this program.

While the example is super simple, the moral is general. *Computational rules determine actions whose execution depends on the local properties of symbols to which they are applied.* The rules themselves are blind to the meaning of those representations.

If reasoning in human and nonhuman animals proceeds in this way, it ought to be possible to explain understanding and meaning by positing "dumb" computational engines whose components lack the florid mental powers they render possible.

The artificial intelligence pioneers Herbert Simon and Allan Newell argued, accordingly, that treating minds as "physical symbol systems" whose state transitions are governed by syntax-sensitive rules is a scientifically fruitful way of explaining how humans and animals think and offers clues for producing artificial intelligences implemented on similar lines (Newell & Simon 1976).

Embodied cognitive science, by contrast, draws inspiration from computational prowess exhibited in biological systems which exhibit no symbolization. Its proponents argue that the preconditions of intelligence can emerge from local interactions between relatively dumb agents (like ants or neurons) and their environments without a planner or "thinking subject" to choreograph their activities; and without the need for computational rules like the branching if/else statement. Swarm intelligence is one example of such emergent computation. It is exhibited where a population of interacting agents – for example, ants, robots or software entities – displays a problem-solving capacity that is not possible for any individual within the population working in isolation. For example, Deneubourg *et al.* (1990) showed that colonies of Argentine ants (*Irido-myrmex humilis*) were able to discriminate a nearer food source from a more distant one by utilizing a simple positive feedback relation between pheromones deposited by ants and the hard-wired tendency of ants to head towards the greatest concentrations of pheromone. Since pheromones evaporate with time, the trails left by ants returning from nearer food sources tend to have greater concentrations, thus *recruiting* more ants for foraging and catalyzing recruitment by further biasing the density of the pheromone trail. Here the problem-solving power of the hive "super-organism" *emerges* from the positive feedback between ant recruitment and pheromone signals. This is one of many cases in which component inter-actions induce *self-organizing behaviour* in a complex system without the need for a central controller or queenly "hive mind" to choreograph their efforts (see also discussion of neural networks in §4.1).

The classical, symbol-driven approach has also been subject to an extensive critique by embodied theorists like Wheeler, Clark, Rodney Brooks and Susan Hurley. This is motivated by some apparent difficulties facing the Classical account.

One way of understanding these is by distinguishing between a process being *computable* and being *tractably computable*. In the early part of the twentieth century it was shown by Alan Turing and others that not all well-defined mathematical functions are computable. There are functions whose values for particular inputs cannot be calculated by following formal rules for manipulating logical symbols. Turing made the con-ceptual leap from formal logic to computation by showing that inferences in formal systems can be implemented on mathematically defined symbol-manipulating devices (now called "Turing Machines").[1] A Turing machine manipulates symbols according to a machine table (i.e. its pro-gram) specifying how it should behave when reading a particular symbol at a particular memory location on its "tape", when in a particular state. The scanning and machine behaviours are extremely simple operations that can be accomplished by any physical machine which responds dif-ferentially to its internal states. Moreover, since their rules are purely syntax-sensitive we need not ascribe an understanding of meaning to any part of the computer responsible for these operations (Petzold 2008). Many writers use the idea of a Universal Turing Machine – an abstract computer that can read any "program" on its tape and compute the result – to capture the intuitive idea of a mechanical computation. According to this (contested) view, any computation that can be undertaken by a physical information processor can be represented by a program-controlled Universal Turing Machine (Copeland 2000).

However, a Turing-computable function may not be *tractably computable* within real-world constraints on time, memory and energy. Tractability matters for humans, animals or replicant fugitives who must respond fluidly to whatever the world throws at them. According to classical computational theory of mind, they achieve this via a four-stage process dubbed the *Sense-Model-Plan-Act* cycle (SMPA) by Rodney Brooks. The first stage of the cycle is to acquire sensory information from input devices (eyes, cameras, nose, whiskers, etc.). The second is to construct symbolically represented beliefs about the world from the sensory information. The third (Plan) is to infer a series of actions by applying general structure–sensitive rules to the beliefs formed in the second stage. The fourth stage is to generate those actions by transforming the plan into a structured series of movements (Brooks 1991: 140; Wheeler 2005: 67).

Critics of the symbol system approach to understanding cognition, like Wheeler and Hubert Dreyfus, have argued that Steps 2 and 3 are particularly problematic in any complex environment. In particular, both tasks are subject to what has come to be known as "frame problems". Frame problems concern how a cognitive system distinguishes relevant from irrelevant information. Humans and higher nonhuman animals regularly make skillful and occasionally very fast inferences about the state of their world. Here are some examples – the last two due to Churchland (2012):

- There are voices coming from the empty basement – the DVD has come off pause!
- Smoke is coming out of the kitchen – the toast is burning!
- *Artificial* selection of horses, pigeons, pigs, etc. can produce new varieties of creature – evolution is *natural* selection!

Frame problems pose a challenge to classicism because it implies that a sophisticated cognitive system has myriads of belief-like entities internally represented as discrete physical states (like "inner sentences" or file locations in Random Access Memory). Even Fodor, the arch-classicist, concedes that these feats of fluid inference are hard to explain because it requires our brains to put a "frame" around the representations relevant to making the inference – information about the Highway Code or the diameter of the Sun probably won't be relevant to figuring out that burning toast is causing the smoke in the kitchen. Relevance seems to be a holistic property – beliefs are relevant given a context, given our values and in virtue of *relations to lots of other beliefs*.

But which ones? How do our brains know where to kink the frame without first making a costly, unbounded search through all our beliefs, inspecting each for its relevance to the problem?

Suppose that a system must evaluate the consequences of some plan for its world-representation. Unless it first isolates a small subset of relevant beliefs, it will need to iterate through a World Stack, a list containing all its beliefs arranged in no particular order to pick out the ones that will be relevant to the task at hand (the order would be indifferent since prior to evaluation no relevance score can be assigned to them). If its World Stack is very large, the system is liable to have to plough through many entirely irrelevant beliefs, deducing whether it has any implications for its plan. With a very big World Stack, this process may turn out to be computationally intractable. After all, unless there is a time limit on updating, the system may need to review beliefs it has updated earlier in the light of updates of subsequent beliefs in the stack. Maybe the system will clunk away evaluating many irrelevant beliefs before it gets to the ones it needs to reassess in the light of its plan (Fodor 1983: 112–13; Wheeler 2005: 178–82).

As Terrence Horgan and John Tienson point out (using Fodor's analysis) this problem is compounded by the fact that a sophisticated, rational system will also need to be sensitive to non-local properties of a world-representation like simplicity and conservatism (Horgan & Tienson 1994: 314). Horgan and Tienson think that it is quite likely that holistic properties like relevance and non-local properties like simplicity cannot be captured in computationally tractable algorithms.

For critics of classicism, the frame problems are symptomatic of the need for a different approach to understanding the mental – though, even among critics of the physical symbol approach, there is little consensus on what this ought to be (see Churchland 2012; Horgan & Tienson 1994).

Wheeler argues that the frame problem for mental representation arises because the representations in question are presumed *disembedded* from their environmental contexts:

> In typical cases of perceptually guided intelligent action, the environment is not more than i) a furnisher of problems for the agent to solve, ii) a source of informational inputs to the mind (via sensing), and, most distinctively, iii) a kind of stage on which sequences of preplanned actions (outputs of the faculty of reason) are simply executed.
>
> (Wheeler 2005: 45)

This means that the environment only supplies raw material for the construction and updating of inner representations and the occasions for action but *plays no role in mental processing*.[2] How does disembedding mental representation contribute to problems of relevance?

Well, here Wheeler turns to Martin Heidegger's phenomenological critique of rational psychology in his *Being and Time*.

If thought is the manipulation of mental representations according to rules sensitive purely to their physical structure, then context can only figure in thought by being *explicitly represented* by the symbols which refer to objective features of that context like shapes or motions. Otherwise structure–sensitive rules can take no account of it.

Heidegger argues that this Cartesian model of the mind as a repre-sentational system over-intellectualizes human agency. While humans can create explicit representations of objects, their everyday access to the world is that of skillful, engaged coping. In skillful coping we rarely represent objects explicitly, according to Heidegger. More commonly, we are aware of objects in terms of their significance for current tasks (as *zuhanden* or ready-to-hand) while we are aware of our environment primarily as a set of potentials for action (sometimes referred to as "affordances") not as represented bundles of properties and relationships (this idea will be important when we consider the worldly background of interpretative understanding in §3.7).

According to Heidegger, this phenomenology of everyday agency belies the classical picture of a rational subject representing mind-independent properties of an external world in sentences and concepts (Heidegger 1962; Dreyfus 1990).

Heidegger's phenomenologically based insight into the structure of everyday coping can inform an embodied cognitive science by shifting efforts away from representing knowledge in terms of inner symbols and rules and towards the kind of skillful, flexible coping activity that biolo-gical organisms exhibit on their home turf. In AI and cognitive science, for example, this approach is evident in behaviour-based robotics systems which build sparse and temporary representations of their world by sensing the current context and activity of the robot. According to Wheeler, such "action-oriented representations" *build in* value and contextual relevance to the system *because of their dependence on the situation of a robot or organism*. Here the world is "encoded in terms of possibilities for action" much as Heidegger inferred from his phenomenological account of human agency (Wheeler 2005: 197). Relevance does not have to be deduced by com-puting the outcomes of lots of individual facts (spawning the frame pro-blem) since action-oriented representations are inherently value-laden and relevant.

The mind portrayed by the embodied approach is not, then, the Cartesian-internalist mind standing apart from its world, but an externali-zable pattern of bodily interactions, a patterning which, as in ant superorganisms, can emerge from asynchronous interactions between dumb components. According to this "active-externalist" picture, Hayles argues, *there is no classically self-present human subjectivity for the posthuman to transcend.* Mental powers of deliberation, inference, consciousness, etc. are *already* distributed between biological neural networks, actively sensing bodies and artefacts (Hayles 1999: 239, 286). *Pace* Descartes, humans are not self-transparent subjects but beings that appear remarkably inept at understanding their nature. Never mind posthumans – humans are already weird amalgams of machines. We just don't know it yet.[3]

Deconstruction

What of the deconstructive attack on the autonomous subject that Hayles takes to complement that of cognitive science? As we saw in §1.4, Derrida argues that subjectivity depends on generalized writing or general textuality, where the notion of a "general text" refers to a highly abstract set of conditions for the production of "sense" or "meaning" which any signifying item must satisfy. For example: any semiotic or semantic theory must assume a distinction between sign tokens and ideal types which each repetition or "iteration" of a sign instances. But, Derrida argues, iteration cannot be repetition of stable semantic essence, for any significant particular can always be detached from its context and "grafted" into a new one in which it means something different. In Derrida's later work this undecidable logic assumes a broader ethical significance. Iterability implies that the text is *both* context-bound *and* transcends any *given* context, supposing "both that there are only contexts, that nothing exists outside context … but also that the limit of the frame or the border of the context always entails a clause of nonclosure. The outside penetrates and thus determines the inside" (Derrida 1988: 152). Any application of a moral or legal principle is thus potentially an act of reinterpretation or invention: "Each case is other, each decision is different and requires an absolutely unique interpretation, which no existing, coded rule can or ought to guarantee absolutely" (Derrida 2002: 251).

If iterability is a condition of thought or meaning as such, as Derrida argues, it implies that both have an open-textured temporal structure. The subject of thought, experience and intentionality is, accordingly, an "effect" of a mobile network of signifying states (or traces) structurally open to modification or recontextualization. Derrida's neologism *différance* captures this essential openness by capitalizing on the homonymy between the French verbs for differing and deferring. The identity or stability of the system of traces is differed-deferred because it is "vitiated by the mark of its relation to the future element" (Derrida 1984: 13–17).

The posthuman subject

For Hayles, the "autonomous liberal subject" she identifies with humanist theory is distinct from the conceptually ordered world in which it works out its plans for the good (Hayles 1999: 286). The *posthuman subject*, by contrast, is problematically individuated, because its agency is embedded and embodied in that world (*as per* active externalism) and because of the open, ungrounded materiality – or "iterability" – of language (Derrida 1988: 152; Hayles 1999: 264–5). The decentred posthuman subject is no longer sufficiently distinct from the world to order it autonomously as the subject of liberal theory is required to do.

But is this right?

Let's suppose, along with Hayles and other proponents of embodied cognitive science, that the skin-bag does not fix the boundary between agent and world or between the mental and non-mental. Nonetheless, even if thinking is a pattern of bodily and extra-bodily processes, this does not render thought or action less evaluable in terms of the rationality standards we apply to deliberative acts. As Badmington shows with respect to Descartes, rationality seems like a capacity that is manifested in our mental and *bodily functioning* (§1.5). An agent whose rational functioning depends on states of affairs beyond their skin is no less rational for all that. So even if the humanist subject is a swarm of bodily and extra-bodily agencies, this metaphysical dependence (or "supervenience") need not impair its capacity to subtend the powers of deliberation or reasoning liberal theory requires of it.[4]

If we accept his arguments, Derrida's account of general textuality nuances this picture by entailing limits on the scope of deliberation in the face of the "outside" or exception which infects any rule-governed system (Derrida 1988: 152).

But there is a difference between being ahead of oneself and being beheaded. The posthuman, in Hayles's critical sense of the term, *is not less human* for confronting the fragile and open-textured temporality of its cognitive and moral powers (see Chapter 6). The problem of how reason deals with the particular, the one-off, the exception, for example, is presaged in Aristotle's account of practical reason as well as Kant's account of aesthetic judgment: both insisting on the need for judgement to accommodate the singular or exceptional without resort to rules.

What Derridean deconstruction adds to this venerable tradition – as Martin Hägglund has emphasized recently – is the claim that these textual structures generalize beyond the sphere of the human. Concepts such as iterability and *différance* – (differing/deferring) originate in Derrida's readings of the philosophies of subjectivity but their sphere of application generalizes beyond this to all manner of machinic system: social institutions, living cells, computer programs and biological nervous systems

(Derrida 1978, 1998: 9; Hägglund 2008; Roden 2004b). But the fact that human subjectivity depends on structures shared by other biological or technical entities in no way levels functional differences between human and nonhuman (§1.4). After all, the traditional philosophical materialist will insist on a very similar thesis: "Humans are not special metaphysically. They are made out of the same fundamental particles, fields and forces that everything else is made out of." The fact that humans are made out of the same protons, quarks or electrons that everything else is made out of does entail that they are the same as everything else: to reason otherwise is to commit the fallacy of composition.

This is not to say that there is no merit in the model of the hybrid, open-textured self that Hayles and others present under the rubric of "the posthuman subject", or that it has no implications for "pre-critical" speculative posthumanism elaborated here. It does. I will argue in Chapter 4 that – far from being antithetic – critical and speculative posthumanism are complementary. A naturalistic position structurally similar to Derrida's deconstructive account of subjectivity can be applied to transcendental constraints on posthuman weirdness.

It will argue that a "naturalized deconstruction" of subjectivity widens the portals of posthuman *possibility* whereas it complicates but does not repudiate human actuality (Roden 2005, 2013). Understanding human agency in terms of iterability and *différance* leads to a moderately revisionary (but still interesting) account of what human rationality and agency consists in. But this leads us beyond the human by suggesting how rationality and agency depend on structures that are shared by nonhuman systems that may lack the capacities associated with human agency, or have other powers that humans do not enjoy (as an example of a loose application of the iterability argument to nonhuman systems, see my discussion of AI goals in §4.3).[5]

I conclude that the anti-humanist argument does not succeed in showing that humans lack the powers of rational agency required by ethical humanist doctrines such as cosmopolitanism. Rather, critical posthumanist accounts of subjectivity and embodiment imply a *cyborg-humanism* that attributes our cognitive and moral natures as much to our cultural environments (languages, technologies, social institutions) as to our biology. But cyborg humanism is compatible with the speculative posthumanist claim that our wide descendants might exhibit distinctively nonhuman moral powers (Roden 2010a; see Chapter 4, §§4.3, 8.2).

2.2 The technogenesis argument

Let's consider the second dismissal of SP – which begins from the claim that the human is "always already" technically constituted. In "Wrestling with Transhumanism", Hayles argues that transhumanists are wedded to a *technogenetic anthropology* for which humans and technologies have existed and co-evolved in symbiotic partnership. Future transhuman enhancement would be technogenetic processes, according to this story; but so are comparable transformations in the deep past (Hayles 2011).

Human cultural and technical activity has, for example, equipped some with lactose tolerance or differential calculus without monstering the beneficiaries into posthumans (Laland *et al*. 2000)! Clark frames *the technogenesis argument* against posthumanism in his book *Natural Born Cyborgs* particularly well:

> The promised, or perhaps threatened, transition to a world of wired humans and semi-intelligent gadgets is just one more move in an ancient game …
> We are already masters at incorporating nonbiological stuff and structure deep into our physical and cognitive routines. To appreciate this is to cease to believe in any post-human future and to resist the temptation to define *ourselves* in brutal opposition to the very worlds in which so many of us now live, love, and work.
>
> (Clark 2003: 142)

Clark is famous for promulgating a variant of embodied cognitive science/ active externalism known as the *extended mind thesis* (Chapter 5). Proponents of the extended mind thesis like Clark and Chalmers argue from a principle of "parity" between processes that go on in the head and any functionally equivalent process in the world beyond (Clark & Chalmers 1998).[6] The parity principle implies that mental processes need not occur only in biological nervous systems but in the environments and tools of embodied thinkers. If some chalk marks on a blackboard with which I record the steps of a length calculation make a cognitive contribution to my thinking, *they are as much part of my mental activity as the activation patterns in my brain*.

For Clark, humans are particularly adept at offloading processing demands onto external resources like written symbols and smart phones. Like Dennett (1991), Clark thinks these "hybrid mental representations" may account for our capacity to reflect on our own thoughts and thought processes – for example, via the use of embedding sentences such as "Joan believed that Bill is the culprit" (Clark 2008: 58; Bermudez 2002). If this is right, then skills like philosophical reflection and deliberation are the product of our technical-cultural activity rather than habits of bare brains. Rationality would already be due to a *cyborg coupling* of biological and cultural systems (though, as argued in the previous section, no less rational for all that – see Chapter 6, §6.5).

Clearly, if we restrict the evidence for the technogenesis argument to cases where technological change has not resulted in one species or group splitting off from another, we are likely to infer that this is not liable to happen in the future. However, even allowing for this constraint, the fact that the game of self-augmentation is ancient does not imply that the rules cannot change.

Some pre-human divergence had to have happened in our evolutionary past and it is at least plausible – given Clark's cyborg anthropology – that technologies such as public symbol systems were a factor in the "hominization process" (see, in particular, Deacon 1997).

So there is evidence that one cultural-technological system may have been an evolutionary spur for the divergence of modern humans from their primate ancestors. Taking our cue from Churchland's proposal for centipedal cognition, it is conceivable that a cognitive augmentation of a similar order might accomplish a similar trick for posthumans were it to replace public language with a more flexible or potent medium of metarepresentation (§4.1). This is entirely compatible with Clark's hybrid account of biological/cultural representation since it involves the withering of a cultural component of one kind of hybrid mental state and its replacement with a new kind of hybrid mental state. Thus technogenetic anthropology is conceptually compatible with at least one scenario for the divergence of posthumans from humans. If technogenesis is conceptually compatible with one kind of posthuman/human divergence, it might be compatible with others (say, Vingean singularities).

Thus the technogenesis dismissal of SP invalidly infers that because technological changes have not monstered us into posthumans thus far, they will not do so in the future.

2.3 The materiality argument

Another of Hayles's objections to futurist visions of posthuman succession is their supposed denial or repression of the materiality of human embodiment and cognition: *the materiality argument* (this was discussed in §1.4). Computer simulations can help us understand the self-organizing capacities of the natural world, but this does not entail that any natural system can be fully *replicated* by a computational system that emulates its functional architecture or simulates its dynamics. The fact that cosmologists can simulate the evolution of galaxies with cellular automata does not mean that galaxies *are* cellular automata (Piccinini 2010: 279).

As we have seen, some transhumanist and speculative posthumanist scenarios presuppose a functionalist account of mind because they claim that minds could be fully emulated on computational soul engines (§1.3). This objection applies to a fairly restricted (if oft-cited) class of posthuman itineraries, however. SP is not committed to the singularity hypothesis; it is not committed to the possibility that humans could become digitized immortals.

It merely states that some of our wide descendants (human, machine, cyborg, etc.) might cease to be human in consequence of technological alteration (§1.4).

Perhaps, as Hayles hints in the opening of *How We Became Posthuman*, substrate neutrality collapses and beings differently embodied would also be differently minded (§1.4). If this was the case then uploading might not be possible, or if possible in some loose or extended sense, might not be consistent with the ethical humanity of the uploadee.

Thus the materiality of embodiment argument works in favour of the pre-critical posthumanist account (SP), *not against it*. It implies that weird morphologies can spawn weird mentalities.[7] On the other hand, Hayles may be wrong about embodiment and substrate neutrality. Mental properties of things may, for all we know, depend on their computational properties because every other property depends on them as well. To conclude: the materiality argument suggests ways in which posthumans might be very inhuman. It is, if anything, an argument for speculative posthumanism, not an argument against it (I will pursue this idea further in Chapter 3, §§3.1, 3.2).

2.4 The anti-essentialist argument

I turn, finally, to a dismissal that is perhaps implicit in some of the arguments considered above but which is worth considering for its speculative payoff. I refer to this as *the anti-essentialist argument*.

The anti-essentialist objection to SP starts from a particular interpretation of the disjointness of the human and the posthuman. This is that the only thing that could distinguish the set of posthumans and the set of humans is that *all posthumans would lack some essential property of humanness* by virtue of their augmentation history. An essential property of a kind is a property that no member of that kind can be without. If humans are necessarily rational, for example, then it is a necessary truth that if x is human, then x is rational.[8] It follows that if there is no human essence – no properties that humans possess in all possible worlds – there can be no posthuman divergence or transcendence.

This is a potentially serious objection to speculative posthumanism because there seem to be plausible grounds for rejecting essentialism in the sciences of complexity or self-organization that underwrite many posthumanist prognostications. Some philosophers of biology hold that the interpretation of biological taxa most consonant with Darwinian evolution is that they are not kinds (i.e. properties) but individual populations (see §6.4 for a fuller discussion). An individual or proto-individual can undergo a self-organizing process, but an abstract kind or universal cannot. Thus, the argument goes, evolution happens to species *qua* individuals (or proto-individuals) not species *qua* kinds. To be biologically human on this view is *not* to exemplify some set of necessary and sufficient properties, but to be genealogically related to earlier members of the population of humans (Hull 1986).[9]

Clearly, if biological categories are not kinds and posthuman transcendence requires the technically mediated loss of properties essential to membership of some biological kind, posthuman transcendence envisaged by pre-critical posthumanism is metaphysically impossible.[10]

However, the anti-essentialist objection assumes that the only significant differences are differences in the essential properties demarcating natural kinds.

But why adhere to this philosophy of difference? The view that nature is articulated by differences in the instantiation of abstract universals sits poorly with the idea of an actively self-organizing nature underlying the leading edge cognitive and life sciences cited by Hayles, Haraway and other proponents of critical posthumanism. A view of difference consistent with self-organization would locate the engines of differentiation in those micro-components and structural properties whose cumulative activity generates the emergent regularities of complex systems (§5.4).

For example, we might adopt an immanent and particularist ontology of difference for which individuating boundaries are generated by local states of matter: such as differences in pressure, temperature, miscibility or chemical concentration. For immanent ontologies of difference, like the assemblage theory we explore in Chapters 5 and 6, the conceptual differences articulated in the natural language lexicons are asymmetrically dependent upon active individuating differences, not overbearing forms or transcendental subjects (Deleuze 1994; DeLanda 2002: 10).

In short: we can be anti-essentialists (if we insist) while being realists for whom the world is profoundly differentiated in a way that owes nothing to the transcendental causality of abstract universals, subjectivity or language.[11] But if anti-essentialism is consistent with the mind-independent reality of differences – including differences between forms of life – there is no reason to think that it is not compatible with the existence of a human–posthuman difference which subsists independently of our representations of them.

Looking forward

I have argued that critical posthumanists provide few convincing reasons for abandoning "pre-critical" posthumanism (SP).

The anti-essentialist argument just considered presupposes a model of difference that is ill-adapted to the sciences that critical posthumanists cite in favour of their naturalized deconstruction of the human subject.

The deconstruction of the humanist subject implied in the anti-humanist dismissal complicates rather than corrodes philosophical humanism – leaving open *the possibility of a radical differentiation of the human and the posthuman*. The technogenesis argument is just invalid. The materiality argument is based on metaphysical assumptions which, if true, would preclude only some scenarios for posthuman divergence while ramping up the weirdness factor for most others.

As we shall see in the following chapter, the main threat to SP is transcendental humanism since – in certain forms – it suggests that significantly powerful or self-optimizing forms of life would need psychologies or phenomenologies that conform to ours. Consequently, we shall explore transcendental humanism further in Chapter 3, considering some of its variants in the work of Kant (its originator), contemporary analytic philosophy, and phenomenology. In Chapter 4 I will develop some arguments that, I hope to show, unbind the constraints of transcendental anthropology.

However, this is just the beginning of an elaboration of SP and its philosophical implications. In Chapter 5 I will spell out the concept of what a posthuman is with greater precision in the form of the disconnection thesis. This will also develop an assemblage model of posthuman difference derived from DeLanda/Deleuze's account of immanent difference introduced in the last section. From there on we will be in a position to articulate the claim that posthumans would – for all their unbounded weirdness – be a kind of life.

Notes

1 The table specifies which operation the machine carries out when in a particular machine state (say, q_0) and a particular symbol is lying on the square currently being scanned. The table may, for example, specify that if the machine is in q_0 and a "0" is on the current square, then it should erase "0", replace it with a "1", move right, and enter another state (e.g. q_2). These simple "read", "erase", "write" operations can manipulate the contents of the tape, can generate an output corresponding to the value of a function when appropriately choreographed by the machine table – for example, the binary expression of a fraction.

2 Of course, even in classical cognitive science, the body and environment remain as "boundary conditions" for proper functioning of internal mental processes (Keijzer & Schouten 2007: 114).

3 This position has been explored in fiction in R. Scott Bakker's thriller *Neuropath* (2010) and in the work of philosophers such as Thomas Metzinger, whose views on what I call "dark phenomenology" will be considered in Chapter 4.

4 The notion of supervenience is used by non-reductive materialists to express the dependence of mental properties on physical properties without entailing their reducibility to the latter. Informally: M properties supervene on P properties if a thing's P properties determine its M properties. Suppose culinary properties supervene on physical properties: then if x is physically identical to y and x is tasty, y must be tasty.

5 We will also need to consider ethical complications arising from the temporal exposure of subjectivity to complex socio-technical systems in Chapters 7 and 8.

6 "Parity Principle. If, as we confront some task, a part of the world functions as a process which, were it to go on in the head, we would have no hesitation in accepting as part of the cognitive

process, then that part of the world is (for that time) part of the cognitive process" (Clark & Chalmers 1998: 8). The PP is, in large part, a trivial consequence of functionalism. If mental states are individuated by their roles, then only the role and not the location of a state is relevant to it being mental. It is also open to the objection that the functional roles relevant to the individuations of cognitive processes are not borne by external representations (Rupert 2009). However, I will not adjudicate on this debate here since it has little impact on my thesis.

7 The argument may militate against the transhumanist dreams of virtual immortality alluded to above, but, as many have pointed out, this is a humanist or "hyper-humanist" scenario, not a posthumanist one (see Badmington 2003).

8 Another way of putting this is to say that in any possible world in which humans exist they are rational. Other properties of humans may be purely "accidental" – for example, their colour or language. It is not part of the essence of humans that they speak English, for example. Insofar as speaking English is an accidental property of humans, there are possible worlds in which there are humans but no English speakers.

9 David Hull points out that the genealogical boundaries between species can be considerably sharper than boundaries in "character space" (Hull 1986: 4). The fact that nectar-feeding hummingbird hawk moths and nectar-feeding hummingbirds look and behave in similar ways does not invalidate the claim that they have utterly distinct lines of evolutionary descent (LaPorte 2004: 44).

10 This objection is overdetermined because the possibility of successfully implementing radical transhumanist policies seems incompatible with a stable human nature. If there are few cognitive or body invariants that could not – in principle – be modified with the help of some hypothetical NBIC technology – then transhumanism arguably presupposes that there are no such essential properties for humanness.

11 For an excellent but somewhat neglected exploration of this idea in the context of contemporary anti-realism, see Farrell (1996).

3 The edge of the human

Introduction

In Chapters 1 and 2 I suggested that one of the distinctions between SP and transhumanism is that the former position allows that our "wide human descendants" could have minds that are very different from ours and thus be unamenable to broadly humanist values or politics. Vinge's speculations about the technological singularity provides an example of a posthuman weird tale (§§1.3, 1.4). But maybe there are constraints on posthuman weirdness that would restrict any posthuman–human divergence of mind and value. The possibility of an ontological catastrophe resulting from posthuman technologies will be reduced. SP would be correspondingly "bounded" because the scope for posthuman difference would be much less than some hope or fear.

But if there are significant constraints on posthuman possibility, how are we to find out what they are?

One potential source of information might be our current knowledge of the physical world or of information processing and computation. I will argue that, in the absence of actual posthumans, there is no evidence for significant constraints in these areas.

This will motivate the search for other "future-proof" constraints on posthuman possibility that we can know before evidence about the nature of actual posthumans is in.

The most coherent philosophical account of such *a priori* knowledge is to be found in the post-Kantian transcendental tradition. Some transcendentalists claim that worlds must be thinkable or experienceable for beings like ourselves; entailing that the form of the world is correlated with the structure of human subjectivity (Meillassoux 2010). If there are reality-constraints imposed by transcendental anthropology, these must also constrain the scope of posthuman weirdness. Transcendental humanism thus entails an *anthropologically bounded* SP. This chapter will attempt to formulate a plausible set of transcendental constraints of posthuman possibility with the help of central thinkers in the transcendental tradition such as Kant, Davidson, Husserl and Heidegger. This serves as a prologue to Chapter 4 in which I will argue against anthropologically bounded posthumanism.

3.1 Bounds on posthuman possibility

I have argued that there are reasons for thinking that there could be nonhuman descendants of humans that have become nonhuman because of some technical alteration history. I have suggested that we should think of descent in "wide" terms in view of the likelihood that such relations will be technically mediated to an arbitrary degree. Finally, I have given reasons why the speculative posthumanist thesis SP does not commit us to a conception of the human that is unwarrantedly essentialist, which fails to reckon with the co-evolution of humans and technique, the nature of embodiment, or with the open-textured nature of subjectivity (§2.4 – this position will be honed considerably in Chapter 5). Some of the objections to SP promulgated by critical posthumanists have been shown to rest on confusion between SP and transhumanism, or on precipitate claims about the implications of theories such as deconstruction or embodied cognitive science (§2.1).

However, even given SP – given *that there could be posthumans* – it does not follow that every conceivable posthuman is a possible one. If some posthumans are impossible, that is presumably because there are real constraints on the kinds of beings that are possible in this world. If we could discover some of these constraints, we could begin to narrow down the field of our possible technological successors. If any of these are necessary constraints, we will also be able to say something about what posthumans would have to be like. Thus exploring potential constraints on posthuman life seems like a method for developing a more positive account of the posthuman even in the face of their dated nonexistence.

We can make this idea more precise by considering the collection of physically and technically possible histories whereby posthuman wide descendants of humans could emerge on this planet – *posthuman possibility space* (PPS).

Recall that wide descent is technically mediated to an arbitrary degree. So PPS could include many different paths to posthumanity corresponding, perhaps, to prospective NBIC technologies. The only thing that these itineraries need share is that they are the result of feasible technologies. For example, if faster than light (FTL) travel is impossible in our universe – as general relativity suggests – then no posthumans will be able to FTL. If machine AGI is – for whatever reason – impossible, then PPS will not include any paths to posthumanity involving AGI, and so on (§1.2).

As yet we know very little about PPS. We saw in Chapter 1 that it is legitimate to conceive becoming not human in essentialist or anti-essentialist terms. That is, we may think that there are properties necessary to being human that posthumans lack. But we may also deny essentialism and consider human–posthuman differences to be historically emergent relations of some kind.

Though we know nothing about them, as yet, we can think of these possible posthumans as corresponding to the posthuman states of the world in PPS.

For all we know, PPS contains nothing at all.[1] This would mean that posthumans – however conceivable – could not occur in a world like our own. Alternatively, it may be thronging with inhuman histories. Perhaps you will occupy one of these histories, either because you will become posthuman or you will encounter them in your future.

At this point in our investigation, it need not concern us which of these alternative scenarios is true. All that we need assume is that PPS exists and is either empty or nonempty.

3.2 Natural constraints on PPS

Whether PPS is empty or nonempty depends on what is possible in our world or any world whose structure or laws are similar. I will refer to this broad notion of possibility as "natural possibility".

However, SP is primarily concerned with technological possibility. A technologically impossible posthuman would be impossible *period*. Not every naturally possible state need be technologically possible. For example, sustained nuclear fusion might only be producible by gravitational confinement in a star.

It might seem that some technological possibilities can be discerned *a priori* – by consulting reliable conceptual "intuitions" about the extendible powers of current technologies. For example, a being like Skynet – the genocidal military computer in James Cameron's *Terminator* films – seems a plausible occupant of a PPS timeline; whereas Sauron, the supernatural dark lord of Tolkien's *Lord of the Rings*, does not. However, since the work of Saul Kripke in the 1970s many philosophers have come to accept that there are *a posteriori* natural possibilities and necessities that are only discoverable empirically. That light has a maximum velocity from any reference frame upsets common-sense intuitions about relative motion and could not have been discovered by reflecting on pre-relativistic concepts of light (Fine 2002).

Claims about hypothetical technological possibility may be as vulnerable to refutation as naïve physics. States like the US and China employ computers to co-ordinate military activities so a Skynet seems the more plausible posthuman antagonist. But the fact that there are computers but no dark lords does not entail that their capacities could be extended in any way we imagine. Light bulbs exist as well as computers, but maybe a Skynet is no more technologically possible than Byron the intelligent light bulb in Thomas Pynchon's fabulist novel *Gravity's Rainbow* (see §5.6).

This prescription for epistemic modesty is supported by a recent study of past predictions about the future of artificial intelligence. Stuart Armstrong and Kaj Sotala have collated expert predictions regarding the nature and timeline of key advances in AI, suggesting that these are contradictory and barely distinguishable from the predictionsArmstrong & Sotala 2012). On this basis, they argue that it remains unclear whether revolutions in AI development will require just more hard work and money ("grind") or some new "insight" (pp. 64–5).If it is the latter, any predictions about shape and nature of the machine minds of the posthuman future are liable to be highly error-prone.

Perhaps drawing on *a posteriori* physical possibilities that have been discovered as our guide to technological possibility will give us clues about some possible occupants of PPS as well as some possible constraints on membership. Anders Sandberg (1999) suggests that any intelligent system will need to store and transform information in a physical medium.[2] Perhaps the physical limits of data processing will apply to all denizens of PPS.

There are physical constraints on the data that can be stored in a given kind of medium, and constraints on the speed and accuracy with which that information can be transformed. According to Eric Drexler, computer memories that code bits at the atomic level may enable data to be stored at a density of approximately a billion million million bits per cubic metre if the storage medium approached the density of diamond (Drexler 1992, cited in Sandberg 1999). MP3 players and smartphones are technically possible because hard disks can store in the order of ten billion bits per cubic metre (Walter 2005). Thus current data storage operates many orders of magnitude below the theoretical limit available in ordinary matter.[3]

Any physical limits on information storage density and processor speed will presumably constrain all occupants of PPS unless fundamental physical laws or powers can change. These numbers suggest that current information processing capacities may be many, many orders of magnitude below the maximum allowed in nature.

Even apart from physical constraints of the kind just mentioned, one can ask what kinds of system can perform such computation. Jiří Wiedermann cites results from his research suggesting "amorphous systems" made up of independent units forming into ad hoc networks (e.g. tiny nanomachines or genetically engineered microbes) could have universal computing power: that is, in principle, such a system could compute any program that a universal Turing machine could compute (Wiedermann 2012: 83–4; §2.1).

However, as noted above, not all programs that are computable (in the Turing sense) are *tractably computable*. Some computations – like generating all the sequences of sixty different things – may be simple enough to program, but still take longer than the lifetime of physical universe to complete (Biermann 1997: 374–5). Inferences that take account of holistic properties of representations may – for all we know – be computable in a purely mathematical sense[4] but the relevant programs may not be performable under real world time constraints (§2.1; Horgan & Tienson 1994; Eliasmith 2002).

Given these uncertainties about the computational basis of mind, it is hard to derive strong *a priori* constraints on the contents of PPS from constraints on physical information processing or efficient computation. The results reviewed here suggest only that there may be natural scope for information processors that are much faster and fatter than humans.

Are there any philosophical principles that suggest how the space of possible minds might be constrained by factors over and above the physical constraints considered?

We have already considered two opposing accounts of the relationship between embodiment and mind in our discussion of Hayles's materiality claim in the last chapter. She asserts that a computational emulation of a being with a mind – which matches the causal-functional roles of all that being's components (e.g. neurons, inter-neuronal connections, and chemical modulators) – could never duplicate its mental states. The opposing view, of course, is that mental states could be duplicated if the being's components were emulated at a sufficiently fine grain.

Hayles fails to support the materiality claim; but *it is* supportable. The argument assumes a metaphysical distinction between the *dispositions* or *powers* of a thing and the way in which those dispositions are manifested in disparate contexts. As John Heil points out, we ordinarily describe a disposition by its manifestation – for example, elasticity, sonorousness, solubility, irritability, though the disposition itself could have manifested differently in a different environment.[5] How a power gets to manifest itself thus depends on triggering conditions (see Heil 2003: 83). Thus it does not follow from the fact that we describe dispositions in terms of what they do that they are just the sum of what they do; or even that powers claims are equivalent to conditional claims about possible manifestations (Molnar 2006: 83–92).

It follows that a system whose input–output behaviour was relevantly similar to a human might still have different powers to a human by virtue of its different composition and structure.[6] For example, suppose that my brain and body were emulated to a fine level of detail on "computronium" – a form of programmable matter like the materials anticipated by Drexler – which encodes information at enormous densities and allows information processing with speeds several orders of magnitude greater than any current information processor on Earth. Call this functional duplication $David_C$.

Let us assume a substrate neutrality sufficient for consciousness, intentionality and other key mental properties to be realized on non-organic as well as organic substrates (§1.3). $David_C$ might start out with mental states with a similar structure and content – the same beliefs, desires, etc. – as my biological duplicate. However, $David_C$'s computronium body is capable of thinking a billion times faster than those of his biological friends. So, rather than engage in tiresome social interaction with them, he delegates his human public relations to a further (human-speed) emulation $David_E$ running on a tiny volume of his computronium core. Even if $David_C$ starts out as a functional duplicate of David Roden, his powers would be significantly different by virtue of his accelerated thought processes. Once $David_C$ includes $David_E$ as a public relations module, we no longer have a system that is plausibly identical to David Roden at a functional or computational level. Because of his $David_E$ homunculus he could outwardly behave much like I behave in human social contexts (responding the same way to the same questions or prompts from his human friends) but his appearance would be deceptive.

If the time-window required for thinking is relevant to making assessments of psychological similarity, then people running on radically different computational substrates are unlikely to be psychologically similar because their powers – including their ability to alter their own functional structure – will be different (Chapter 6). We can only produce psychologically similar copies of ourselves on alternative substrates where the powers of those copies are relevantly similar (call this the *power-identity assumption* – PIA).

The PIA implies that creating a functional duplicate of a human on a more or less efficient computational substrate would not necessarily duplicate their psychology (see Eliasmith 2002). If this is right, people-emulations on digital computers or other non-biological substrates may be different in ways that we cannot yet predict because the powers that they have in virtue of differences in computational speed or efficiency are not ours.

As observed in the previous chapter, the metaphysical constraint represented by PIA does not make the future shapes of mind any easier to predict – if true, it is metaphysically and ethically salutary but provides no hard information about PPS. It suggests that predicting posthuman lives is harder because minds embodied in different substrates will not be psychologically identical (see §5.6).

To be sure, if fine differences in substrates were always relevant to gross behaviour, computer modelling would be impossible. Reality would not be decomposable into chunks whose stability in the face of lower level differences can be assumed (DeLanda 2011: 13–14).[7] However, short of emulating a sophisticated mind on some actual computational substrate, it remains unclear whether powers-differences between biological humans and their uploaded or emulated counterparts would be negligible in technologically feasible cases.

3.3 Kant and transcendental humanism

If we seek bounds on posthuman weirdness, perhaps we should look for knowledge that is truly *a priori* knowledge: non-trivial information about the future that can never be disconfirmed by subsequent evidence. By "non-trivial" I mean that such knowledge would have to ascribe properties to posthumans not already implied in some concept of posthumanity we have constructed. If we specify in advance that posthumans are nonhumans, it follows trivially that no posthuman (thus conceived) will be human.

The claim that we could have non-trivial *a priori* knowledge of the nonhuman world runs contrary to the minimal realist assumptions that: 1) the nonhuman world exists and 2) its nature or structure is independent of our representations of it (Devitt 1991: 32–3). If the world is mind-independent, as the realist claims, it can always be other than minds represent it as being.

Descartes' evil demon thought experiment is, of course, one way in which we can make the realist idea of the autonomy of reality vivid (§1.4).

Kant – who believed that the *a priori* is necessary for science – bites this bullet by rejecting the realist construal of knowledge as bearing reference to a mind-independent reality, as well as the sceptical problematic that arises from it. His startlingly original conclusion is that *objects must conform to their representations in certain ways to be knowable at all.* Meanwhile subjectivity – in particular, our experience of being a unitary self over time – is only possible if it refers to objects (Kant 1978: B133). Mind and world are thus not mutually independent, as Descartes thought, but inseparably related. "Transcendental" knowledge is the part of philosophy that is concerned with the subjective conditions for the human–world relation (B25).

Kant holds that knowledge would not be possible unless the transcendental subject already interprets its experience as about a common, objective world. Descartes thought that knowledge could be founded by retreating to an inner world whose ideas are clear and immediately evident to the experiencer (§1.4). But Kant denies that we could be aware of mental events prior to giving some of them objective content. We cannot be aware of changes in our "inner" states, according to Kant, unless we can identify something outside ourselves to which these occur (1978: A181/B224–5; Guyer 2006: 106–08). This objective purport comes about by *synthesizing* our disparate sensations into conceptually ordered experiences using high-level concepts known as "categories".

For example, to observe that a melting block of ice persists across the changes in its sensory appearance, I apply the concept *substance*. To judge that these changes result from exposure to a heat source, I use the concept *cause*. The first synthesis makes my experience of change possible by attributing it to a persistent thing. The second gives succession a deter- minate order in time, since if a relation between events is causal, one follows as a necessary consequence of the other (Longuenesse 2005: 25, 158). Without this categorical ordering, these experience could only concern disparate sensations or features; which is just to say that they would not be experiences of a being aware of its mental life or the world around it (see §4.1).

This provides the transcendental warrant for the Kantian argument. If the application of the categories is a condition of self-awareness in human subjects, then from the fact that we are self-conscious we can infer that the empirical world of ice blocks, galaxies and prospective posthumans does indeed conform to human categories.

Kant accepts that there are mind-independent things-in-themselves – *noumena* – that do not conform to this human-imposed structure. How- ever, he denies that we have knowledge of them because we only have access to the empirical world generated by our categorical activity. These are ineluctably ordered in a single space and time, which, he argues, are the outer and inner forms of human sensory experience rather than mind-independent "things-in-themselves" (Kant 1978: B37, A23). So the properties of things that we can know about are not properties of *noumena* but properties of *phenomena* – categorically ordered things in space and time.

For transcendental synthesis to occur there must be an entirely non- representational relationship between categories and the content of experience, since the sensations organized by synthesis have no objective content of their own – the category cannot match or conform to the sen- sory manifold it unifies. Kant's explanation is that the mind applies a "schema", a rule for ordering experience that conforms to a concept (Kant 1978: A140/B180). Truth, then, is not a correspondence between an inner mental realm and an outer nonmental one, as it is for the realist. For the judgement "The popcorn has been cooked" to be true there must be both empirical cooking and transcendental cooking. The popcorn needs to have been heated. But it must also be possible for any human observer to generate an experience that would allow us to concur with this claim (Braver 2007: 50).

As Braver points out, this interpretation of truth as intersubjective agreement would fail to justify belief in a unique empirical reality unless transcendental subjectivity is stable across observers. Suppose you have an alien cognitive nature that employs different categories to connect your perceptions. None of the judgements I could make about my world could be true of your world – or vice versa. We would experience distinct worlds without common points of reference. Attributing a common human nature to subjects means humans cook up a shared phenomenal world even if they do not hook up to noumena (*ibid.*: 49).

Thus, as advertised in Chapter 1, Kant's position is a drastically new form of humanism: transcendental humanism. It implies that humans are distinctive in virtue of being the transcendental architects of the human–world correlation.

3.4 Pragmatism and phenomenology

Philosophers who followed in Kant's transcendental footsteps – for example, Hegel, Husserl, Heidegger and Davidson – have advanced recognizably transcendental claims which identify the conditions of possible knowledge or meaning with facts about human subjectivity. However, most of these successors have argued that the idea of the noumenal beyond is unintelligible. The only conception of reality we have is of one we can know and access. For example, modern phenomenologists claim that transcendental philosophy must devote itself to the investigation and understanding of "what appears" – bracketing speculative assumptions of the kind found in realist metaphysics. Phenomenology does not treat appearances as mental copies of mind-independent noumena (Heidegger 1962: 51; Braver 2007: 182–5). For Heidegger and for Husserl the phenomenon (that which appears) "shows itself in itself".

Now, making sense of mind-dependence turns out to be as hard as making sense of mind-independence. Kant's original account of transcendental subjectivity is notoriously problematic. For example, Kant admits that he cannot explain how a schema imposes form on an intrinsically formless manifold of sensation.

However, modern pragmatism, like phenomenology, seems well placed to avoid this "scheme content" dualism (Davidson 1984: 183–98). Pragmatists are committed to the claim that conceptual and intellectual powers are grounded in our practical abilities rather than in relations between mental entities and what they represent (Brandom 2006). So while pragmatists buy into the Kantian claim that concepts are cooks, not hooks, they are leery of all the "transcendental psychology" that goes with it (but see §4.1). Modern pragmatists argue that conceptual understanding is exhibited in our practical grasp of public norms of reasoning rather than in mysterious agencies of the mind (Brandom 2001: 6; Sellars 1963).

This results – arguably – in a significant gain in intelligibility and practical import because concepts are now implicated in human social life (Rorty 1980; Levine 2010: 582–3). Language is not a medium for expressing our inner selves or outer realities, but a social matrix that can be revised by the proposing of new paths through the space of reasons (Rorty 1989: 18–19).

3.5 Discursive agency

Pragmatism is an attractive and widely held doctrine because it promises to elucidate difficult notions like meaning and truth in terms of human activities rather than problematic transcendent metaphysics. It is precisely because pragmatism elaborates transcendental humanism plausibly that we need to consider its implications for posthuman possibility.

The first consequence of the pragmatist idea that language is the matrix in which we cooperatively form and revise reasons is what I will call the *discursive agency thesis* (DAT). DAT asserts that agents must have the capacity to use public language in social contexts. If true, DAT would be a significant *a priori* constraint on SP since, until now, we have not assumed that posthumans would have to be language-using or social.

The argument for discursive agency falls out of the broader pragmatist claim that the rational coordination of beliefs, desires and intentions is a social skill:

1) An agent is a being that acts for reasons.
2) To act for reasons an agent must have desires or intentions to act.
3) An agent cannot have desires or intentions without beliefs.
4) The ability to have beliefs *requires a grasp of what belief is* since to believe is also to understand "the possibility of being mistaken" (metacognitive claim).
5) A grasp of the possibility of being mistaken is only possible for language users (linguistic constitutivity).

So a being that lacks the capacity for language cannot be an agent.

Psychological states such as beliefs, desires and intentions (along with hopes, wishes, suppositions, etc.) are commonly referred to as "propositional attitudes" because they are expressed as an attitude towards the content of a declarative sentence embedded in a "that" clause (for example, I believe that *Lima is the capital of Peru.* You hope that *Manchester United will win the European Champions League*).

Many philosophers take propositional attitude psychology to be the core conceptual framework with which humans predict and interpret each other in interpersonal life. Davidson accepts this, but argues that the social activity of attributing and evaluating beliefs serves a function comparable to the transcendental categories in Kant (§3.3). It allows us to understand objectivity. For Davidson, our grasp of objectivity and truth falls out of the "triangular" situation in which "two (or more) creatures each correlate their own reactions to external phenomena" (Davidson 2001b: 129).

This idea informs the first of the two strong assumptions in the DAT argument, which I have referred to as "the metacognitive claim" because it asserts that having mental states *about* mental states (in this case, a concept of what a belief is) is essential to having beliefs. For Davidson, belief is an attitude of "holding" true some proposition: for example, that there is a cat behind that wall. But if belief is *holding true* it seems to require a grasp of truth and falsity and thus of belief itself. Thus we cannot believe anything without grasping that others could have beliefs about the same topic (Davidson 1984: 170; 2001b: 104 – though see §4.1).

This leads us to Premise 5 (linguistic constitutivity). For Davidson, the intersubjective triangle between the subject, another person and the world is only accessible to a being which can actively attribute beliefs (Davidson 2001b: 129; Briscoe 2007: 140–41). But for triangulation to occur, there must be a common framework in which two or more beings can compare and evaluate their respective takes on the world through dialogue. According to Davidson, language provides this dialogic framework for representing differences, similarities and relations between beliefs:

> Our manner of attributing attitudes ensures that all the expressive power of language can be used to make such distinctions. One can believe that Scott is not the author of *Waverley* while not doubting that Scott is Scott; one can want to be the discoverer of a creature with a heart without wanting to be the discoverer of a creature with a kidney. One can intend to bite into the apple in the hand without intending to bite into the only apple with a worm in it; and so forth. The intensionality we make so much of in the attribution of thoughts is very hard to make much of when speech is not present. The dog, we say, knows that its master is home. But does it know that Mr Smith (who is his master), or that the president of the bank (who is that same master), is home? We have no real idea how to settle, or make sense of, these questions.
>
> (Davidson 1984: 163)

However, if language is necessary for belief, and beliefs are necessary for agency, Davidson's position is both transcendentally humanist and strongly anthropocentric. Language is a condition of possibility for rationality, objective thought and agency (rationality is a "social trait", Davidson claims).

Non-language using animals may be sentient but, as Robert Brandom puts it, they are not *sapient* (Brandom 2001: 157; Wennemann 2013: 47). They cannot be answerable to reasons, identify themselves as the thinkers of several thoughts over time, or have any grasp of being in the world of objective things.

Davidson's account of linguistically mediated rationality thus reformulates the transcendental humanist thesis that humans constitute the world and are not just things in it. This process is now seen in terms of inter-subjective dialogue rather than Kant's hoary transcendental psychology. We have a relationship to a world only if we trade propositions in common linguistic coin. Davidson does not think that this communicative structure requires common linguistic conventions; but it does require the capacity to impute reasons to others' verbal behaviour, even where, as with Lewis Carroll, James Joyce or Mrs Malaprop, their speech deviates from the norm (Davidson 1986). Humans are animals with the social capacity to be "gripped" by concepts and norms of reasoning (Brassier 2011).

The DAT implies that the occupants of posthuman possibility space (PPS) will need to be subjects of discourse if they are to be agents. Daryl Wennemann makes this assumption in this book *Posthuman Personhood*. Wennemann adopts the traditional Kantian idea that agency consists in the capacity to justify one's actions according to reasons and shared norms. For Wennemann, a person is a being able to "reflect on himself and his world from the perspective of a being sharing in a certain community" (Punzo 1969, cited in Wennemann 2013: 47). And this is a condition of posthuman agency as much as of human agency:

> In a posthuman age, the moral community is constituted by all beings of a kind that are capable of moral reflection and thus agency. Human beings are one such kind. There may be other kinds as well (computers, robots, aliens). So, to identify morally with the members of the moral community in a posthuman environment is to identify morally with all beings of a kind capable of agency.
>
> (Wennemann 2013: 49 – citation modified[8])

It follows that posthuman agents will need concepts, desires and intentions expressible in the social idiom of sentences: the full panoply of propositional attitudes. This is a problem if we still entertain the idea of the radically *weird* posthumans that Vinge holds out for in "The Coming Technological Singularity". For the DAT implies that we can know *a priori* that the *structure* of posthuman thought and agency would be discursive, even if posthumans have strange bodies or social habits. Such differences seem superficial in the light of the deep transcendental structures entailed by the DAT. After all, humans differ in gender, skin colour and physiognomy; and people from different cultures often live according to contrary conceptions of the good life. These differences are politically important in isolated cases where conceptions of the good life clash, or where sexists, racists and xenophobes make them so; but they do not run particularly deep. If so, it is hard to see how mere differences in appearance of substrate could have distinctive metaphysical or moral import attributed to SP, let alone carry the eldritch promise of the radical weird.

3.6 Pragmatism and anti-realism

Unlike Kantian transcendental philosophy, pragmatism seems compatible with the mind-independent *existence* of the world and thus with one half of realist claims that the nonmental world is existentially independent of our minds and has a nature independent of our cognitive activity (§3.3; Devitt 1991). After all, it is committed to practices and thus to their material supports like pencils and power lines. However, we shall see that pragmatism is not compatible with an independent nature because it implies that the way the world is articulated or "contoured" depends on discursive practices.

If so, pragmatism implies a second *a priori* constraint on PPS. If posthumans are agents and subjects of discourse (from DAT) their world is discursively articulated, even if the practices by which they carve up the world might differ from ours. In the next section I use considerations of mutual interpretability to argue that a pragmatist world is not an aggregate of things (lumps) but an open-textured "horizon" differentiated by the activity of speaking (human, posthuman, alien) subjects. This is clearly a form of what Meillassoux entitles *correlationism* (§1.4). It implies that posthuman and human lives would be co-correlated with the *same* world horizon.

In modern analytic philosophy the rejection of the second plank of realism inaugurated by Kant's turn is referred to as "anti-realism". We lack space to consider all the varieties of pragmatic anti-realism, so in what follows I'll consider a relatively clear cut anti-realist doctrine that Hilary Putnam refers to as "internal realism" (IR).

First, to understand why IR is not really realism, we need to introduce Putnam's influential analysis of traditional realism – or *metaphysical realism* (MR).

MR is not one thing, according to Putnam, but a bag of interrelated claims about the mind–world relationship. The key components of MR are 1) the *independence thesis*; 2) the *correspondence thesis*; 3) the *uniqueness thesis*.

The *independence thesis* states that there is a "fixed totality of mind-independent objects" (the world) (Putnam 1981: 49).

The *correspondence thesis* states that there are determinate reference relations between bits of language or mental representations and the bits of the world to which they refer.

The *uniqueness thesis* states that there is a single theory whose sentences correctly describe the states of these objects. This implies a singular correspondence between the terms belonging to this theory and the objects and properties that they refer to.

MR is a package deal. The correspondence thesis needs objects (independence) for the mental and linguistic bits to correspond to. There must be mind-independent objects for there to be a single correct way in which the One True Theory corresponds to the world (uniqueness entails independence and correspondence).

Putnam presents this idea in terms of a branch of mathematical logic known as "model theory". Model theory is an abstract way of understanding the links between formal languages and the "world" their sentences are about. A model is a set of objects. These can be material things like cats and elementary particles, or abstract objects like sets or numbers. In model theory, a formal language (a collection of uninterpreted symbols organized by a grammar and rules of inference) is given an interpretation by assigning elements or subsets of the model to its symbols. This assignment is called an *interpretation function*.

In model-theoretic terms, MR is just the claim that there is a unique description of the world *hooked up to that world by a single interpretation function*. The singularity of the interpretation function is crucial because if there was more than one way of interpreting the terms of the One True Theory there would not be a single correct description of the world. Uniqueness (thus MR) would fail.

What virtues could help us distinguish the One True Theory from competitors? According to Putnam, it would need to satisfy the "operational constraints" that ideally rational inquirers would impose on such a theory. If one imagines science progressing to an ideal limit at which no improvements can be made in its explanatory power, coherence, elegance or simplicity, etc., then the One True Theory would have to be as acceptable to ideally rational enquirers as that theory (Putnam 1981: 30, 33).

However, Putnam argues that even if we were to find a theory that satisfied these constraints at the ideal limit, it would be possible to find another with the same scientific virtues just as true as it is and equally as consistent with our practices of speech and justification. Thus – failing other facts that could distinguish an ideal theory as God's Own – uniqueness fails and, with it, MR.

Putnam's argument against MR is supported by a theorem of model theory. This states that for any language whose referring expressions are mapped onto objects in a range of possible worlds (each associated with a "fixed totality of objects") by an interpretation function I, there will always be a second interpretation function J that maps the same expressions onto different objects picked from the same world which preserves the truth/falsity of all the sentences of the language (pp. 217–18). Thus the general term "cat" might refer to the set of cats under I but to the set of cherries under J. This will not affect the truth value of a sentence like "Fred is a cat" so long as the new interpretation J maps "Fred" onto a member of the set of cherries.[9] So "Fred is a cat" will remain true under J but will mean something different.

Thus even a theory that satisfies the ideal of operational virtue is convertible to a second *equally good* theory in the same world by shuffling around the meanings of its symbols. The second theory is equally good because the truth values[10] of all of its sentences in the language are retained under J. Any observation sentence that supports the theory under I will support it under J. Any true prediction that follows from the theory under I will follow under J, etc.

If this is right, for every true theory of the world, there is at least one other true theory. Metaphysical realism fails because uniqueness fails: even God, it seems, cannot have a preferred way of describing the world.

Some might object that uniquely intended interpretations can be mentally imposed by our beliefs or ideas. So on this account theories are not interpretable formal languages but intrinsically meaningful thoughts in our minds. This might appear to block the conversion of the first good theory to another because the model-theoretic argument applied to languages, not to thoughts.

However, it can be objected that this response just assumes there can be a "magic language" of self-interpreting mental signs (Wheeler 2000: 3). But the same argument can be applied to a thought as can be applied to the terms of a formal language so long as we assume that thoughts are expressed in some medium or other (e.g. "mentalese"). Thoughts, on this account, are just mental signs. Mental signs do not interpret themselves and wear their meaning on their sleeves any more than anything else (Putnam 1983: 207). The problem is not that there are no correspondences between signs and things. There are too many to secure a unique interpretation-independent meaning for even the best of theories (Putnam 1981: 73; Moran 2000: 78). Thus appealing to "inner" or mental signs to fix the intended meanings of our theories reruns the problem of indeterminacy all over again.

So, for Putnam, the possibility of gerrymandering new interpretations from old implies that MR is false. There is no single theory that uniquely describes the realist's mind-independent world and thus no non-interpretation-relative way the world is.

Rather than aspiring to the idealized God's Eye View of metaphysical realism, Putnam argues we should recognize that truth, reference and objectivity are properties that our languages have because of "our" social practices of inference, confirmation and observation (pragmatism again). To assert "'Cow' refers to cows" is not to make a claim about some determinate relationship between word and world but to make a normative claim about how a competent speaker of English should use "cow" around these parts (Putnam 1978: 128, 136). This does not reflect some metaphysical insight into the mind–world relationship but our tacit grasp of a particular form of human life (p. 137).

Before going on to consider the implications of this anti-realist position for pragmatist conceptions of understanding and worldhood, it should be pointed out that there are lines of attack open to those who wish to retain some version of realism. Some, like Fodor, argue that there are semantic truths about what refers to what that are interpretation-independent (Fodor 1990; Hale & Wright 1999). Thus the existence of alternative interpretations of a theory does not entail that they are equally acceptable. Perhaps the world is differentiated in one way rather than another and a One True Theory would hook onto those differences regardless of whether alternative referents were assignable to its sub-sentential terms. For example, any theory could be given a model consisting of sets and set-theoretical structures. It does not follow that set theory is just as good an interpretation of some part of physical theory as one which posits elementary particles or fields.

More interestingly, one might claim that MR is just a logician's caricature of realism to which the metaphysical realist need not be committed. For example, Devitt denies that realism is really committed to uniqueness – the view that there is exactly "one true and complete description of the world" (Devitt 1984: 229). We might also demur from the assumption that the world consists of objects or only objects that enter into semantic relationships with bits of language or mind. Structural realists, for example, argue that reality *is* structure and that this is precisely what approximately similar theories capture – regardless of their official ontological divergences (Ladyman & Ross 2007: 94–5). Some speculative ontologies deny the correspondence assumption, holding that the world contains entities that cannot be fully represented in any theory: for example, powers, Deleuzean intensities, or Harman-style objects (see §6.6).

Perhaps, the correspondence assumption just replicates the Kantian view that entities must conform to linguistic modes of representation

(§3.3). If, as I argue in Chapter 4, we have no secure grounds to make such wide-ranging transcendental claims, then the scope of Putnam's argument can also be deconstructed from within.

It is not clear, however, that any of these responses are open to pragmatists, for whom formal semantic facts like those captured in model theory are ultimately mystified expressions of our communal or idiomatic practices. So I want to consider how pragmatists might square the failure of uniqueness with the requirement that communication and interpretation take place in a shared world. Is the pragmatist entitled to a unique world and, if so, what manner of world is it?

3.7 From pragmatism to phenomenology: Davidson, Husserl and Heidegger

Putnam's anti-realism implies that we have no better conception of what the truth of a sentence or belief consists in other than its acceptance by ideally rational inquirers when all the evidence is in. Davidson is on record as rejecting this epistemic conception because it appears to relativize truth to languages (Davidson 2001b: 186–7). However, whether this charge is justified is irrelevant for our purposes. Davidson, as we saw in §3.5, is committed to the claim that each believer has the concept of an objective world about which she or others can have "true" or "false" beliefs:

> Communication depends on each communicator having, and correctly thinking that the other has, the concept of a shared world, an intersubjective world. But the concept of an intersubjective world is the concept of an objective world, a world about which each communicator can have beliefs.
>
> (Davidson 2001b: 105)

Putnam's conception of truth at the limit of enquiry may (or may not) be weaker than Davidson's, but *it has to furnish a conception of an intersubjective world*. For grasping it must allow me to understand that my beliefs may not be confirmed under ideal conditions by smarter creatures with access to more evidence. The concepts of truth and intersubjectivity are thus as interconnected in Putnam as in Davidson.

This is also the case with Davidson's account of meaning. Davidson thinks that the best way to illuminate the notion of meaning in philosophy is to characterize what we know that allows us to interpret fellow language users. Davidson claims that an interpretation can be represented using the logical machinery devised by Alfred Tarksi to derive the truth conditions for any sentence in a formal language (Davidson 1984: 17–36).

The argument for the adequacy of truth theories for encoding our linguistic competence is justified in terms of a thought experiment which envisages a field linguist interpreting an alien language from scratch: the ideal of *radical interpretation* (pp. 125–37).

Davidson argues that the criterion of hermeneutic success in radical interpretation is that the truth theory correctly predicts circumstances of utterance for arbitrary utterances by stating what would make them come true. For example, a correct truth theory for English would state (in its language) that the sentence "Snow is white" is true if and only if snow is white.

If Davidsonian truth theories capture a competent speaker's grasp of meaning, no part of a language – for example, the predicate " … is white" – can be understood unless we understand the truth conditions of all the sentence in which it occurs ("Snow is white", "Cotton is white", etc.). But the connections ramify, since these sentences will also depend on other parts ("Snow") whose meaning requires still other truth conditions to be spelled out ("Snow is a form of water").

The upshot of this is the holist thesis (familiar from Saussure's structuralism and some versions of inferential role semantics) that the meaning of any term in a language depends on its interrelationships with all the other terms in a language (Davidson 1984: 21; Evnine 1991: 120; Brandom 2007).

Davidson's meaning holism also implies *psychological* holism for, as the DAT implies, sentence meaning and psychological content are interdependent (Malpas 1992: 86–7). Our capacity for belief and agency depends on our capacity to interpret utterances in the light of novel speech behaviour. No belief content and no content of any other psychological state can be fixed in isolation:

> If someone is glad that, or notices that, or remembers that, or knows that, the gun is loaded, then he must believe that the gun is loaded. Even to wonder whether the gun is loaded, or to speculate on the possibility that the gun is loaded, requires the belief, for example, that a gun is a weapon, that it is a more or less enduring physical object, and so on. There are good reasons for not insisting on any particular list of beliefs that are needed if a creature is to wonder whether a gun is loaded. Nevertheless, it is necessary that there be endless interlocked beliefs. The system of such beliefs identifies a thought by locating it in a logical and epistemic space.
>
> (Davidson 1984: 156–7)

One of the important (and contested) conclusions that Davidson derives from the metatheory of radical interpretation is that a prospective interpreter must adopt a regulative principle of charity by assuming that speakers of the language under interpretation are rational and not systematically mistaken. Were speakers systematically duped about their world, their public utterances would reveal nothing about their truth conditions or their beliefs. Charity is not an ethical embrace of cultural otherness but a recognition that the mind needs the world to furnish its content (Davidson 1984: 137). Descartes' *internalist* claim that we could be locked in our minds by an Evil Demon (ditto: mad neuroscientists or godlike aliens from another reality) is incoherent (§1.4). Although any particular belief can turn out false, massive error would deprive us of the transactions with things that give our beliefs worldly purport (Davidson 2001b: 153).

As well as opposing scepticism, Davidson's account seems to furnish an argument against the possibility of radically alien minds: no alien conceptual scheme, it seems, could be so strange as to resist interpretation since, as in the case of global scepticism, such beings *would lack the rational and coherent environmental transactions that could qualify them as thinkers at all* (§§5.7, 8.1). So, again, Vinge's tremulous speculations about radical weirdness seem off the mark.

Davidson's semantics, then, entails that the grounds for adhering to semantic theories are exhausted by the public facts about use accessible to a radical interpreter, and thus that incompatible theories of meaning could be equally consistent with the same observational data about what folk say, when. But if that is right, what meaning can be attached to the "shared world" about which speakers compare and contrast beliefs?

The obvious and intuitive answer is to respond that the shared world is just all the things there are. However, this universe of things would be raw material for interpreting a worldview via the incorporation of its members into different models. Both thinkers accept that there is no pragmatic way of ruling out the construction of multiple theories in line with Putnam's model-theoretic argument (see Davidson 1984: 235, 239–40). There could be (if we accept Putnam's metaphysical assumptions) no uniquely true theory related to it and thus we can make no sense of the idea that the unique, shared world is the collection of things in it.

Perhaps we might hope to live with this – accepting that the world is a determinate collection of lumps interpretable according to different lights. But this assumes without justification that the second-order vocabulary of terms like "object", "number" or "set" is uniquely assigned somehow even if first-order terms like "cat" and "cherry" are subject to disparate assignments. But which practices are supposed to "fix" the meanings of terms like "object"? As Putnam points out:

> "Object" itself has many uses, and as we creatively invent new uses of words, we find that we can speak of "objects" that were not 'values of any variable' in any language we previous spoke. (The invention of "set theory" by Cantor is a good example of this.)
>
> (Putnam 1988: 120)

Thus the indeterminacy that arises from the pragmatist conception of meaning applies recursively to the understanding of worldhood. Saying that the world is a model or a collection of lumps does not, as we had hoped, fix the contours of the real in a way that could explicate the idea of "world" presupposed by the possibility of radical interpretation and discursive subjectivity.

The claim that our shared world is *not* a lump presents obvious difficulties. First, radical interpretation means determining things like cats and rocks that form the topics of beliefs and statements. Thus this non-thing-like world must be compatible with the existence of determinable objects while not *being* those objects.

Such a world must also be unique in order to be shared. This is because, according to pragmatist theories of meaning such as Davidson's, agents qualify as believers by virtue of publicly interpretable transactions with a shared environment. If there are ghosts or intelligent cosmic dust clouds, then their actions might leave few detectable traces that humans can attune to. But such traces would have to be *interpretable in principle* by any intelligent interpreter given unbounded resources or time (see §§5.7, 8.1).

Thus a shared world in which the discursive subject operates must contain determinables and interpretables (texts) and it must be unique.

What could the shared world be if *not* a lump? Well, one plausible proposal derives from the holism thesis according to which every utterance or belief content is fixed by its relations to all the others (see above). These relations cannot be given in the way that the world according to MR is given. They are potentially infinite and also subject to differing but equally valid interpretations.

Some readers of Davidson – notably Jeff Malpas (1999) and Bjorn Ramberg (1989) – have employed the phenomenological idea of a horizon to explicate the idea of the world that underlies this pragmatic, interpretation-based account of meaning and mind.

As we saw, phenomenology is concerned with things as appearances and the conditions of that appearing. One general structure of givenness acknowledged by all phenomenological traditions is that a thing appears in a "wider structure of possible appearing" (Malpas 1999: 266). For example, Husserl claims that any perception of a thing is partial. If I see a hammer, I see it from a certain viewpoint, or hear it falling off a workbench as the cat passes by. If I think of it, I may represent it as a force amplifier or a birthday present. However, each thought or experience implies the possibility of nonactual perspectives. The hammer cannot be reduced to any of these: it is not determinate but, rather, *determinable* since its objectivity consists of being always *in excess* of its appearances (Mooney 1999). According to Husserl, this opening up of transcendence is made possible by the complex nature of temporal presence, which always carries the anticipatory horizon of a new "now" (we will consider this account critically in §4.2).

In *Donald Davidson and the Mirror of Meaning*, Malpas argues that interpretation must have this horizontal structure. All interpretation occurs in a context fixed by certain interests and projects. Any particular project can be frustrated or break down (Malpas 1992: 128). Any project must, moreover, open onto the constitution of a new project, just as each view of the hammer implies the possibility of other views. Thus it is a normative assumption of this "interpretationist" position that each project of understanding is "nested" within further possible projects which extend to the totality of the psychological at an ideal limit.

This normative interleaving of interpretative projects is correlatively an interleaving of *things*. As we have seen, the pragmatist account of meaning cannot easily make sense of a *uniquely determinate* world with determinate representations of all the things in it. Beliefs cannot be identified independently of the determinables that believers interact with. By the same token, the identification of salient collections of objects and events occurs against the background of the interpreter's experience and interests. The nested structure of projects described by Malpas thus constitutes a plausible candidate for a non-reified "world" – a world not of things, but of potential "correlations" between intentional agents and determinable objects.

However, this interleaving is only intelligible if we assume each project to have a hermeneutic structure referred to as "fore-having" within the hermeneutic tradition. Each interpretation must potentially fan out onto future revisionary interpretations (Caputo 1984: 158). Without an appeal to anticipatory structure, there is little content that can be given to the idea of a single intersubjective world that Davidson and the other pragmatic-interpretationists must appeal to.

It is precisely at this point, according to Malpas, that the static concepts of the world (such as model theory) seem wholly inadequate and the *temporalized* models of intentionality and understanding developed in the phenomenological/hermeneutic tradition – represented by Husserl, Heidegger and Gadamer – assume importance.

Like Kant's philosophy, Husserl's mature phenomenology is a transcendental philosophy that supposes that any description of the world is a perspective of a transcendental subject that constitutes the sense of the world as an object of intentional experience (Mohanty 1989: 153). In his later writings, Husserl argues that our scientific and metaphysical theorizing is grounded in an unbreakable correlation between subjectivity and a perceptual "life-world" in which objects manifest themselves in relationship to our embodied activity. The various world concepts that have emerged in the history of science all depart from this life-world, but tend to overlay it with metaphysical interpretations that estrange us from it. For example, Descartes and Galileo's separation of sensations like touch or colour from the allegedly "objective" geometrical properties of things seems like a natural assumption given the history of modern physics.

Husserl argues that this obviousness is a historical artefact which obscures the fact that the ideal shapes of geometry are not evident in our experience of perceptual objects. Whereas geometrical shapes are precise and distinct, the precision of ordinary objects is contingent upon our practical interests and technologies. The relation of geometrical abstractions to the life-world can, thus, be understood *historically* in terms of the practical privilege accorded linear or planar forms and the extension of this perfecting process in the thought of *ideal geometrical objects* (Husserl 1970: 26).

The Husserlian life-world is thus not a collection of lumps (a Putnam model) but something more like a "text" or field of determinables: a meaning or sense of an intentional experience (Rorty 1985).

Heidegger extends Husserl's accounts of time and the lifeworld by considering our non-cognitive relations to things, creatures and other people. He accepts that we represent the world as containing objective "present-at-hand" (*vorhanden*) things with bundles of properties. As we saw in Chapter 2, though, he also holds a version of the pragmatist claim that our cognitive access to the world depends on our noncognitive comportment in it (Okrent 2006). Heidegger conceives *Dasein* (the human agent) as essentially related to an environment of ready-to-hand (*zuhanden*) *equipment* which is practically "articulated" prior to any representation of their objective properties (Heidegger 1962: 98, 189; Okrent 2006). Thus in our regular dealings with it, the hammer is given in terms of its function, not represented as a bearer of objective properties that it could have independently of its function. A hammer is *something for* "producing, repairing or improving something". A car is *something for* transporting something (Heidegger 1995: 214). Novel applications – like using a car as a virility symbol (or murder weapon) – occur against the background of social norms prescribing the proper use of equipment (Okrent 2006).[11]

Equipment norms exhibit a *practical holism* that mirrors the psychological and semantic holisms in pragmatist theories of meaning. Hammers and nails belong to networks of functionally interrelated entities such as workbenches, planks and fences (Heidegger 1962: 120; 1995, 214; Dreyfus 1990: 62–3). Heidegger refers to these as "involvement totalities" (Heidegger 1962: 189; 1995: 215). We do not choose our involvement networks, according to Heidegger. They provide the context in which meaningful choices can be made and in which objects can come into view as salient topics of assertion. Each *Dasein* finds itself "thrown" into a socially meaningful context that it has not chosen but which allows certain things and actions to show up as salient possibilities for it. However, throwness requires that each *Dasein* is already absorbed into a background of shared concerns, activities and norms that *inter alia* grounds the normativity encountered in equipment (Heidegger 1962: 162).

Malpas argues that these structures furnish a "non-propositional horizon" against which entities "show up" as conforming or as failing to conform to our assertions about them. Meaning-holism and psychological holism reflect the structural openness of local constellations of practices to the things with which they are engaged. In particular, the presupposition of a common world which constitutes the horizon of radical interpretation is construed by him as inherent in the structure of disclosure itself:

> The appearing of something is the picking out (intending) of that thing from the wider structure (the horizon) of which it is a part. The wider network of possibilities is itself apparent (and then never completely) only when the project breaks down or is disrupted. In that disruption other possibilities come into view, even if only momentarily, as the project is reconstituted or as a new project arises. In that "moment" of truth the many possibilities of appearance (possibilities which can never be given complete specification) are freed up, only to be closed off again in the re-establishment of the project. What is shown in that moment, however, is the way in which things are within the horizon and the possibilities in which that horizon consists. Truth is the event of freeing up of possibilities which is also an opening up of possible appearances.
>
> (Malpas 1992: 257)

The practical-temporal structure outlined here unpacks the transcendentalist claim that subject and world are correlative rather than distinct. It also unpacks the active externalist view that the mental cannot be conceived other than as a unified pattern of activity on the part of situated, embodied agents (see also §2.4).

Looking forward

Our search for constraints on posthuman possibility did not yield much when confined to empirically refutable claims about the kinds of minds or information processing that might be possible in the physical world (§§2.1, 2.2). However, our search for potential *a priori* constraints seems initially promising. Two of the successors to Kantian transcendental humanism – pragmatism and phenomenology – seem to provide rich and plausible theories of meaning, subjectivity and objectivity which place clear constraints on 1) agency and 2) the relationship – or rather correlation – between mind and world.

These theories place severe anthropological bounds on posthuman weirdness for, whatever kinds of bodies or minds posthumans may have, they will have to be discursively situated agents practically engaged within a common life-world. In Chapter 4 I will consider this "anthropologically bounded posthumanism" critically and argue for a genuinely posthumanist or post-anthropocentric unbinding of SP.

Notes

1 If so, PPS = the empty set ∅.
2 This constraint obviously assumes the falsity of Cartesian dualism or similar doctrines (§1.4).
3 According to Sandberg, these limits are themselves far below the density of information that could be stored in the super-dense, degenerate matter found in collapsed stars.
4 Meaning that there is a universal Turing machine that could perform the operation given unbounded time and indefinite storage on its tape!
5 The disposition that we describe as the "sonorousness" of a metal tuning fork will be manifested differently in different atmospheric conditions. At sea level atmospheric pressure, the tuning fork that resonates at concert A will disturb the air around it and produce an audible pitch corresponding to the A above middle C on a piano (440 Hz). In a vacuum, there is no medium to disturb, thus no audible sound – though the fork will still resonate. However, the behaviour of the tuning fork will differ in each context because the friction caused by the air will "damp" its vibrations. Thus the harmonic properties and overall shape of the vibrations produced in the vacuum will be significantly different in each case.
6 Biological properties of nervous systems such as the noisiness of neuronal responses might be emulatable up to a point, but no further.
7 For example, functional differentiation in animal neural networks can be simulated without coding intracellular flows of ions for each "software neuron". This is because the learning processes that partition these networks into representational units depend on mechanism-independent principles such as the "Hebb rule" relating synaptic strength to the frequency of joint stimulation ("neurons that fire together, wire together").
8 Wennemann appends "human" and "posthuman" with a "B" superscript to indicate that "human" means *biologically human* rather than *morally human* and that "posthuman" entails *not biologically human*. This is because posthumans as agents would be *morally human* in his terminology.
9 Putnam makes the proviso that the interpretation function I must be "non-trivial" in that it assigns at least one predicate in the language F an extension (the set of things to which it applies) that is neither empty nor universal. If this holds we can use the *same universe of objects* over which I is defined to construct an "isomorphic" interpretation J in which every object in the extension of F is mapped one-one to some object belonging to F's different extension under J; thus the truth value of a sentence interpreted under I will be preserved under J while its meaning changes (Putnam 1981: 217). If F is universal and finite only an identity mapping can construct a set which maps one-one to the original extension to build the isomorphic interpretation by shuffling around or "permutating" objects from the same universe. This is trivially the case if F's extension is empty, since only the empty set has the same number of members as itself. However, non-triviality seems a fairly conservative assumption given that any minimally interesting theory about the world is liable to have some concepts which do not refer to everything or nothing. See Button (2013: 227–40) for a very well-illustrated discussion of the metamathematics of Putnam's "permutation argument".
10 That is, True or False.
11 The idea that environmental things are functionally typed in this way will be taken up again in my discussion of Jacques Ellul's philosophy of technology in §7.1.

4 Weird tales

Anthropologically unbounded posthumanism

Introduction

In this chapter I will argue that the *a priori* bounds on posthuman possibility space (PPS) elaborated with the resource of pragmatism and phenomenology in Chapter 3 evaporate on further inspection.

The argument has two stages. In the first part (§4.1) I will show that the argument for the discursive agency thesis (DAT) given in §3.5 is unsound.

The second stage is more complex. In Chapter 3 we saw that pragmatist accounts of meaning, like Davidson's and Putnam's, presuppose a shared world that cannot be understood as a set of objects or a model. The most plausible account of worldhood, thus conceived, I argued, is provided by the phenomenological account of the world as a common temporally-structured horizon or lifeworld.

However, in §4.2, I will argue that this requires a commitment to the methodology of transcendental phenomenology and that this is fatally flawed. As trailed in Chapter 2, the strategy is broadly deconstructive. The argument takes inspiration from some early Derridean texts which propose that the interpretation of phenomenological theory is incompatible with the doctrine of evidence for that interpretation (see, for example, Derrida 1978: 154–68; Roden 2005: 78) – though it does not employ their specific argumentation. The problem of interpretation arises because there are empirical and theoretical grounds for holding that some phenomenology is "dark". *Dark phenomenology* is experienced; but experiencing it offers no standard for its own description or interpretation.

In the course of this chapter I consider two cases of darkness: the first arising in the phenomenology of perception, the second (and most important) from the phenomenology of time. If phenomenology cannot tell us what phenomenology is *a priori*, then phenomenological investigation cannot secure knowledge of phenomenological necessity. In particular, *we have no grounds for holding that we understand what it is to occupy a world that any sophisticated cognizer must share with us.*

Thus we cannot know in advance whether alien or posthuman phenomenologies must coincide with the human "world" in any respect. The anthropologically bounded posthumanism of Chapter 3 must be rejected. In §4.3, the speculative and ethical implications of this anti-transcendental conclusion are prefigured in a discussion of Charles Stross's post-singularity science fiction novel *Accelerando* and Omohundro's work on AI goals.

4.1 Discursive agency – another look

Let's begin by restating the DAT argument considered in §3.5:

1) An agent is a being that acts for reasons.
2) To act for reasons an agent must have desires or intentions to act.
3) An agent cannot have desires or intentions without beliefs.
4) The ability to have beliefs *requires a grasp of what belief is* since to believe is also to understand "the possibility of being mistaken" (metacognitive claim).
5) A grasp of the possibility of being mistaken is only possible for language users (linguistic constitutivity).

So a being that lacks the capacity for language cannot be an agent.

There I presaged my account of Davidson by pointing out that the argument for discursive agency is cast in the idiom of propositional attitude (belief-desire) psychology. If we abandon this constraint, the central claim that sophisticated cognition must be linguistically constituted (Premise 5) appears less persuasive. As in Chapter 2, I focus on the metacognitive claim and the linguistic constitutivity claims.

Perhaps the most intuitive argument for the metacognitive claim is that belief is an attitude of "holding true" towards a statement, claim or a proposition. One might think that a being that does not have a grasp of truth, and is unable to single out truth bearers like claims or propositions, could not adopt the attitude of belief. But this is far from obvious. According to so-called "deflationary accounts" of truth, to assert that a proposition is true is just to assert the proposition. Thus the capacity to *hold true* may not require mastery of a distinct concept of truth or a grasp of the kinds of entities to which truth and falsity adhere (sentences, statements or propositions being the usual suspects).

We can press this point. If holding true could be implicit in public practices such as assertion, it could also be implicit in other cognitive operations. Hilary Kornblith makes this case well:

> Now the idea that a creature can only have beliefs if it understands the possibility of being mistaken has some initial plausibility. But there are weak and strong readings of this idea. Norman Malcolm's dog, who is found

barking up the wrong tree, certainly comes to understand that it has made an error when the squirrel suddenly darts away from behind a neighbouring bush. The ability to respond to mistakes and make corrections in light of them is, without doubt, a feature of animal learning.

(Kornblith 2002: 88)

Thus there are grounds for questioning the metacognitive assumption that only beings with the concept of belief (or truth) qualify as believers. Its plausibility rests on the assumption that adopting a position regarding the way the world is requires an explicit truth concept. But a creature with the capacity for revising its models of the world in the light of evidence must be credited with some position regarding the way its world is, even if it cannot make this explicit.

Perhaps, though, there is a gulf between the ability to assay better and worse representations and the full-dress relationship to a common world discussed by Davidson, Husserl and Heidegger. While something like belief is possible for non-language users, perhaps really sophisticated cognition requires the ability to compare better or worse positions regarding commonly identified objects (see §3.5). That is to say, our challenge to the metacognitive claim does not show that advanced post-humans with florid agency powers would not need to understand what it is to be mistaken by being able to using the common coin of sentences.

So we need to consider Premise 5:

A grasp of the possibility of being mistaken is only possible for language users (linguistic constitutivity).

The claim that language provided humans with the ability to disseminate and reflect upon beliefs and inference patterns seems plausible (see §6.5): what is at issue is whether language is *necessary* for thinking about thoughts.

Suppose there were cognitive states that a) could represent other cognitive states and their epistemic status and b) were not dependent on the mastery of language. This fact would support the claim that language is unnecessary for metacognition even if (in humans) it seems to be a powerful catalyst and contributor to it.

The fact that humans can notice that they have forgotten things, evince surprise, or attend to suddenly salient information (as with the ticking clock that is noticed only when it stops) implies anecdotally that our brains must have mechanisms for representing and evaluating (hence "metacognizing") their states of knowledge and ignorance. Moreover, some metacognitive processes are arguably necessary for language acquisition and thus part of the pre-linguistic scaffold for cultural transmission in humans. For example, Michael Tomasello argues that a human-specific capacity for joint attention and (thus pre-linguistic shared intentionality) explains why human infants are so adept at acquiring languages in the first place (Tomasello 2008; Briscoe 2007).

Churchland thinks that both human and animal brains represent their worlds with activation states of neural networks and, for this reason, argues that we go too far when, as in Putnam's arguments for internal realism, we use sentences and their relationships to represent the structure of thought (Churchland 2012). Much of his argument for the centrality of non-propositional representation hinges on experimental data concerning the representational prowess of *artificial neural networks* (ANNs). Artificial neural networks or "connectionist" systems are a technique for modelling the behaviour of biological nervous systems using software representations of neurons and the strengths of their interconnections (known as "weights"). I will follow Churchland here in assuming that results from connectionist modelling are indicative of the powers of biological networks (or future post-biological cognizers organized on similar lines).

The most common type of ANN is a three-layer net consisting of an input layer where raw data are presented; a *hidden layer* which will parse up the input into categories when the network is trained up; and an output layer which indicates to experimenters how the input has been categorized (e.g. "dog" or "cat"). Categories acquired through training are represented as *prototype regions* within the N-dimensional space representing all the possible activations of N neurons in the hidden layer (Churchland 2012: viii, 77, 81, 103, 105).[1] The trained-up network thus compresses unrepresented similarities in the input onto a small number of "prototype" regions that categorize or represent those similarities. Prototypes for categories are coded by distances and relative positions in activation space.

Representations in neural networks are thus *geometrical* (like maps) rather than propositional or sentence-like (Churchland 2012). They may hook onto observational differences between objects (e.g. dog, cat, mouse, child) or highly abstract differences, such as functional differences. For example, Jeffrey Elman's work on connectionist language learning suggests that different degrees of grammatical embedding among sentences could be represented in terms of distances within the activation space of a *recurrent* neural network rather than, say, the syntactic structure of "linguaformal" internal representations (Elman 1995).

Such representations can capture propositional information, but need not represent or encode it propositionally. For one thing, the stored information in the weights of the network need not exhibit the functional discreteness of sentences, each of which can be independently present or absent. In most neural net architectures *all* the inter-neural weightings of the trained-up network are involved in generating its discrepant outputs (Ramsey *et al.* 1990).

Artificial neural networks can monitor the states of other neural networks, providing the basis for a form of non-propositional metacognition. A basic self-monitoring network can be built up from a "first-order" network trained to categorize stimuli on the basis of the activations of its input layer and a second-order network trained to recognize salient activation states or trajectories (corresponding to different kinds of mental process) in the first-order net (Cleeremans *et al.* 2007: 1034). Evidence from modelling conducted by Cleeremans *et al.* using coupled NNs suggests higher-order networks can learn to monitor the hidden layer processing occurring in lower-level networks and to evaluate the representational success of the first-order network. These results suggest possible mechanisms by which higher associative networks in a biological brain monitor and evaluate processing taking place in other parts of the nervous system.

This hierarchical approach to neural computation is exhibited in "predictive coding models" of animal perception. These assume that our experience depends on the work of competing generative models which represent real world features by simulating their future effects on sensory input (Clark 2013: 183). They imply that the model (or hypothesis) that the brain assesses as most probable, given the way that its internal states alter over time, determines the content at any stage in processing. The selection of the winning model is determined by two factors: how well it predicts activity lower in the hierarchy; and its "prior probability" – measured by how well its own activity is predicted by models further up in the hierarchy (Hohwy *et al.* 2008: 688–9; Clark 2013: 183). Interpretation of sensory features consists of a series of recurrent "top-down" responses to a cascade of bottom-up "driving signals". Some top-down evaluations may code relatively abstract properties of the world in terms of the prior probabilities of certain coincident features – such as that changes in objects are typically caused by changes in other objects. As Clark observes in his useful survey of this topic, these abstract "hyperpriors" have some of the organizing features that Kant attributes to transcendental synthesis (Clark 2013: 196; see §3.3).[2]

If this outline is on the right tracks, then the brain is filled with higher-order networks evaluating the output of lower-order networks and being evaluated by still higher-order networks. Since some of these representations are highly abstract as well as hierarchical, it suggests that sophisticated non-linguistic metacognition is ubiquitous.

It might be argued that this does not suffice to throw doubt on linguistic constitutivity because we have not shown that non-symbolic representations could enable something like Davidson's triangulation and the consequent grasp of an objectivity that we might expect to be necessary for sophisticated agency (see 3.5, though also see §6.1). Languages seem to be uniquely placed to mediate social or intersubjective relationships because (unlike the hidden states of our biological neural networks) symbols are culturally repeatable and reidentifiable of their nature. One explanation for this might be that, unlike neural activation patterns, symbols are *finitely differentiated* (Goodman 1968: 135–6). A mark can only count as a symbol if it is possible to determine which symbol it is. This property allows us to recognize instances of common symbols across empirical variations in sound or shape (cat, cat, cat, etc.).

This is clearly important to the cultural replicability of language patterns for creatures like us. Symbols are the gold standard for public repeatability. However, it is wrong to assume that only finitely differentiated types are culturally repeatable: images or melodies are culturally repeatable but not finitely differentiated. So, as Derrida has argued, repeatability (or iterability) need not be the repeatability of abstract form: a difference intervenes on every repetition (Derrida 1988). Finite differentiation is only necessary to the extent that some differences need to be disregarded. Posthumans with computing power to burn might not need to ignore the contextual differences between culturally ambient patterns in the way that humans do. Their thought might occur in a "non-symbolic workspace" in which contextual differences between patterns play a larger role in their interpretation and evaluation. Such patterns would be non-linguistic by virtue of being non-symbolic. Thus it might not be possible or appropriate to understand them as propositional attitudes.

If Paul Churchland is right and "neuralese" is more map-like than sentence-like, one way in which this symbolic workspace might arise is via the use of brain–computer interfaces proposed in his centipedal thought experiment (see Introduction).

In the Introduction, I suggested that the interfacing technology required for Churchland's neuroculture could be one kind of posthuman-difference maker. One way of expressing this is to concede to pragmatists that language and propositional thinking is constitutive of human forms of culture and thought. We can allow that language provides an important tool for metacognition in humans (we will review more evidence for this claim in Chapter 6, §6.5). Dennett and Clark characterize this in terms of hybrid representational couplings between bare brains and culturally transmitted symbols (Dennett 1991; §2.2), while Davidson's theory of triangulation may explain how language mediates human thought and agency.

It does not follow that language and propositional thinking is constitutive of sophisticated thought in general. Suppose that neural activation states can furnish higher-order representations of other neural activation patterns and that this property could provide the basis for a non-symbolic neurocultural workspace. Successors to humans habituated to this non-sentential format for thinking and communicating might form a semiotically isolated population that could "bud off" from humans, just as reproductively isolated biological species bud off from their predecessors. We can call the claim that this scenario is possible "instrumental eliminativism". Churchland (1981) proposed the theoretical elimination of propositional attitude (or "folk") psychology in favour of a biologically based theory of the dynamics of cognition more consonant with the emerging sciences of the brain. However, instrumental elimination is a literal *replacement of the folk*, not a transition between theories. For this reason, it is a conceivable mechanism for the technogenesis of posthumans (see Chapter 5).

The widespread evidence for non-language-mediated metacognition implies that that we should be dubious of the claim that language is constitutive of sophisticated cognition and thus – by extension – agency. Neurocultures and non-symbolic workspaces may not be possible; but current research into neural computation suggests that we have no grounds to dismiss them *a priori*. Thus the metacognitive claim should be suspended in the form that supports the discursive agency thesis. For even if metacognition is necessary for sophisticated thought, this may not involve trafficking in sentences. Thus we lack persuasive *a priori* grounds for supposing that posthumans would have to be subjects of discourse.

I will now turn from considering discursive constraints on agency and subjectivity to considering phenomenological constraints on the relationship between posthumans and their worlds ("being-in-the-world" or *Dasein*, to repeat the Heideggerian terms). Would sophisticated posthumans have to be subjects aware of their unique identity over time? Would each posthuman be embedded in the unitary world horizon sketched out in Chapter 3?

4.2 Naturalizing phenomenology and the rejection of transcendental constraints

In Chapter 3, I argued that pragmatist accounts of meaning and mind require a notion of a shared world, and that the notion most consonant with the pragmatism derives from the phenomenological tradition. As Malpas argues, this supports a pragmatist approach to ontology by allowing that conceptions of what the world contains can develop through interpretative understanding. Phenomenology and the pragmatist approach to meaning and mind converge at this point because the latter seems to require a phenomenological conception of a temporal horizon that structures activity in the common "lifeworld".

Now, if phenomenology is going to warrant *a priori* constraints on posthuman possibility space (PPS) it will have to go one better than just descriptive psychology. It will need to provide access to the *necessary structure of subjectivity*. This requires it to be a transcendental study of the conditions of possible experience (§§3.3–3.7).

But transcendental phenomenology has its own commitments! One of these is the rejection of global naturalism. Phenomenological worlds are *a priori* structures that we must be able to share with any other transcendental subject, even if their practices and concepts are initially opaque to us. So if we have warrant to reject phenomenology's transcendental dimension, both phenomenologist and pragmatist would have to rescind the claim to have captured the essence of any subject–world correlation. The proposed transcendental constraints on PPS would then have to be rejected. *A priori* at least, PPS would be wide open!

In what follows I will set out a view of phenomenology that supports its naturalization. This will provide us with a second, independent basis for rejecting transcendental-anthropological constraints on PPS and thus on the scope of SP. The argument will be applied initially to a Husserlian conception of phenomenology, but I will argue that its application to other kinds is relatively unproblematic.

The claim that phenomenology is apt for "naturalization" is contentious because many philosophers regard it as *epistemically closed* to findings of disciplines with different doctrines of evidence (call this *the closure assumption*). For example, speculations about the physical basis of conscious experience are frequently held to be irrelevant to describing "how it feels". The closure assumption implies that a neural network model explaining how our experience of time is generated could throw no light on what that experience *is like*. Given closure, we cannot need a theory to tell us what it is like.

For transcendental phenomenologists the meaning of claims about physical entities of the kind posited in some naturalistic ontologies can be adequately explained only in terms of our possible modes of awareness of them. These can be phenomenologically described by suspending ordinary assumptions about the mind-independent existence of objects (the "natural attitude") and directing attention to how we are aware of objects *as mind-independent*. The "world" of modern natural science, thus understood, is just one way of interpreting the culturally moulded lifeworld that forms the horizon of any possible interpretation (Husserl 1970: 51, 111). This methodological suspension is called the *epoché* or "bracketing".

If the *epoché* is possible, the arrows of epistemic pressure at most run from phenomenology to science. The phenomenologist can advise the cognitive scientist about what it means to say that the brain "is a thing" but no reciprocal wisdom can be forthcoming from cognitive science.

Like the naturalization claim, the normative claim for closure requires a justifying doctrine of evidence. One form of this is that phenomenological claims don't have to be scientifically or theoretically informed as long as the things they describe are pre-theoretically or "intuitively" given to the conscious subject.

This putative theory-independence seems to explain transcendental phenomenology's claim to methodological priority over purely conceptual or speculative philosophy. One of the consequences of pragmatism – as Putnam and Davidson argue, and as Quine (1968) argued before them – is that a set of linguistic practices can always be interpreted in different ways consistent with public information about those practices. A scientific theory such as quantum mechanics or the arithmetic of natural numbers can always be glossed in terms of discrepant ontologies even when we know as much as could be known about how to predict or compute using those idioms. If there is no non-theoretical access to "the things themselves" one may reason, as Davidson and Putnam did, that ontology is relative to the model we adopt under radical interpretation: a relativity applying recursively and without end since the ontology applied by the translator will itself be expressible as a theory with multiple models (Davidson 1984: 234–5; §§3.6–3.7).

The discipline of phenomenology suggests a way out of this model-theoretic labyrinth. If intuition obviates regress to a background theory, perhaps it will help us recover the "authentic" meaning of philosophical or scientific claims – including that of naturalism itself![3]

Of course, the claim that anything can be "given" or intuited this way is contestable and has been extensively contested from Kant, through to Hegel and subsequently in the work of pragmatists like Rorty, Davidson and Sellars. It follows that any substantive interpretation of the notion of intuition may cede ground to the anti-naturalist unnecessarily.

Fortunately, we do not need a substantive conception of intuition to understand its role in the debate between phenomenological naturalists and phenomenological anti-naturalists. "Intuition" *can be a placeholder for whatever (real or imagined) epistemic organ allows the phenomenological domain (experience) to provide a yardstick for its own description.*

An anti-naturalistic phenomenology would be *well founded*, then, if its justifications were closed under appeal to intuition (thus understood). The only legitimate challenge to a phenomenological description would be to make a better job of intuiting (Mohanty 1989).

Conversely, a phenomenology that is not well founded would be subject to challenge from non-intuitive sources of evidence, including empirically supported models derived from empirical disciplines like computational neuroscience or artificial intelligence. Theories in naturalistic philosophy of mind, for example, are informed by developments in psychology, neuroscience and AI but also frequently inform research in those areas. In a naturalized philosophical discipline, the arrows of inference and constraint are reciprocal. Non-well-founded phenomenology would be naturalized phenomenology.

Phenomenology would be closed (well founded) only if its domain were completely intuitable. The domain of phenomenology is experience in the broadest sense of the term. This could include perceptual experience, the experience of thinking about sets or posthumans or the embedded, embodied absorption in the world that Heidegger describes in the opening of *Being and Time* (1962: §§2.1, 3.7).

But it is at least conceivable that this domain is not wholly intuitable. Let's call a feature of experience "dark" if it confers no explicit or implicit understanding of its nature on the experiencer. Intuitable phenomenology confers an implicit understanding of its nature on the experiencer, even if this must be subsequently clarified in phenomenological reflection. For example, Husserlian phenomenologists claim that "concepts" under which we grasp objects have implicit entailment structures that can be promoted to objects of awareness in reflection (see e.g. Tieszen 2002: 371–5). Dark phenomenology would be epistemically resistant to such a process. Having experiences in which it figures would not constitute or produce an understanding of its nature that could be explicated at a later date. Dark phenomenology is thus intuition-transcendent.

This is not to say that dark phenomenology would be *ipso facto* inaccessible. A dark phenomenon could influence the dispositions, feelings or actions of the experiencer without improving her capacity to describe them. Theories of dark phenomenology could be adduced to explain these effects.

Our access to the dark side would thus be as theoretically and technically mediated as our access to the humanly unobservable universe. The criteria for evaluating theories of dark phenomenology would presumably be those applying in other areas of empirical enquiry (instrumental efficacy, simplicity, explanatory unity within wider science).

At this point some phenomenologists might object that the dark side is just another posit of speculative/naturalistic thinking and does not lie within the domain of phenomenology as first philosophy. Since it falls short of the ideal of intuitability, the hypothesis of dark phenomenology could be bracketed for purposes of phenomenological description.

However, the bracketing objection assumes that the dark domain is disjoint from the intuitable domain and does not impinge on it in some way. I will call this *the disjointness assumption*.[4]

If disjointness fails, there may be phenomenological structures that are incompletely intuitable because their "visible" relations or entities are conjoined with dark relations or entities. If they are incompletely intuitable, then even intuition could be utterly misleading about their nature.

For example: suppose there are phenomenological structures like colour or pitch continua that are intuitively accessible at a coarse grain but not at a fine grain. Any inference from their coarse structure to their fine structure might be prone to the fallacy of division and unrectifiable as long as closure under appeal to intuition is enforced.

On the other hand, specialists in empirical disciplines such as cognitive science might have access to observational techniques that obviate limits on intuition. If their claims could be supported, *phenomenology would be subject to revisionary pressure from those disciplines* and the methodological injunction "to naturalize" sustained.

How should we understand this possibility? One way to do this is by drawing on an analogy from the history of science. We could compare phenomenological claims based on intuition to studies in electromagnetism, thermodynamics or genetics whose interpretation is largely descriptive or instrumental rather than mathematical or mechanistic. When faced with a theoretical explanation of a phenomenon that is more consilient with other areas of science than a descriptive one, there is typically a dialectical relationship whereby questions can be raised about the metaphysical and explanatory heft of either theory. For example, some claim that Mendel's classical genetics is better understood as a theoretical refinement of instrumental claims about how to obtain different kinds of plants and animals through breeding than as an ontologically revealing account of the underlying mechanisms of heredity (Griffiths & Stotz 2006). Clearly, there are other ways of allocating ontological significance here. Some might argue that classical genetics is "eliminated" or reduced by molecular genetics while those who favour the instrumental interpretation might claim molecular and classical genetics are too different in their aims for the former to be eliminable by the latter (Kitcher 1984).

If this analogy holds, then evidence for dark phenomenology would open up transcendental phenomenology to a dialectic similar in at least some respects to those in other areas of science. According to the epistemic model introduced earlier, this would be a *de facto* naturalization since the claims of intuition would already be susceptible to epistemic pressure from natural science.

But are there any grounds for belief in non-disjoint, dark phenomenology? In the remainder of this section, I will consider some candidates. The first belong to the area of perceptual phenomenology: pitch, colour and timbre perception. The second (and arguably most conjoint of all) is the phenomenology of time. I will argue that both provide ample evidence of phenomenological darkness, thereby undermining the closure of phenomenology under intuition and supporting my naturalization gambit.

Perceptual phenomenology

If intuiting supports the evaluation of phenomenological descriptions, intuition must supply conceptual content. So intuition plausibly includes a recognitional component: if we cannot recognize tokens of some type, we are in no position to evaluate descriptions of it. It follows that any phenomenology that transcended our subjective recognitional powers would be *dark*.

There is some evidence for phenomenological darkness of this kind. Psychophysical work suggests that the human capacity to discriminate musical pitch differences is more fine-grained than the human ability to identify pitch intervals (Raffman 1995: 293–308). In the case of colour perception, the apparent gulf between discrimination and type identification is vast, with discriminable colour differences numbering around ten million as compared with a colour lexicon of around thirty (Mandik 2012).

Diana Raffman uses the evidence for dark phenomenology to rebut a standard physicalist objection to the claim that conscious states are irreducibly subjective, introspectable properties of experience (*qualia*). The objection goes something like this: "[There] are no irreducibly subjective facts; rather, there are simply different ways of knowing ordinary physical or functional facts about the mind-brain" (Raffman 1995: 293).

One detailed proposal for explaining this difference is that conscious states only seem to have irreducibly subjective properties because they are introspected under direct recognitional concepts which track them via some *reliable internal scanning mechanism* (pp. 293–300). The scanning mechanism allows us to recognize phenomenal states as being of a certain kind without exploiting a description or theory of what these states are like. A complete physical description of these scanning mechanisms would not allow one to infer a subjective description that conveys how *red-31* feels simply because no such descriptions are to be had: phenomenal concepts designate phenomenal properties without describing them. The "irreducible subjectivity" of phenomenal states is thus a cognitive illusion generated by their idiosyncratic mode of presentation (a similar position is supported by Thomas Metzinger, as we shall see).

For Raffman, the moral of the psychophysical data on the gulf between discrimination and identification is that any account of phenomenal recognitional concepts is liable to hit a bottleneck on our capacity to remember concepts of phenomenal states that allow tokens of the same phenomenal types to be subsequently recognized. For the psychological data indicate that recognitional schemas simplify the memory task by omitting fine-grained differences in perception. We are not capable of recognizing the refined qualitative states that we nonetheless *appear* to introspect. Suppose the production of phenomenal concepts reflects this coarse-coding strategy (p. 296). If a phenomenal state of seeing *red-31* is more determinate than any available phenomenal recognitional concept, there can be no type-identifying mentalese predicate '*red-31* experience' available to track the corresponding brain states through the memory bottleneck (p. 299). However, *we are introspectively aware of refined qualitative perceptual states.* Thus the disparity between identifying concepts and refined sensory discriminations implies that the introspected character of phenomenal experience is not explicable by way of special-purpose phenomenal concepts.

If the grain of the "memory schemas" that track phenomenal types is coarser than the underlying phenomenology some of this phenomenology will go unrecognized and unremembered (pp. 295–6). If so, then, as Ned Block has argued, phenomenology cannot depend on accessibility to working memory.[5] Corroborating evidence for this is provided by well replicated experiments like those of George Sperling who found that subjects reported seeing all or almost all elements of an alphanumeric array of twelve characters presented for 50 milliseconds, though they were only able to identify around four elements of the array following the presentation (Block 2007). Block uses these findings to argue that phenomenology *overflows* attentional availability. Conscious experience thus cannot depend on informational links between sensory modules and the working memory circuits in the front of the head (p. 492 – see Introduction).

However, the hypothesis that some phenomenology confers no understanding of its nature is not committed to the view that dark phenomenology is too raw or rich for our conceptual capacities. This is just one possible kind of phenomenological darkness. Michael Cohen and Daniel Dennett report variations on the Sperling experiments where elements of the alphanumeric array are altered (letters replaced with pseudo-letters, for example) although the subjects report seeing "only letters". Such change-blindness in Sperling-type situations and elsewhere suggests that subjects can impute richness to the reported phenomenology that is not informationally present (Cohen & Dennett 2011: 360).

This possibility that dark phenomenology could be a lack or a plenitude is further illustrated in Thomas Metzinger's appropriation of Raffman's argument in *Being-No-One: The Self-Model Theory of Subjectivity* (Metzinger 2004). Rather than using dark phenomenology to motivate belief in *qualia*, he co-opts her argument from constraints on working memory to motivate an epistemological argument *against* classic *qualia*.

According to philosophical lore, the classic *quale* is a simple, intrinsically subjective, intuitable property of experience such as a determinately red hue in some part of my visual field or the never to be repeated sensation of a refined cheese.

"Raffman *qualia*" – Metzinger's term for the simplest perceptual dis-criminations – cannot be intuited because, as with very fine pitch intervals, they lack subjective identification conditions.

It does not follow that they are wholly inaccessible or unrepresentable from a third-person point of view, however, or that they are the sensory simples of legend. It is possible to attend to them non-conceptually – as in experiments involving "just noticeable differences" between pitch or colour samples. They can also be functionally identified by their envir-onmental causes and contributions to behaviour. Raffman *qualia*, accord-ingly, are functionally individuated content fixations whose recognition *requires organs other than phenomenological intuition*. The classic *quale* must be a purely theoretical entity because the simplest forms of perceptual con-tent fixation are necessarily intuition-transcendent (thus dark). If *qualia* must be introspected nonconceptually, knowledge of them cannot, as he puts it, "be transported out of the specious present" (p. 82). For such states, Metzinger quips, "Neurophenomenology is possible; phenomenology is impossible."

Thus a good case can be made for "dark" perceptual grains and invo-lutes nestling in the intuitable phenomenological uplands. If so, a portion of its structure *is not intuitively accessible* and a solely "phenomenological" account of phenomenology will be liable to mischaracterize it (see Roden 2005, 2013).

The phenomenology of time

Temporality is a central ingredient in most phenomenological accounts of reality or transcendence. As we saw in §3.7, Husserl understands the objectivity of the physical thing as an excess over any of its temporally structured aspects: "The thing itself is always in motion, always, and for everyone, a unity for consciousness of the openly endless multiplicity of changing experiences and experienced things, one's own and those of others" (Husserl 1970: 164).

As with the case of Raffman *qualia*, committing this structure to the dark side would not entail its inaccessibility to other epistemic organs. However, if temporality has a dark underbelly this would be a transcen-dent thing, not *a transcendental condition of thinging* (§3.3). There would be no reason to accord it a different epistemological status to ice blocks or cats. The distinction between the *transcendental* structure of experience and the entities whose contents it articulates would be irreparably undermined. If temporality can no longer be regarded as a topic for transcendental claims, however, phenomenological claims about the unitary structure of possible minds or lives must be regarded as tentative empirical generalizations at best, *not future-proof constraints on posthuman possibility.*

Is there any reason to believe that temporality is dark?

For representationalist philosophers of mind who believe that the mind is an engine for forming and transforming mental representations there is good reason to be sceptical about the supposed transcendental role of time (§2.1). If temporality is a property of mental representations, then there can obviously be a phenomenology of temporal relations and relata, but only if it is represented by another representation.

What aspect of the temporality of experience could be captured by such higher-order representations? This depends on what the salient represented properties of temporality are. Whatever these turn out to be, there is no reason to think that the higher-order representations that generate phenomenology (if such there be) capture all the features of the lower-order representation of temporal experience. Thus representationalism implies that phenomenology could not possibly be well founded – closed under appeal to intuition – because it would always be the case that representations of content-relevant properties of mental states could be epistemically deficient.

Of course, any good naturalist should concede that representationalism could be a false or otherwise "bad" theory of mind, while all good Husserlian or Heideggerian phenomenologists reject it anyway. So the argument from representationalism suggests at most that first-person insight into temporality *might not be* well founded. It is hardly a conclusive argument.

However, there may be reasons internal to phenomenology for considering theories of temporality to be in need of clarification from wider science. They concern the relationship between phenomenological ontology and the doctrine of evidence that motivates its closure. *For where a phenomenological ontology transcends the plausible limits of intuition* its interpretation would have to be arbitrated according to its instrumental efficacy, simplicity and explanatory potential as well as its descriptive content.

We can get a schematic idea of how what we might call the "argument from intuitive overreach" works for specific phenomenological ontologies by considering the ontological commitments of Husserl's theory of temporality (§3.7). Husserl's theory of temporality builds on the assumption that the content of our experience of objective succession depends upon the organization of subjective time. He thinks this organization must be continuous and non-atomistic. If our experience was made up of disconnected atoms, the persistence and unfolding of objects required for the transcendental theory of the world would have no basis in experience. We would not hear the melody famously described by Husserl in §16 of the *Phenomenology of Internal Time Consciousness* but a series of unrelated notes.

Husserl explains the capacity of subjectivity to generate a unified temporality by describing the experiential "now" in terms of three indissociable aspects of its intentional content: 1) an intending of the current phase of the object – for example, the falling of the fourth to the third of the scale; 2) a "retention" or primary remembrance of the previous experience; 3) a "protension" which anticipates the content to come:

> The "source-point" with which the "generation" of the enduring Object begins is a primal impression. This consciousness is engaged in continuous alteration. The actual [*leibhafte*] tonal now is constantly changed into something that has been; constantly, an ever fresh tonal now, which passes over into modification, peels off. However, when the tonal now, the primal impression, passes over into retention, this retention is itself again a now, an actual existent. While it itself is actual (but not an actual sound), it is the retention of a sound that has been.
>
> (Husserl 1964: 50)

Why might we consider this triple structure to be a speculative description of an intuition-transcendent object rather than the non-objective condition of thinging that phenomenology requires it to be? Because, like the physical thing, the entity that Husserl describes has a structure that must exceed intuitability if it is to do the job of unifying objects. The now or temporal source point, as Husserl claims, must be *continuously modified into retention*. Lacking continuity, the operation would have gaps, as on the atomistic model (p. 62). If temporal experience could possess gaps, phenomenology would be committed to a dark phenomenology in any case; thus ceding to naturalistic modes of inquiry for the reasons we have already discussed.

However, suppose every segment of a continuum is divisible into a further segment with the same non-discrete characteristics. Unless intuition can handle infinite complexity, apprehending the structure of temporality appears as much an endless task as the apprehension of any physical thing (§3.7).

We might try to rescue Husserl by thinking of the continuum as a potential or virtuality rather than as a complete thing. Perhaps I am making an elementary error in treating the temporal continuum as a complex object with a real infinity of occurrent parts. Perhaps intuiting the continuum is more like figuring out a rule by which a virtual present is transformed into a virtual past. It is probably correct to say that Husserl did not think that the temporal continuum was composed of independently subsisting pieces (p. 62). Robert Dostal puts this well: "The present, for [Husserl], is not the nondimensional point of the instantaneous now. Rather, we might say that the present is 'thick' to the extent that, *within* the present, we find both the past and the future; that is, we find all three dimensions of time" (Dostal 1993: 125).

However, his reason for denying that phenomenological temporality can be broken down into points is that it replicates the triple dependence structure at every grain. The question still arises: over what regions and at what phenomenological scales does this rule apply? The claim that this operation can be applied at any scale of the temporal flow entails that it has no gaps and that the triplicate structure is replicated ad infinitum at every scale. Yet, no finite phenomenological subject could ever carry out a complete investigation of this nested structure. It is, as David Wood has argued, a pure metaphysical posit made on epistemological rather than phenomenological grounds (Wood 2001: 78–9).

Thus experiential temporality is dark in representationalist accounts and in a rival phenomenological account that rejects representationalism. If phenomenology has anything interesting to say about temporality, it concerns a crepuscular structure with both light and dark aspects. It must, therefore, provide an incomplete account of that structure that requires supplementation through other modes of enquiry.

If phenomenology is incompletely characterized by the discipline of phenomenology, though, it seems proper that methods of enquiry such as those employed by cognitive scientists, neuroscientists and cognitive modellers should take up the interpretative slack. If phenomenologists want to understand what they are talking about, they should apply the natural attitude to their own discipline.

Now, it could be objected that my anti-transcendentalist argument depends on understanding temporality in Husserl's sense and that the argument may not generalize to all phenomenologies of time (phenomenology's Hydra-headedness). Husserl's account of temporality is unable to determine the nature of its object (time, or whatever) because it is committed to structures unintuitable in terms of its doctrine of evidence. But Heidegger's phenomenology – it can be countered – does not rest on an ideal of intuitability because it is not a descriptive but a *hermeneutic* phenomenology which seeks to interpret structures of experience whose meaning is already foreshadowed in our ordinary dealings with things (Caputo 1984: 158; §3.7). Interpreting experience does not require that we aspire towards a final interpretation of being or experience. It follows that hermeneutic phenomenology, unlike descriptive phenomenology, cannot overreach.

However, the concept of intuition employed in the argument of this section is general enough to accommodate an interpretative approach to phenomenology since this must also presuppose a phenomenon which guides interpretation and which interpretation may capture more or less faithfully (Mohanty 1989: 54–5).

Two further summary points need to be stressed here. Heidegger's philosophy of time is importantly different from Husserl's in ways that might appear to avoid overreach. Husserl's seems well adapted to describing our encounters with things which Heidegger describes as "present-at-hand" (*vorhanden*): persistent objects like melodies and their properties (key, cadential structure, etc.). Husserl's time requires a continuous modification of the now, leading to the difficulty that it is unable to decide what it is about so long as it remains a transcendental theory.

Heidegger thinks that encountering objects in time, as Husserl describes it, requires the still deeper backdrop that immerses Daseins (human agents) in the ready-to-hand (§3.7). However, this background and the horizon structure it manifests would not be possible but for *Dasein*'s inherent temporality, which Heidegger understands in terms of a capacity to "project" ahead of itself beyond the meanings generated in a given context. Projection is not, Heidegger insists, the property of a detached Cartesian subject, but integral to a fundamental immersion in things as a whole which Heidegger calls "care" (*Sorge*). *Dasein is* the care-structure since it is by virtue of this "non-cognitive openness to beings" that anything ready or present-to-hand can be encountered at all (Critchley *et al.* 2008: 92–3; Heidegger 1962: 236–7, 371).

Projection is also the basis for the unity of *Dasein* since – as is required for transcendental conditions of thinging – it is not a thing but a kind of temporal process or potentiality. As Bernard Stiegler puts it, the *who* (*Dasein*) "is to be radically distinguished from the *what*" – the realm of beings that it discloses (Stiegler 1998: 240). This disclaimer is of course familiar from other transcendental accounts (e.g. transcendental subjectivity is not in the world, but a condition of there being a world, etc.). However, whereas the temporal structure of Husserl's subject requires a dynamic continuity, *Dasein*'s fundamental temporality consists of distinct "ecstases" which do not require a synthesis in the present (Heidegger 1962: 377; Dostal 1993: 135). This structure consists of a futural dimension towards which *Dasein* projects; a "having been" which gives the context in which projection occurs (thrownness); and a "present" constituted by our preoccupation with other people or equipment (Critchley *et al.* 2008: 104–05; Ricoeur 1990: 83).

The common-sense conception of time as a series of nows from which Husserl takes leave is, according to Heidegger, dependent on this deeper triplication, since without the projection it makes possible nothing would be disclosed or encountered – there would no world in the sense of "world horizon".

Heidegger's time is thus not Husserl's time, and it might be thought that his account is not subject to the overreach argument because it does not require dynamic continuity. However, two qualifications need to be made here. First, Heidegger's time does not supersede Husserl's present-to-hand time. It is a deeper condition of possibility for presence. So his account of time does not obviate Husserl's difficulties.

Second, it can be argued that Heidegger's phenomenology of time is subject to issues of scope and interpretation similar to those that afflict Husserl's. To take just one example: deconstructionist readings like those of Stiegler, Hägglund and Paul Cilliers argue that the differential or "ecstatic" model of temporality generalizes well beyond transcendental subjects to the structures of "generalized writing", which we alluded to in §§1.4 and 2.1. Following Derrida's lead,[6] Stiegler and Hägglund argue that temporality as *différance* is a characteristic of mobile networks of signifying traces that ramify at all levels of biological and technological existence (Stiegler 1998; Hägglund 2008, 2011; see Chapter 7). Cilliers (again following Derrida 1978: 196–231) shows that this differential conception of time can be fruitfully used to understand content in neural networks by complicating the geometric conception at the heart of the state space model we discussed in §4.1 (Cilliers 2002; Roden 2005).

At this point our discussion of dark temporality converges on the topic of dark perceptual phenomenology. There we noted Metzinger's claim that phenomenology is impossible for rudimentary perceptual experience despite the fact that it *has* a phenomenology. If, as Derrida and his materialist followers claim, differential temporality operates below the level of the subject or *Dasein*, then it may be a feature of dark phenomenology. Applying the phenomenological method, however, will be no help in determining whether this is so.

As a final illustration of this non-phenomenologically accessible phenomenology consider an eight-second extract from Iannis Xenakis's pioneering granular composition *Concret Ph*.[7] The music consists of fleeting differences in density, pitch and timbre of very short microsounds (grains). While the detailed patterns cannot be recalled in the way that a tonal melody can, humans can distinguish the macro-patterns assumed by the grain clouds from one moment to the next. For example, most listeners can distinguish an eight-second sequence from *Concret Ph* and a loop that repeats the first one-second slice of it for eight seconds because of the obvious repetition in pitch and dynamics in the loop.

Telling the looped sequence from the non-looped sequence is not, however, the same as acquiring subjective identity conditions that would allow us to recognize the *extra structure* distinguishing the non-looped from the looped sequence in a different context (e.g. within the entirety of *Concret Ph*). What is intuited here is a fact about the shortfall between type-identifiable light phenomenology and dark phenomenology. It does not provide any obvious insight into the structure or nature of the latter and thus does not constitute an exception to Metzinger's claim.

As an illustration of this, the mere awareness that there is missing structure in the loop does not help settle whether the content fixations which compose our experience of the grain cloud are "ecstatic" (involving a temporal difference without a synthesis) or consist in atomistic representations of discrete sonic properties. It is plausible to suppose that the perceptual awareness of the missing structure in the Xenakis loop consists of virtual contents – a representation of tendencies in the developing sound rather than something like a constantly updated encoding of occurrent sonic events. As phenomenologists, we can only "suppose" since this structure is too complex to be recalled out of the present. However, there are empirical reasons for thinking that the fine structure of the experience is virtual because this accords with the widely held assumption that our representation of temporal structure is accomplished via recurrent neural architecture that modulates each current input by feeding back earlier input (Van Gelder 1999). Cilliers thinks that this tendency is also an instance of *différance* and thus ecstatic since the activation of hidden nodes in a recurrent neural network is deferred "until its own activity (and those of others) has been reflected back on it" (Cilliers 2002: 82).

In Chapter 6 I will also argue that the differential model of temporality used in Derrida and Deleuze's work can be usefully attributed to a range of impersonal complex systems or assemblages. But for the moment I wish to stress the epistemological burden that waylays transcendental phenomenology. Dark phenomenology undermines the transcendental anthropologies of Heidegger and Husserl because it deprives them of the ability to distinguish transcendental conditions of possibility such as *Dasein* or Husserl's temporal subject (which are not things in the world) from the manifestation of things that they make possible. They are deconstructed insofar as *they become unable to interpret the formal structures with which they understand the fundamental conditions of possibility for worlds or things*.

This deconstruction is also naturalistic, however, because the reasons cited for attributing differential temporality to *whats* as opposed to *whos* draw on empirically based models of the evolution of material systems such as neutral networks just as the phenomenological/deconstructive model contributes to thinking in areas like physics and the science of complex systems (Cilliers 2002). Thus there is good reason to think that dark phenomenology is pervasive. If time is dark, then phenomenological investigation cannot provide a theory of temporality closed under appeal to intuition. A naturalized account of temporality might be possible but the epistemic status of temporality would then be that of a thing in the world rather than a condition of worlding or thinging.

As bruited, this failure of transcendentalism is crucial for our understanding of SP. If there is no *a priori* theory of temporality, there is no *a priori* theory of worlds and we cannot appeal to phenomenology to exclude the possibility that posthuman modes of being could be structurally unlike our own in ways that we cannot currently comprehend. Neither – given the argument of §4.1 – can we reasonably appeal to the assumption that intelligent nonhumans would require discursively structured intellects, even if we allow that they would require metacognitive resources of some kind. A naturalistic account of temporality moreover would provide no *a priori* warrant regarding the structure of the shared world required by pragmatist theories of meaning and mind (§§3.5–3.7).

Thus both the routes to a posthumanism bounded by transcendental anthropologies considered in Chapter 3 can be rejected (there might be other viable options, but pragmatism and phenomenology arguably saturate the field at the moment). If this failure is systemic – as I believe it is – then we have no future-proof grounds for assuming that humans and posthumans would belong to structurally similar worlds. This is not the same as saying that they would not belong to the same reality or universe. But we cannot unpack what belonging to the same reality means in terms of potentially shared world horizons.

Humans and posthumans might, for all anyone knows, have coincident ways of being in the world. It is conceivable that all highly optimizing intelligent life forms will need to have phenomenologies and thoughts much like our own. However, this fraternity of intellects would need to be observed and encountered rather than deduced from our armchairs. Failing supplementary arguments, transcendental philosophy should not be regarded as setting bounds on posthuman possibility (Chapter 8).

4.3 The analytic of the vile

The implications of transcendentally unbounded posthumanism for our understanding can be illustrated by considering the fictional case set out in Charles Stross's science fiction novel *Accelerando* (Stross 2006).

Accelerando provides a vivid and blackly funny portrayal of a transition from a merely transhuman to an utterly posthuman world. The Singularity has arrived by the twenty-second century. The self-improving AIs that now run the world are "wide human descendants" of human corporations and automated legal systems, which achieved both sentience and a form of legal personhood back in the twenty-first. As Stross's narrator observes, the phrase "smart money" has taken on an entirely new meaning!

Eventually, these "corporate carnivores" – known by the epithet "Vile Offspring" – institute a new form of capitalism (Economics 2.0) in which supply and demand relationships are computed too rapidly for those burdened by a "narrative chain" of personal consciousness to keep up.

Under Economics 2.0 first-person subjectivity is replaced "with a journal file of bid/request transactions" between autonomous software agents.

E 2.0 is so remorselessly efficient that it comes to dominate the major part of the solar system, whole planets pulverized and diverted to fast-thinking dust clouds of smart matter "blooming" around the sun (Stross 2006: 208–10).

This post-singularity scenario certainly seems bad for humans. Even their souped-up transhuman offspring prove incapable of functioning within E 2.0 and can only flee to the outer solar system and beyond as their worlds are "ethnically cleansed".

At the same time, it is not clear that E 2.0 is really "good" for post-humans in a way that might conceivably outweigh its bad impact on humans. If the Vile Offspring lack a linear, narrative consciousness of the kind that Husserl describes, can their form of existence be worthy of ethical consideration?

Well, their lack of linear consciousness seems to imply that the Vile Offspring would not be persons in at least one philosophically important sense of the term. Locke defined a person as "a thinking intelligent being that has reason and reflection and can consider itself as itself, the same thinking thing in different times and places" (Locke 1990: XXVII, §9).

If Locke is right about the psychological preconditions for personhood, then the Vile Offspring cannot count as persons because their phenomenology lacks the narrative centre that a being needs to consider itself the same thing at different times.[8] A Vile Offspring would be incapable of experiencing a life that might go better or worse for it (we might regard it as *Dasein*less as well as selfless, for this reason). It is hard to see how such entities could form an idea of the good and act in accordance with it. Vile Offspring would not be morally autonomous – in the way that is normally understood – because they could not choose the principles that govern their lives (see Chapters 5 and 6).

If humanists are right to say that persons have special moral worth and we add to this the claim that there could be no nonpersons with greater or equivalent moral worth than persons, then very weird posthumans such as Vile Offspring who lack personal phenomenology would not be as worthy of moral consideration as humans or transhumans.

Posthumans lacking personhood but possessing equivalents of pleasure or pain could be granted an equivalent status to nonhuman animals that also lack the psychological prerequisites of personhood. Posthumans lacking personhood and the capacity for pleasure and pain would, thus, not be sources for any kind of moral claim. Posthuman (or post-singularity) ethics would then be possible only in an etiolated form though it would not be applicable where our wide human descendants departed radically from human phenomenological invariants.

Perhaps this is what accounts for the "Vileness" of the Offspring. They are not "subjects" (*whos*) with plans for their lives and conceptions of the good but super-intelligent realizers of inchoate drives – like H. P. Lovecraft's blind, idiot God, Azathoth.

However, this analysis of posthuman vileness is premature.

It assumes that there is a moral hierarchy mapping onto a psychological or phenomenological hierarchy. But the fact that persons have morally considerable psychological properties does not entail that all beings lacking these properties must be morally inferior, or vile. For it is conceivable that there could be intelligent beings whose experience lacks some prerequisites for personhood but have phenomenological attributes that are not morally inferior to those of persons.

We humans might find it hard to conceive what such impersonal phenomenologies could be like (to say of them that they are "impersonal" or *Dasein*less is not to commit ourselves regarding the kinds of experiences they furnish). However, as I have argued above, our first-person understanding of our phenomenology is limited by the fact that light phenomenology is conjoined with a "dark side" which yields no such insight. Since this means that we have no first-person grasp of what our phenomenology is we cannot credit ourselves with understanding the space of possible phenomenologies.

According to Metzinger the existence of the dark side is a result of the computational limitations of the higher order representational system that generates subjectivity in humans. Human personal experience, he argues, is a dynamic and temporally situated model of the world, which represents the modeller as a distinct and always present ("untranscendable") part of the phenomenological scene. The phenomenal world model thus includes a phenomenal self-model (PSM). However, neither model represents the subpersonal cognitive processes that implement them. To borrow a phrase from Michael Tye: the phenomenal world- and self-models are "transparent" – we *seem* to look through them into an immediately given world out there and a self-present mental life "in here" (Metzinger 2004: 131, 165). However, this is a cognitive illusion generated by the brain's inability to look under its own hood.

Metzinger calls this constraint "autoepistemic closure". The world "out there" and our "inner" life appear not to be models or simulations only because we are not aware of the processes that generate them. Autoepistemic closure explains selfhood and being-in-the-world (*Dasein*) as a specific computational strategy. If selfhood is a higher-order model (akin to the second-order neural network in §3.1), there is a rationale for keeping the representational load incurred by the modelling process to a minimum. A system that modelled itself then attempted to model that modelling process in turn, and so on, would have to be infinitely large.

A real-world system existing under urgent time constraints needs to concentrate on essential tasks like keeping important data in working memory and ensuring that its sensory feedback conforms to expectations generated by its action emulators:

> Any self-modeling system, operating under real-world constraints and evolutionary pressures, will have to constantly minimize the computational resources needed to make system-related information available on the level of conscious experience. Because, as I have just pointed out, self-modeling possesses a potentially infinite and circular logical structure, it has to find an efficient way to break the reflexive loop. One simple and efficient way to interrupt a circular structure is by introducing an untranscendable *object*. My hypothesis is that the phenomenon of *transparent* self-modeling developed as an evolutionary viable strategy because it constituted a reliable way of making system-related information available without entangling the system in endless internal loops of higher-order self-modeling. Any biological system on the path to self-awareness must find a solution to this problem, or it will greatly diminish its reproductive success.
>
> (Metzinger 2004: 338)

Our subjectivity seems to exist in a spatial-temporal pocket: a situated, embodied self along with the dynamically evolving present so patiently described by Husserl and subsequent phenomenologists. Moreover, it is characterized by a bivalent distinction between self and other, non-mine and mine and a sense of temporal newness – or presentationality – "a virtual window of presence" that gives us a baseline with which to distinguish actuality and simulated possibility (pp. 42, 96). But according to the self-model account, the dynamically altering "now" described in Husserl, or the projecting of *Dasein* described by Heidegger, are aspects of the way in which creatures *like us* represent their relation to their environment. The usefulness of this representational scheme may depend on the fact that our sensory and motor systems are bundled "in a very small region of physical space, simultaneously establishing dense causal coupling" (Metzinger 2004: 161).

Other kinds of life – "conscious interstellar gas clouds" or Vile Offspring – might have to concoct phenomenologies of a radically different nature (Metzinger 2004: 161).

A super-swarm intelligence (see §2.1) like the Vile Offspring might need to find very different higher-order modelling strategies to cope with its spatial extent and the fact that its sub-agents might all have to deal with different problems occurring on multiple time-scales (making a single window of presence impracticable and potentially disastrous). A physically distributed entity with computing power to burn might support a "multi-threaded" and "multi-level" phenomenology that tracks the adventures of distributed located nodes while providing varied, but equally distributed, perspectives on its cognitive processing.

Now, it might be objected that there are certain rational norms that we are entitled to generalize from actual humans to hypothetical posthumans simply on the grounds that the latter would be intelligent, goal-driven systems. Such beings might not be *Lockean* persons equipped with a sense of subjective mineness or self-hood, but could, supposedly, be *Kantian* rational persons able to evaluate their behaviour according to explicit goals and generalizable rules (Brassier 2011).

Steve Omohundro has argued on such grounds that there is scope for predicting the overriding goals of even post-singularity entities. For example, systems that can alter their software or physical structure would have an incentive to make modifications that would help them achieve their goals more effectively. A concomitant of this, he argues, is that such beings would want to ensure that such improvements do not threaten their current goals:

> So how can it ensure that future self-modifications will accomplish its current objectives? For one thing, it has to make those objectives clear to itself. If its objectives are only implicit in the structure of a complex circuit or program, then future modifications are unlikely to preserve them. Systems will therefore be motivated to reflect on their goals and to make them explicit.
>
> (Omohundro 2008)

I think this conception of a self-present value-system reposing in the physical or computational component of a machine-self is questionable in a way that is instructive for speculations about a "general economy" of values within PPS and the role of our restricted concept of life within it (see §§6.1, 8.2).

Omohundro requires that there could be internal systems states of post-singularity AIs whose value content could be legible for the system's internal probes. Obviously, this assumes that the properties of a piece of hardware or software can determine the content of the system states that it orchestrates independently of the external environment in which the system is located. This property of non-environmental determination is known as "local supervenience" in the philosophy of mind literature (§2.1). If local supervenience for value-content fails, any inner state could signify different values in different environments. "Clamping" machine states to current values would entail restrictions on the situations in which the system could operate as well as on possible self-modifications.

Local supervenience might well not hold for system values. But let's assume it does. The problem for Omohundro is that the relevant inner determining properties are liable to be holistic. The intrinsic shape or colour of an icon representing a station on a metro map is arbitrary. There is nothing about a circle or a square or the colour blue that signifies "station". It is only the conformity between the relations between the icons and the stations in the metro system it represents which does this (Churchland's 2012 account of the meaning of prototype vectors in neural networks utilizes this analogy – see §4.1).

Hence once we disregard system–environment relations, the only properties liable to anchor the content of a system state are its relations to *other states* of the system. The meaning of an internal state s under some configuration of the system must depend on some inner context (like a cortical map) where s is related to lots of other states of a similar kind (Fodor & Lepore 1992).

But relationships between states of the self-modifying AI systems are assumed to be extremely plastic because each system will have an excellent model of its own hardware and software and the power to modify them (call this attribute "hyperplasticity"). If these relationships are modifiable then any state could exist in alternative configurations. It might function like homonyms within or between languages, having very different meanings in different contexts.

Suppose that some hyperplastic AI needs to ensure a state in one of its value circuits, s, retains the value it has under the machine's current configuration: v^*. To do this it must avoid altering itself in ways that would lead to s being in an inner context in which it meant some other value (v^{**}) or no value at all. It must clamp itself to those contexts to avoid s assuming v^{**} or v^{***}, etc.

To achieve clamping, though, it needs to select possible configurations of itself in which s is paired with a context c that preserves its meaning.

The problem for the AI is that all $[s + c]$ pairings are just more internal systems states which might assume different meanings in different contexts. To ensure that s means v^* in context c it needs to have done to some $[s + c]$ what it had been attempting with s – restrict itself to the supplementary contexts in which $[s + c]$ leads to s having v^* as a value and not something else.

Now, a hyperplastic machine will always be in a position to modify any configuration that it finds itself in (for good or ill). So this problem will be replicated for any combination of states $[s + c \ldots + \ldots]$ that the machine could assume within its configuration space. Each of these states will have to be repeatable in yet other contexts, etc. Since each concatenation of system states is a system state to which the principle of contextual variability applies recursively, there is no final system state for which this issue does not arise.

Clamping any arbitrary s requires that we have already clamped some undefined set of contexts for s and this condition applies to the clamping of that set.

So when Omohundro envisages a machine scanning its internal states to explicate their values he seems to be proposing an infinite task that has already been completed by a being with vast but presumably still finite computational resources.

Metzinger suggests that the human self-model is embedded in a maximally transparent phenomenal representation of the state of the organism – for example, the orientation of our musculoskeletal structure, visceral and cutaneous states – and its sensory responses to objects coded in cortical maps within the brainstem (Metzinger 2004: 310; Parvizi & Damasio 2001). These representations are transparent (or dark) because we are not aware of them as representations. By contrast, humans can be aware of thoughts as structured representations which they represent, in turn, as having an intentional relationship to the content of the transparently given "world" (Metzinger 2004: 400). Thus the "core-self" modelled in the sub-cortical structures is not accessible to humans *as such* (*as* the referent of a phenomenal model) but, on Metzinger's account, provides the phenomenological context in which we can compose, analyse and alter more "opaque" representational structures which we are aware of as representations (thoughts, sentences or mental images).

I take it that this functional partition could not apply to hyperplastic AIs. It might at first seem, then, that their "experience" (unlike ours) would be one of beings capable of recognizing that their phenomenology is a representation (Metzinger 2004: 565). However, my argument suggests that we may be whistling in the phenomenological darkness when we try to conceptualize such beings in advance of their manifestation. Such entities may have multi-threaded or selfless (*nemocentric*) models of reality, but given that the internal legibility of systems states may depend on some illegible background, hyperplastic entities may "experience" modes of illegibility that have little in common with our experience of embodied self-hood or mineness.

Likewise, we are not in a position to determine whether they could be selfless rational *subjects* in the grip of socially expressible concepts (Brassier 2011), for this may presuppose a congealed background of practical inferential know-how that could be serially *uncongealed* by hyperplasticity (§4.1). As Vinge avers, a post-singularity disconnection where such beings operated would be "a point where our old models must be discarded and a new reality rules" (Vinge 1993: np).

As in the octopus and centipedal cases, our inability to grasp hyperplastic phenomenology is not an intimation of its impossibility or unreality (see Introduction). Such a phenomenology might employ different strategies for modelling relationships between the modeller and its environment. It would be misleading to describe such a strategy as involving a project contextualized by a world horizon – as in Malpas's account of the context of radical interpretation – because the very idea of a project of understanding presupposes a single agent whose project it is and a congealed background against which an agent's possibilities show up.

Likewise, the phenomenological conception of world in Husserl and Heidegger presupposes that there is a single time in which the subject anticipates or projects into the future. But such a structure could be entirely inappropriate for understanding the variant phenomenologies of highly self-optimizing nonhumans. Such beings might not have projects because it might not profit them to represent themselves as agents. Thus they would not experience the world as a unitary horizon of possible horizons.

Now we do not have to buy all the details of Metzinger's representationalist account to support its deflationary implications for *anthropologically bounded posthumanism*. While his "self-model" account of subjectivity may or may not be on the right tracks, my general argument for dark phenomenology supports it indirectly by showing that there are no *a priori* grounds for excluding his hypothesis or the possibility of hyper-optimizing non-Lockean and non-Kantian intelligences.

Looking forward

Contrary to the thesis of transcendentally/anthropologically bounded posthumanism, I have argued that SP implies no *a priori* constraints on what being posthuman could be like. This is not to say, of course, that there are no constraints on PPS. But if they exist, they can only be discovered *a posteriori* – by exploring whatever posthuman life is technically within reach.

Posthuman minds may or may not be weirder than we can know. We cannot preclude maximum weirdness prior to their appearance. But what do we mean by such an advent? Given the extreme space of possible variation opened up by the collapse of the anthropological boundary, it seems that we can make few substantive assumptions about what posthumans would have to be like. Still, as I will argue in the next chapter, we can provide a formal analysis of the concept of posthuman life which explains why we must lack a substantive conception of it prior to meeting it in the wild.

Notes

1 Learning in ANNs usually involves reducing the error between the actual output of the network (initialized randomly) and the desired output, via adjustments to the "weights" or connection strengths between neurons. In ANNs there are *supervised learning algorithms* that tweak the NNs' weights until the error between the actual output vector and the vector desired by the trainers is minimized. It is important for the biological plausibility of connectionist models that some

ANNs (for example, Kohonen Self-Organizing Feature Maps) use *unsupervised learning* algorithms to generate useful output such as pattern identification, without that pattern having to be pre-identified by a trainer (see Churchland 2012). One example is the "Hebb Rule" which adjusts connection weights according to the timing of neuron activations (neurons that fire together, wire together). So ANNs don't have to be spoon-fed information but can self-organize in the face of structured input. Like ant colony "superorganisms", ANNs can latch onto real structure in the input data by local rules relating connection strength and neuron firing times.

2 Though it remains to be seen whether any hyperpriors are transcendental – i.e. necessary for any possible experience.

3 This insight or hope seemed to animate the main practitioners of phenomenology as a method of philosophical explication. Husserl's interest in the "origin of geometry" was motivated by the realization that a purely formalist account of geometric theories could not satisfactorily explain the meaning of geometrical claims or account for the ontological status of its posits (Husserl 1970: 44–5, 366–7).

4 Note that disjointness is rejected by any strong phenomenological realism. The ontology of *conjoint phenomenology* is not a correlate of our means of accessing it.

5 Where working memory is the cognitive ability to retain contents of experience for wider cognitive tasks such as reflection, categorization, planning and the production of verbal reports.

6 See Derrida's remarks on the role of generalized writing in cybernetics and molecular biology (Derrida 1998: 9).

7 These can be heard at http://enemyindustry.net/blog/?p=4356.

8 The conception of selves as narrative centres of gravity is from Dennett (1991).

5   The disconnection thesis

Introduction

I have characterized posthumans in very general terms as hypothetical wide "descendants" of current humans that are *no longer human* in consequence of some history of technological alteration" (§1.4). Speculative posthumanism is the claim that such beings might be produced as part of a feasible future history (§3.1).

We have also considered examples of hypothetical posthuman conditions – Vinge's singularity and Churchland's centipedal culture, to name but two. These suggest that the arrival of posthumans would be a significant event for us or our descendants, thus that we have a moral interest in exploring the implications of speculative posthumanism.

This chapter will seek to clarify the nature of this concern. To do this, however, we need to sharpen up our concept of the posthuman. The schematic formulation of speculative posthumanism given in Chapter 1 leaves us with some serious questions about the qualifications for posthuman status. What is the "humanity" to which the posthuman is "post"? Does the possibility of a posthumanity presuppose that there is a "human essence", or is there some other way of conceiving the human–posthuman difference? Without an answer to this question we cannot say, in general, what it is to become posthuman and thus why it should matter to humans or their wide descendants. In short, we require a theory of *human–posthuman difference*.

In this chapter I argue that the difference should be conceived as an emergent *disconnection* between individuals, not in terms of the presence or lack of essential properties (see Introduction, §2.4). I also suggest that these individuals should not be conceived in narrow biological terms but in "wide" terms permitting biological, cultural and technological relations of descent between human and posthuman.

If, as I claim, the posthuman difference is not one between kinds but emerges diachronically between individuals, we cannot specify its nature *a priori* but only *a posteriori* – after the emergence of actual posthumans.

The ethical implications of this are somewhat paradoxical. Given the dated non-existence of posthumans, we are unable to evaluate any post-human condition. Since posthumans could result from some iteration of our current technical activity, we have an interest in understanding what they might be like. If so, we have an interest in making or becoming posthumans.

5.1 The posthuman impasse: accounting and discounting

If we assume SP it seems we can adopt either of two policies towards the (so far) dimly intimated posthuman prospect. First, we can *account* for it: that is to say, assess the ethical implications of contributing to the creation of posthumans through our current technological activities.

However, the fictive avatars of posthumanity that have occupied us in the preceeding chapters suggest that the differences between humans and posthumans could be so great as to render accounting impossible, or problematic in the cases that matter. The differences stressed in Vinge's essay on the technological singularity are mainly cognitive: posthumans might be so smart that we could not understand their thoughts or anticipate the transformative effects of posthuman technology. There might be other very radical differences. Posthumans such as centipedes or hyperplastic AIs might have experiences so different from ours that we cannot envisage what living a posthuman life would be like, let alone whether it would be a worthwhile or worthless one.

For this reason, we may just opt to *discount* the possibility of post-humanity when considering the implications of our technological activity: considering only its implications for humans or for their modestly enhanced transhuman cousins. We can refer to the latter using Ray Kurzweil's coinage "MOSH": Mostly Original Substrate Human (Agar 2010: 41).

However, humans and MOSHs seem to have a *prima facie* duty to evaluate the outcomes of their technical activities with a view to maxi-mizing the chances of achieving the good posthuman outcomes or at least avoiding the bad ones. It is, after all, their actions and their technologies that will antecede a posthuman difference-maker such as a singularity, while the stakes for humans and MOSHs will be very great indeed.

From the human/MOSH point of view some posthuman dispensations might be transcendently good. Others could lead to a very rapid extinc-tion of all humans and MOSHs, or worse. Stross's *Accelerando* has humans and MOSHs being "ethnically cleansed" by descendants of capitalist financial instruments (Chapter 4, §4.3). But we might have mentioned the *Terminator* movies or Harlan Ellison's short story "I Have No Mouth, and I Must Scream" in which a vengeful AI tortures the remnants of humanity forever (Ellison 2012).

Thus *accounting* for our contribution to making posthumans seems obligatory, but may be impossible in the cases that really matter; while discounting our contribution to posthuman succession appears irresponsible and foolhardy.

We can call this double bind "the posthuman impasse".

If the impasse is real rather than apparent, then there may be no principles by which to assess the most significant and disruptive long-term outcomes of current developments in NBIC (and related) technologies.

One might try to circumvent the impasse by casting doubt on the thesis of speculative posthumanism. It is conceivable that further developments in technology, on this planet at least, will never contribute to the emergence of significantly nonhuman forms of life. I do not deny this. However, speculative posthumanism is a significantly weaker hypothesis than any single posthuman prognosis and thus more plausible. For example, it is a much weaker claim than Vinge's singularity hypothesis (§1.4). Vinge specifies one recipe for generating posthumans and it is one that is taken seriously by leading philosophers, futurists and scientists – Vinge himself and David Chalmers, to name but two. But there might be posthuman difference-makers that do not require recursive self-improvement (we will consider some of these in due course). Moreover, we know that Darwinian natural selection has generated novel forms of life in the evolutionary past since humans are one such. Since there seems to be nothing special about the period of terrestrial history in which we live it seems hard to credit that comparable novelty resulting from some combination of biological or technological factors might not occur in the future.

So there seem to be no *a priori* grounds for circumventing the claims of SP. They are sufficiently plausible in the light of current technological trends to merit consideration.

Is there any way round the impasse that is compatible with SP?

In this chapter and in the final chapter I will begin to outline a framework for approaching our posthuman prospects and thus to avoid the impasse. However, to understand how the impasse can be avoided we must first consider what SP entails in more detail.

As a first step towards this clarification, let us summarize the schematic possibility claim SP:

(SP) *Descendants of current humans could cease to be human by virtue of a history of technical alteration.*

SP has notable features which, when fully explicated, can contribute to a coherent philosophical account of posthumanity.

First, the SP schema defines posthumanity as the result of a process of technical *alteration*. Value-laden terms such as "enhancement" or "augmentation", which are more commonly used in debates about transhumanism and posthumanism, are, as advertised, to be strenuously avoided (§§1.2, 1.4). I shall explain and justify this formulation in §5.2.

Second, it represents the relationship between humans and posthumans as a historical successor relation, *wide descent*, introduced in Chapter 1 (§1.4). Recall that the concept of wide descent was introduced because posthuman making could be mediated by disparate technologies and to an arbitrary degree. Entities qualifying as posthuman might include our biological descendants or beings resulting from purely technical mediators (e.g. artificial intelligences, synthetic life-forms or uploaded minds). The concept of wide descent will be further explained in §5.3.

As we shall see in §5.3, wide descent also bears on a foundational problem confronting a general account of the posthuman: what renders posthumans *nonhuman*? Is SP committed to a "human" or MOSH *essence* that all posthumans lack, or are there other ways of conceiving the difference?

Before going there, it will be helpful to further distance the idea of technical alteration introduced in SP from more widely used notions of enhancement and augmentation that regularly feature in bioethical discussions of the posthuman.

5.2 Value neutrality

SP states that a future history of a general type is metaphysically and technically possible. It does not imply that the posthuman would *improve on* the human or MOSH state, or that there would be a commonly accessible perspective from which to evaluate human and posthuman lives. Posthumans may, as Vinge writes, be "simply too different to fit into the classical frame of good and evil" (Vinge 1993: np).

It could be objected that the value-neutralization of the historical successor relation in the SP schema is excessively cautious and loses traction on what distinguishes humans from their hypothetical posthuman descendants: namely, that posthumans would be in some sense "better" by virtue of having greater capacities.

One of the most widely used formulations of the idea of the posthuman – that of transhumanist philosopher Nick Bostrom – is non-neutral. He defines a posthuman as a "being that has at least one posthuman capacity" by which is meant "a central capacity greatly exceeding the maximum attainable by any current human being without recourse to new technological means". Candidates for posthuman capacities include augmented "healthspan", "cognition" or "emotional dispositions" (Bostrom 2008: 108).

While this is not a purely metaphysical conception of the posthuman it is, it might be argued, not so loaded as to beg ethical questions against critics of radical enhancement. As Allen Buchanan points out, "enhancement" is *a restrictedly value-laden notion* insofar as enhancing a capacity implies making it function more effectively but does not imply improving the welfare of its bearer (Buchanan 2009: 350, n6).

Moreover, it could be objected that "alteration" is so neutral that a technical process could count as posthuman engendering if it resulted in wide descendants of humans with capacities far below those of normal humans (I will address this point in §5.5).

However, it is easy to see that the value-ladenness of "enhancement" is not restricted enough to capture some conceivable paths to posthumanity. To be sure, posthumans might result from a progressive enhancement of cognitive powers – much as in Vinge's recursive improvement scenario. Alternatively, our posthuman descendants might have capacities we have no concepts for while lacking some capacities that we can conceive of.

In the previous chapter we considered the possibility that shared "non-symbolic workspaces" – which support a very rich but non-linguistic form of thinking – might render human natural language unnecessary and thus eliminate the cultural preconditions for propositional and sentential thinking. If propositional attitude psychology collectively distinguishes humans from non-humans, users of non-symbolic workspaces might instrumentally eliminate the non-propositional and thus cease to be human (as I show in §5.4, a "human distinguishing" property does not have to be part of a human essence).

It is not clear that the process leading to this relatively radical cognitive alteration would constitute an *augmentation* history in the usual sense – since it could involve the loss of one central capacity (the capacity for language and thinking with sentences) and the acquisition of an entirely new one. Yet it is arguable that it could engender beings so different from us in cognitive structure that they would intuitively qualify as posthuman.

Star Trek's Borg provide an interesting variation on the theme of the "value-equivocal" posthuman. The Borg-Collective possesses enormous instrumental intelligence and the technical prowess to appropriate and "Borgify" entire planets. However, its powers emerge from the interactions of highly networked "drones", each of whom has had its personal capacities for reflection and agency suppressed.

5.3 Wide descent

In this section I elaborate the distinction between wide descent and narrow descent in term of a distinction between a *narrow* conception of the human *qua* species and a *wide* conception of the human.

Whereas narrow humanity can be identified, if we wish, with the biological species *Homo sapiens*, wide humanity is a technogenetic construction or "assemblage" with both narrowly human and narrowly nonhuman parts.

There are two principal justifications for introducing wide descent and the correlative notion of wide humanity:

First, as I claimed in §1.4, there are many conceivable technical pathways to posthumanity (e.g. mind uploading) consistent with the extension of some or other NBIC technology that involves non-biological relations of descent from humans individuals. Some, like Vinge, argue that posthumans could be descended from human artefacts such as machine robots and computers. Since these conceivable lines of descent are central to our intuitive concept of posthumanity they need to be reflected in a philosophically explicated one.

It follows that when considering the lives of hypothetical posthuman descendants we must understand "descent" as a relationship that can be technically mediated to any degree (§3.1).

Second, "Humanity" is already the product of a technogenetic process.

A plausible analogy for the emergence of posthumans, as Vinge observes, is the evolutionary process that differentiated humans from nonhuman primates.

But there are grounds for holding that the process of becoming human (hominization) has been mediated by human cultural and technological activity. One way of conceiving hominization is in terms of cultural niche construction. Niche construction occurs where members of a biological population actively alter their environment in a way that alters the selection pressures upon it. For example, it has been argued that that the invention of dairy farming technology (around 10,000 BC) created an environment selective for genes that confer adult lactose tolerance. Thus the inventors of animal husbandry unwittingly reconfigured the bodies of their descendants to survive in colder climes (Laland *et al.* 2000; Buchanan 2011: 204). The anthropologist Terrence Deacon proposes that the emergence of early symbolic practices produced a symbolically structured social environment in which the capacity to acquire competence in complex symbol systems was a clear selective advantage. Thus it is possible that the selection pressures that made humans' brains adept at language learning were a consequence of our ancestors' own social activity even as these brains imposed a learnability bottleneck on the cultural evolution of human languages (Deacon 1997: 322–6, 338).

If this model is broadly correct, hominization has involved a confluence of biological, cultural and technological processes. It has produced sociotechnical "assemblages" where humans are coupled with other active components: for example, languages, legal codes, cities and computer-mediated information networks.

The term "assemblage" will figure extensively in the remainder of the book because it is a central concept in the ontological framework for speculative posthumanism. Here is a quick gloss on the topic (we will explore its implications further in Chapter 6).

The concept of assemblage was developed by the poststructuralist philosophers Gilles Deleuze and Félix Guattari (1988). Its clearest expression, though, is in the work of the Deleuzean philosopher of science Manuel DeLanda. For DeLanda, an assemblage is an *emergent* but *decomposable* whole and belongs to the conceptual armory of the particularist "flat" ontology I will propose for SP in §5.4. Assemblages are *emergent* wholes in that they exhibit powers and properties not attributable to their parts but which depend (or "supervene") on those powers. Assemblages are also *decomposable* insofar as all the relations between their components are "external": each part can be detached from the whole to exist independently (assemblages are thus opposed to "totalities" in an idealist or holist sense). This is the case even where the part is functionally necessary for the continuation of the whole (DeLanda 2006: 184; see §6.5).

Biological humans are currently "obligatory" components of modern technical assemblages. Technical systems like air-carrier groups, cities or financial markets have powers that cannot be attributed to narrow humans but depend on them for their operation and maintenance much as an animal depends on the continued existence of its vital organs. Technological systems are thus intimately coupled with biology and have been over successive technological revolutions.

However, this dependency runs in the other direction: the distinctive social and cognitive accomplishments of biological humans require a technical and cultural infrastructure. Our capacity to perform mathematical operations on arbitrarily large numbers is not just due to an innate number sense but depends on our acquisition of routines like addition or long division and our acculturation into culturally stored numeral systems. Our species-specific language ability puts us in a unique position to apply critical thinking skills to thoughts expressed in public language, to co-ordinate social behavior via state institutions or record information about complex economic transactions (Clark 2003, 2008: 44–60; see §6.5).

These considerations lend support to the claim that the emergence of biological humans has been one aspect of the technogenesis of a planet-wide assemblage composed of biological humans locked into networks of increasingly "lively" and "autonomous" technical artefacts (Haraway 1991; §1.4). It is this wider, interlocking system, and not bare-brained biological humans, that would furnish the conditions for the emergence of posthumans. Were the emergence of posthumans to occur, it would thus be a historical rupture in the development of this extended socio-technical network.

However, while the emergence of posthumans *must* involve the network, the degree to which it would involve modifications of biological humans is conceptually open (see above). Posthumans may derive from us by some technical process that mediates biological descent (such as a germ-line cognitive enhancement) or they may be a consequence of largely technological factors.

I shall refer to this human socio-technical assemblage as the "Wide Human" (henceforth WH). An entity is a Wide Human just so long as it depends for its continued functioning on WH while contributing to its operations to some degree. Members of the biological species *Homo sapiens*, on the other hand, are *narrowly* human. Thus, domesticated animals, mobile phones and toothbrushes are Wide Humans while we obligatory biologicals are both *narrowly* and *widely* human.

Having outlined the patient and the generic process of becoming posthuman, we now state a recursive definition of Wide Human descent:

> An entity is a Wide Human descendant if it is the result of a technically mediated process:
>
> A) Caused by a part of WH – where the ancestral part may be wholly biological, wholly technological or some combination of the two.
> B) Caused by a wide human descendant.

A is the "basis clause". It states what belongs to the initial generation of Wide Human descendants without using the concept of wide descent. B is the recursive part of the definition. Given *any* generation of Wide Human descendants, it specifies a successor generation of Wide Human descendants.

It is important that this definition does not imply that a Wide Human descendant *need be human* in either wide or narrow senses. Any part of WH ceases to be widely human if its wide descendants go "feral": acquiring the capacity for independent functioning and replication outside the human network (see §6.1 for an analysis of this functional relationship). SP entails that with becoming posthuman this would occur as a result of some history of technical change.

Becoming posthuman would thus be an unprecedented discontinuity in the hominization process. WH has undergone revolutions in the past (like the shift from hunter-gatherer to sedentary modes of life) but no part of it has been *technically altered* so as to function outside of it.

It follows that a Wide Human descendent is a posthuman if and only if:

> I. It has ceased to belong to WH (the Wide Human) as a result of technical alteration.
> II. *Or is a wide descendant of such a being (outside WH).*[1]

I refer to this claim as the *disconnection thesis*.

Put more informally, the disconnection thesis proposes that posthumans would be cases of former Wide Humans *becoming feral*: becoming able to fulfil an independent career as an agent outside the human socio-technical assemblage WH. This intuitive sketch will have to do for now. In Chapter 6 we will consider the agency conditions for disconnection at greater length.

5.4 Disconnection and anti-essentialism

My formulation of what it means to cease to be human will seem strange and counter-intuitive to some. We are used to thinking of *being human* not as a part–whole relation (being a part of WH in this case) but as instantiating a human nature or "essence" (see Introduction, §2.4).

An essential property of a kind is a property that no member of that kind can be without. If humans are necessarily rational, for example, then it is a necessary truth that if x is human, then x is rational.[2]

To say that a human essence exists is just to say that there is a set of individually necessary conditions for humanity.

Anthropological essentialism (the claim that there is a human essence) implies that the technically mediated loss of even one of these would export the loser from humanity to posthumanity. As metaphysical formulae go, this has the immediate appeal of simplicity.

It also provides a nice clear method for resolving the *posthuman impasse*. We can call this the "apophatic method": after the method of apophatic or "negative" theology. Apophatic theologians think that God is so mysterious that we can only describe Him by saying what He is not (Tuggy 2010). By extension, anthropological essentialism, if true, would allow us to identify each path to posthumanity with the deletion of some component of the human essence. This, in turn, would allow us to adjudicate the value of these paths by considering the ethical implications of each loss of an anthropologically necessary property.

For example, an essentialist may claim on either *a posteriori* or *a priori* grounds that humans are necessarily *moral persons* with capacities for deliberation and autonomous agency. If so, one sure route to posthumanity would be to lose those moral capacities. Put somewhat crudely, we could then know that *some* conceivable posthumans are non-persons. If persons are, as Rawls claims, "self-authenticating sources of valid claims" and non-persons are not, then *this* posthuman state involves the loss of unconditional moral status (Rawls 2005: 33). This particular path to posthumanity would, it seems, involve unequivocal loss.

The disconnection thesis does not entail the rejection of anthropological essentialism but it renders any reference to essential human characteristics unnecessary. The fact that some Wide Human descendant no longer belongs to the Wide Human implies nothing about its intrinsic properties or the process that brought about its disconnection. However, we can motivate the disconnection thesis and its mereological (part–whole) conception of wide humanity by arguing against essentialism on general grounds.

The most plausible argument for abandoning anthropological essentialism is naturalistic: essential properties seem to play no role in our best scientific explanations of how the world acquired biological, technical and social structures and entities. At this level, form is not imposed on matter from "above" but emerges via generative mechanisms that depend on the amplification or inhibition of differences between particular entities (for example, natural selection among biological species or competitive learning algorithms in cortical maps).[3] If this picture holds generally, then essentialism provides a misleading picture of reality.

DeLanda refers to ontologies that reject a hierarchy between organizing form and a passive nature or "matter" as "flat ontologies". Whereas a hierarchical ontology has categorical entities like essences to organize it, a flat universe is "made exclusively of unique, singular individuals, differing in spatio-temporal scale but not in ontological status" (DeLanda 2002: 58; §§6.2, 6.3).

The properties and the capacities of these entities are never imposed by transcendent entities but develop out of causal interactions between particulars at various scales. Importantly for the present discussion, *a flat ontology recognizes no primacy of natural over artificial kinds* (Harman 2008).

It is significant that one of DeLanda's characterizations of flat ontology occurs during a discussion of the ontological status of biological species in which he sides with philosophers who hold that species are individuals rather than types or universals (DeLanda 2002: 59–60). For example, Ernst Mayr's "biological species concept" (BSC) accounts for species differences among sexually reproducing populations in terms of the reproductive isolation of their members. This restricts gene recombination and thus limits the scope for phenotypic variation resulting from gene flows, further reinforcing discontinuities between conspecifics (Okasha 2002: 200).

Motivated by such anti-essentialist scruples, Nicolas Agar has argued that differences between humans and prospective posthumans can be conceived in terms of membership or non-membership of a reproductively isolated population as conceived by the BSC (Agar 2010: 19). Posthumans would arise where (and only where) radical enhancement created reproductive barriers between the enhanced and the mainstream human population.

Agar's proposal illustrates one variant of the flat ontological approach. However, importing the BSC neat from the science of the evolutionary past is problematic when considering the ontology of *technogenetic* life forms. Biotechnologies such as the artificial transfer of genetic material across species boundaries could make the role of natural reproductive boundaries less significant in a posthuman or transhuman dispensation (Buchanan 2009: 352, n10). If these alternative modes of genetic transmission became routinely used alongside "regular" sex, the homeostatic role of reproductive barriers would be significantly reduced.

While BSC has a clear application to understanding speciation in sexually reproducing life forms, it has no applicability to non-sexually reproducing life forms. Likewise, the distinction between the genetics lab and nature cannot be assumed relevant in a posthuman world where biotechnology or post-biological forms of descent dominate the production of intelligence and the production of order more generally (*ibid.*). The flat ontological injunction not to prioritize natural over artificial sources of order provides a more reliable methodological principle than Agar's misguided ethical naturalism.

The distinction between wide and narrow humanity broached earlier in this chapter accommodates this possibility by distinguishing between the narrow human (which can be understood in terms of the BSC) and the socio-technical assemblage WH which fully expresses human societies, cultures and minds.

WH has the same *ontological status* as species like *Homo sapiens* – both are complex individuals rather than kinds or essences. However, WH is constituted by causal relationships between biological and non-biological parts, such as languages, technologies and institutions. A disconnection event would be liable to involve technological mechanisms without equivalents in the biological world and this should be allowed for in any ontology that supports speculative posthumanism.

5.5 Modes of disconnection

As mentioned above, Vinge considers the possibility that disconnection between posthumans and humans may occur as a result of differences in the cognitive powers of budding posthumans rendering them incomprehensible and uninterpretable for baseline humans.

For example, something like a centipedal existence or (more drastically) a "vile" or hyperplastic one might be incompatible with a phenomenology associated with the existence of biographically persistent Lockean persons or moral Kantian persons (Introduction, §4.3; see also Vinge 1993).

If non-subjective phenomenology among posthumans is possible, Vinge's worry that these forms of existence might not be evaluable according our conceptions of morality seems warranted. Most public ethical frameworks have maximal conditions. For example, liberals valorize the capacity for personal autonomy that allows most humans "to form, to revise, and rationally to pursue a conception of the good" (Rawls 1980: 525).

Personal or moral autonomy presumably has threshold cognitive and affective preconditions such as the capacity to evaluate actions, beliefs and desires (practical rationality) and a capacity for the emotions and affiliations informing these evaluations. And, as we saw in §4.3, the capacity for practical reason at issue in our conception of autonomy might not be accessible to a hyperplastic being that lacks the stable background phenomenology required for self-evaluation.

As emphasized in Chapter 4, our inability to imagine impersonal phenomenologies may reflect the transparency (cognitive inaccessibility) of *human* phenomenological invariants and their centrality to the ways humans understand the relationship between mind and world, rather than any insight into the necessary structure of worlds and subjects (see §3.3; Metzinger 2004: 213). Metzinger argues that our temporally and spatially centred subjectivity depends on the fact that our sensory receptors and motor effectors are "physically integrated within the body of a single organism" (p. 161). Super-smart fogs or swarms like the Vile Offspring might feel very differently.

Disconnection may take other forms, however.

All that is required for a disconnection from the Wide Human recall is that some part of this assemblage becomes capable of going wild and following an independent career. This is not true of current types of artificial intelligence, for example, which need to be built, maintained by narrow humans and powered by other human artefacts. This is why beings that are artificially "downgraded" so that their capacities are less than human are unlikely to generate a disconnection event (§5.2).

A disconnection could ensue, then, wherever prospective posthumans have properties that make their feasible forms of association disjoint from humans/MOSH forms of association.

I suggested in §4.1 that linguistically mediated propositional attitude psychology might distinguish humans from nonhumans. However, as our excursus into flat ontology shows, the capacity to form propositional attitudes such as the *belief* that Lima is in Peru need not be thought of as a component of a human essence but as a filter or "sorting mechanism" which excludes nonhumans from human society much as incompatibilities in sexual organs or preferences create reproductive barriers between Mayr-style biological species (Agar 2010: 19–28). Wide successors to humans, such as the centipedes, who have a non-propositional format in which to communicate, might not be able to participate in our society just as our unmodified descendants might not be able to participate in theirs. Such disconnections could happen by degrees and (unlike in a Vingean singularity) relatively slowly in terms of individual lifetimes.

There might also be cases where the disconnection remains partial (for example, some non-propositional thinkers might retain a vestigial capacity to converse with humans and MOSHs).

5.6 Are disconnections predictable?

I do not claim that speculations in the previous section reliably predict the nature and dynamics of a disconnection event. For example, we do not know whether greater than human intelligence is possible or whether it can be produced by an "extendible" technological method (Chalmers 2010).

Nor, at this point, can we claim to have knowledge about the feasibility of the other disconnection events that we have speculated about (e.g. the replacement of propositional attitude psychology with some non-linguistic cognitive format).

These scenarios are merely intended to illustrate the *ontological thesis* that posthuman–human difference would be a discontinuity resulting from parts of the Wide Human becoming so technically "altered" they can cut out on their own. The intrinsic properties exhibited by these entities are left open by the disconnection thesis (see §8.2).

This epistemological caution seems advisable given that the advent of posthumanity is a (currently) hypothetical future event whose nature and precipitating causes are *ex hypothesi* unprecedented. There are many conceivable ways in which such an event might be caused. Even if a Vinge-style singularity is conceivable but not possible, some unrelated technology might be a possible precursor to a disconnection. Disconnections are not defined by a particular technical cause (such as mind-uploading) but purely by an abstract relation of wide descent and the property of functional and replicative independence.

Disconnection *can thus be multiply realized by technologies which have little in common other than a) feasibility and b) that disconnection is one of their possible historical effects.*

There are no irrefutable grounds for extrapolating the long-run capacities of actual technologies from their current capacities (as in the Skynet case). This precaution applies more stringently to hypothetical technologies. Thus we can have no reliable grounds for holding that *conceivable* precursors to a disconnection are *feasible* precursors so long as the relevant technologies are underdeveloped. Speculating about how currently notional technologies might bring about autonomy for parts of WH affords no reliable information about posthuman lives, though it may, as here, inform salutary reflections on the scope for posthuman difference. Given the power identity assumption (PIA), the same modesty should attend speculations about digitally emulated or "uploaded" minds (§3.2).

However, once a feasible precursor has been produced, the Wide Human could be poised at the beginning of a disconnection process since the capacity to generate disconnection would be a realized technological power whose powers would be becoming empirically manifest (absent defeaters; see Chalmers 2010). Thus it is plausible to suppose that any disconnection (however technically realized) will be an instance of what Paul Humphreys terms *diachronic emergence* (Humphreys 2008). A diachronically emergent behaviour or property occurs as a result of a temporally extended process, but cannot be inferred from the initial state of that process.

An emergent property of a system is one that depends or "supervenes" on the properties of its components but which is fundamentally different from those properties (§2.1). Classical emergentism was chiefly concerned with synchronic emergence: where the emergent property occurs at the same time as the component properties or interactions that generate it. For example, some philosophers cite consciousness as a candidate for emergent properties on the grounds that the properties of conscious experience clearly depend on the physical properties of the brain and nervous system but are non-physical and have causal powers that are independent of the powers of the physical components. This is an example of the thesis of *strong emergence* because it holds that emergent properties can exert a "downward causal" influence on physical states that is irreducible in some way to the influence exerted by the physical components of the system (Bedau 1997: 376).

Diachronic emergence, on the other hand, is a case of what Mark Bedau calls "weak emergence". Bedau's definition states that a macro-property (P) is weakly emergent only if it can only be derived from P's microdynamics and external conditions via a simulation with relevantly similar properties (1997: 378).

For jobbing scientists, this epistemological formulation neatly sidesteps philosophical issues about "spooky emergent" properties. Emergent macrobehaviour can be exhibited by systems in which it is entirely determined by the simple dynamic rules governing the components. For example, cellular automata such as John Conway's Game of Life are governed by very simple rules, yet simulations in the Life show that complex and unpredictable transitions between cell-configurations can "emerge" over their successive iteration (Bedau 1997: 381–6).

So the claim that disconnections are diachronically emergent is metaphysically modest. Weakly emergent phenomena are scientifically well-attested. Any technology that is disconnection-potent (can produce a disconnection) has properties that have not been exhibited by earlier technologies. Thus predictions about its effects and behaviour could not be reliably inferred from the effects of earlier technologies. Moreover, we have seen that the nature and feasibility of candidates for posthuman-making technologies is highly uncertain (§§1.3, 3.1, 3.2). Thus it seems unlikely that we will be able to discern the nature or the effects of feasible disconnection-potent technologies without building serviceable prototypes.

5.7 Interpreting posthuman others

If disconnections are diachronically emergent phenomena, their morally salient characteristics will not be predictable prior to their occurrence. While this constrains our ability to prognosticate about disconnections, it leaves other aspects of their epistemology open. As Humphrey reminds us, diachronic emergence is a one-time event. Once we observe a formerly diachronically emergent event we are in a position to predict tokens of the same type of emergent property from causal antecedents that have been observed to generate it in the past. Diachronic emergence has no implications for the uninterpretability or weirdness of posthumans since their nature is left open by the disconnection thesis.

I have argued that posthumans might have phenomenologies that are very different to human subjectivity or *Dasein* (Chapter 4). However, the fact that a being might have a very different experience of the world to ours does not entail that we could not come to understand it. We predict and understand nonhumans like octopuses, dogs or nation-states by treating them as agents with reasons for acting – a hermeneutic strategy Dennett (1987) refers to as the "intentional stance" (see also Clark 1994). We adopt the intentional stance to a system by ascribing it the beliefs and desires it seems it ought to have given the kind of system it is; then see if its behaviour is predictable on this basis. Dennett describes how we might apply it to raccoons:

> One can often predict or explain what an animal will do by simply noticing what it notices and figuring out what it wants. The raccoon wants the food in the box-trap, but knows better than to walk into a potential trap where it can't see its way out. That's why you have to put two open doors on the trap – so that the animal will dare to enter the first, planning to leave by the second if there's any trouble. You'll have a hard time getting a raccoon to enter a trap that doesn't have an apparent "emergency exit" that closes along with the entrance.
>
> (Dennett 1995a: 112)

The raccoon's responses to the one-door trap and its seduction by the *two-door trap* justifies the following interpretation of raccoon mental life: that raccoons have beliefs about the numbers of doors in traps and that they are averse to traps with only one door. Raccoons are "intentional systems" in virtue of being predictable from the intentional stance. Using it does not entail understanding *what it is like* for the raccoon to experience an aversion to one-door traps. Phenomenological similarity is not a condition of interpretation.

Maybe there are other preconditions for interpretation that might be absent under disconnection. Raccoon responsiveness to the difference between *one-* and *two-door* traps exhibits a pattern we can pick up on. Could there be mind-like patterns humans could not pick up on, even *in principle*?

But we cannot formulate the concept of necessary uninterpretability for humans without invoking a human essence which imposes necessary limits on what we can interpret. So if we adopt the anti-essentialist flat ontology I have recommended as a basis for the disconnection thesis, we should beware of using terms like "radical alien" or "radically other". For a thing could be radically *other to humans* only if the inability to understand it were a part of the human cognitive essence. If we reject essences wholesale, we must hold that there are no modal facts of this nature. There is no big "O" Other because there is no "hard" organizing structure for it to be other to (Farrell 1996; Roden 2004b).

For pragmatists like Davidson and Dennett, to have content or meaning *just is* to be interpretable as having it. So pragmatism implies that, regardless of the vicissitudes of phenomenology, there cannot be radically alien minds. An uninterpretable entity would lack coherent transactions with the world that could qualify it as a thinker.[4]

However, I argued in Chapter 4 that the idea of a common world – a world as a shared horizon of encounter – cannot be formulated without insights into phenomenological necessity and that the discipline of phenomenology is not in a position to warrant these insights (§4.2). Even if we allow that we live in a common physical universe, this is not the world of common determinables presupposed by a pragmatist hermeneutics (§3.7).

We have baulked at the idea of the radical alien (or Big Other) since it is not clear how to unpack this without recourse to a human cognitive essence. But this suggests at most that a weird posthuman such as a Vile Offspring would not be a cognitive thing-in-itself forever sealed from minds of a different kind. Yet grasping vilese could be as beyond current or future human capabilities as human-inference is beyond any raccoon.[5] A Vile Super-Intelligence might be exquisitely sensitive to perspectival facts that are fully objective yet don't show up for beings with a different kind of *Dasein*. All this could be true without it being true that it is part of our cognitive essence that vilese is incomprehensible to us. For example, if there are no essences – because ontology is flat – then it is not part of the human essence that we are incapable of unpowered flight. Yet humans are incapable of unpowered flight.

What are the implications of this for a posthuman or post-singularity ethics?

Well, we have considered interpretationist grounds for believing that there could be no posthuman minds recalcitrant to interpretation in principle. All this shows is that a posthuman will not be be utterly transcendent – like the God of Negative Theology or Kant's Thing. Thus a post-singularity existence might be interpretable in principle but not by us.[6]

Some posthuman thinking may still be so powerful or so strangely formatted that it would defy the interpretative capacities of wide human descendants *not altered to an equivalent degree*. But this would depend on the contingencies of disconnection – which are, as yet, unknown. If the technology exists to create posthumans, then the same technology might support "interfaces" between human and posthuman beings such as the bi-formatted propositional/non-propositional thinkers mentioned above. Thus where conditions favour it, "Posthuman Studies" may graduate from speculative metaphysics to a viable cultural research program (see Chapter 8).

5.8 A resolution of the impasse?

What are the implications of the disconnection thesis for attempts to negotiate the ethical bind of the posthuman impasse? The impasse is a way of formulating the ethical concern that the posthuman consequences of our own technical activity may be beyond our moral compass. I have conceded that posthumans might be very different from us in diverse ways, but have argued that there is no basis for concluding that posthumans would have to be beyond evaluation.

As argued in §5.6, we may be in a far superior position to undertake a value-assessment once a disconnection has occurred. Thus if we have a moral (or any other) interest in *accounting* for posthumans we have an interest in bringing about the circumstances in which accounting can occur. Thus we have an interest in contributing to the emergence of posthumans or *becoming posthuman* ourselves where this is liable to mitigate the interpretative problems posed by disconnection.

It could be objected, at this point, that we may also have counter-vailing reasons for *preventing* the emergence of posthumans and not becoming posthuman ourselves.

We have acknowledged that some disconnections could be very bad for humans. Since disconnection could go very wrong, it can be objected that the precautionary principle (PP) trumps the accounting principle. Although there is no canonical formulation, all versions of the PP place a greater burden of proof on arguments for an activity alleged to have the potential for causing extensive public or environmental harm than on arguments against it (Cranor 2004; Buchanan 2009: 199–200). In the present context the PP implies that even where the grounds for holding that the effects of disconnection will be harmful are comparatively weak, the onus is on those who seek disconnection to show that it will not go very wrong.

However, the diachronically emergent nature of disconnection implies that such a demonstration is not possible prior to a disconnection event. Thus one can use the PP to argue that accounting for disconnection (assessing its ethical implications) is not morally obligatory but morally wrong.

One might conclude at this point that we have substituted one impasse (the conflict between accounting and discounting) for a second: the conflict between the principle of accounting and the PP. However, this will depend on the different attitudes to uncertainty expressed in different versions of the PP. If the principle is so stringent as to forbid technical options whose long-range effects remain uncertain to any degree, then it forbids the development of disconnection-potent technology. However, this would forbid almost any kind of technological decision (including the decision to relinquish a technology).[7] Thus a maximally stringent PP is self-vitiating (Buchanan 2011: 200–01).

It follows that the PP should require reasonable evidence of possible harm before precautionary action is considered. A selective precautionary approach to the possibility of disconnection would require that suspect activities be "flagged" for the potential to produce bad disconnections (even where this evidence is not authoritative). But if disconnections are diachronically emergent phenomena, the evidence to underwrite flagging will not be available until the process of technical change is poised for disconnection.

To take a historical analogy: the syntax of modern computer programming languages is built on the work on formal languages developed in the nineteenth century by mathematicians and philosophers like Frege and Boole. Lacking comparable industrial models, it would have been impossible for contemporary technological forecasters to predict the immense global impact of what appeared an utterly rarefied intellectual enquiry. We have no reason to suppose that we are better placed to predict the long-run effects of current scientific work than our nineteenth-century forebears (if anything the future seems more rather than less uncertain). Thus even if we enjoin selective caution to prevent worst-case outcomes from disconnection-potent technologies, we must still place ourselves in a situation in which such potential can be identified. Thus seeking to contribute to the emergence of posthumans, or to become posthuman ourselves, is compatible with a reasonably constrained PP.

Looking forward

This chapter has furnished the abstract theory of human–posthuman difference that we required. It is abstract because, as emphasized above, the disconnection relation could be realized or satisfied by disparate forms of human–posthuman difference. The disconnection thesis provides a clear qualification for posthuman status but it is not an informative one, sadly. This led us to conclude that the only way of satisfying our moral concern with our posthuman prospects through posthuman accounting is by seeking to produce or become posthumans. While objections to the policy of posthuman accounting on precautionary grounds have been deflected here, the reader could be forgiven for being dissatisfied by this resolution of the posthuman impasse (§5.1). This resolution is tactical and provisional. However, before we are in a position to provide a more satisfactory resolution, in the form of an ethics of becoming posthuman, we will need to devise a general account of the posthuman autonomy or agency presupposed by the disconnection thesis and consider its general ontological requirements.

Notes

1 The stipulation that WHDs of feral posthumans remain outside the WH avoids us designating as "posthuman" WHDs of feral posthumans that are subsequently re-domesticated or re-humanized into WH. I am grateful to Søren Holm for bringing this to my attention.

2 Another way of putting this is to say that in any possible world in which humans exist they are rational. Other properties of humans may be purely "accidental" – e.g. their colour or language. It is not part of the essence of humans that they speak English, for example. Insofar as speaking English is an accidental property of humans, there are possible worlds in which there are humans but no English speakers.

3 I accept that this is open to contestation. There may be a case, for example, for ascribing essential properties to fundamental particles such as charge or spin that may not supervene on other properties (see Molnar 2006), in which case flat ontology would only have regional application at most.

4 Davidson has famously argued that we can make little sense of the idea of radically incommensurable or untranslatable languages or conceptual schemes (Davidson 1984: 183–98).

5 The Marvel superhero Rocket Raccoon can understand human thought and ways but is, I take it, a wide raccoonish descendant disconnected into postraccoonity.

6 Bear in mind that I'm not using "human" to designate beings with some essential biological or cognitive nature here. According to the disconnection thesis, being human is a matter of belonging to one of two historical entities: WH – a socio-technical assemblage – or the narrow biological species that keeps WH going. Neither has been defined in terms of essential properties.

7 Given our acknowledged dependence on technical systems, the long-run outcomes of relinquishment may be as disastrous as any technological alternative.

6 Functional autonomy and assemblage theory

Introduction

The disconnection thesis offers a clear ontological analysis of the idea of the posthuman, the most important feature of which is that it leaves the nature of posthumans open. The disconnection relation is an example of degenerate multiple realizability/satisfiability: that an entity satisfies the relation tells us nothing about its nature or powers. This is a feature rather than a bug since, as I have argued, it expresses our epistemological state of play with regard to the posthuman. Posthumans, there are none.

Given their dated nonexistence, we do not know what it would be like to encounter or *be* posthuman. This should be the Archimedean pivot for any account of posthuman ethics or politics that is not fooling itself. Nonetheless, I think there are grounds for specifying the concept further by thinking about properties of living and autonomous systems. This is the goal of the present chapter.

I will argue that the disconnection thesis implies that posthumans would be *functionally autonomous* assemblages. A being is functionally autonomous if it can enlist entities as values for functions or accrue functions. We will, however, need to work out a theory of functions and an ecological account of value compatible with the assemblage ontology in which the thesis is cast (§6.4).

We limber up to this account by looking at different views of how the activity and function of living systems are fixed such as the Aristotelian, Kantian and standard causal theories. I argue that the most satisfactory account is one for which functions are determined by contributions to autonomous systems. Unlike Aristotle's approach, the *autonomous systems approach* (ASA) does not require purposes to be fixed by invariant forms or essences transcending the individual systems that instantiate them (§6.2). Contrary to the Kantian approach, it holds that functions or natural purposes are real dependence relations; not artefacts of human explanations of nature. The ASA also provides a more satisfactory account of how a thing's functions depend on its "capture" by assemblages or containing systems than the causal-historical account. Above all, though, it ties function acquisition to agency. Thus it allows us to cash out the idea that post-humans would be living agents where they are not Lockean or Kantian persons (§4.3).[1]

A more delicate issue is whether ASA implies some form of intrinsic teleology. Intrinsic teleology holds that entities have their purposes or functions essentially. The disconnection thesis rejects intrinsic teleology because entities must be able to lose or acquire functions to become posthuman. I argue that a reasonably pluralistic ontology which admits objects as well as events and processes can finesse this issue.

This result comports well with assemblage theory, for the decom-posability of assemblages entails ontological anti-holism (§5.3). Nothing is defined by its role within a larger containing system (things can always "play elsewhere"). While its parts can play crucial roles for an assemblage, none plays that role necessarily. The theory offers a partial non-anthropocentric value-theory and an account of enlistment by functionally autonomous systems which will support later discussion of the ethics of posthuman becoming (§8.2).

The metaphysics of functional autonomy allows an expansion of the schematic characterization of posthumans given in the disconnection thesis consistent with massive multiple realizability. I equate the degree of a system's functional autonomy (its "power") with its ability to couple opportunistically with other systems and hence to its modularity. Thus I finish this chapter by clarifying the idea of modularity, or articulation, involved here and relating it to theories of non-subjective temporality derived from the work of Derrida and Deleuze (§4.2). This will prove important as we move into the final chapters since we need theoretical treatments of posthuman power, posthuman value and the temporal complexity of *becoming posthuman* to evaluate the provisional ethical claims of Chapter 5.

6.1 Moral and functional autonomy

According to the moral philosophy that follows in the wake of Rousseau and Kant, autonomous beings are intentional agents that determine their principles of action by reflecting and deliberating about the desires and principles that they should be moved by. A nonhuman animal may have desires and drives, but lacking rationality it cannot represent those desires to itself or decide to be motivated by different ones (Frankfurt 1971).

Kepa Ruiz-Mirazo and Alvaro Moreno acknowledge the moral and political conception but argue that there is a wider conception of auton-omy that is essential to biological thought. Autonomous beings in the wide sense are those whose agency contributes to the maintenance of their form of life whether or not they represent that form of life or understand themselves as selves (Ruiz-Mirazo & Moreno 2012: 29–34).

First, we need to consider the relationship between autonomy and the posthuman in more detail. Why should the ability to function outside the scope of the Wide Human require autonomy in either sense?

The link between autonomy, life and the posthuman comes about because disconnection entails a kind of functional and existential independence from the Wide Human (WH). We can see better what this involves if we consider how things fall in or fall out of WH as it is presently constituted.

Within WH functional and existential independence are clearly related. Entities belonging to WH are required by biological (narrow) humans. They come to exist in forms that are perpetuated across human generations – although, in the case of technical artefacts, these forms may also be modified drastically (see Chapter 7).

Further, their existences and forms are explained by their contribution to narrow human ends. The current forms of domestic animals such as dogs and pigs are explained by centuries of unnatural selection for humanly desirable traits such as obedience and succulence.

This contribution may be real but relatively indirect. For example, it is arguable that the most stable factors in technological change are not complete artefacts – like cars – but functional components and sub-components of those systems like valves or cathodes (Arthur 2009; §7.4).

We can express the regularity holding between function and existence as a "consequence law" (Cohen 1982) where E is the dated fact that some entity type ε exists in some context σ and (H) is a fact about what tokens of ε are disposed to do (e.g. producing milk or hams) that narrow humans value.

Thus:

$$(E \rightarrow H) \rightarrow E$$

This simple formula represents the fact $(E \rightarrow H)$ accounts for or causes E. A consequence law supports counterfactuals. If $(E \rightarrow H)$ ceased to obtain, the tokens of ε would cease to occur in σ (E would become false).

Technological change generates new functions as well as new kinds of thing and it is quite normal for earlier realizers of those functions to be superseded by new realizers. Cars have superseded horses in many parts of the world because functions associated with horses can be served by cars more effectively. The result is that horses have ceased to occur in the contexts in which they were formerly used (public transport and the provision of motive power).

Objects can also acquire new functions. But E (the contextual existence fact) in the formula will continue to hold so long as there is some human-related function that the type ε things continue to serve in σ.

This is important, as we shall see, since it allows that entities of type ε *might become "unhitched" from σ and come to exist in different contexts.* It also allows that they might become unhitched from any human context since existence in a human context is not a condition of existing *per se.*

The consequence law schema expresses the functional dependence of those Wide Humans that are not narrow humans upon WH. They exist in a given context only so long as there is some narrow human purpose that they fulfil. It also expresses the fact that WH is predicated on the existence of narrowly human individuals. If narrow human individuals – or some good approximation – ceased to exist, so would the functions on which they depend.

As advertised, pigs and cows are Wide Humans because they exist in the way they do in virtue of the human-relative functions they fulfil. If all humans converted to veganism and vegetarianism, cows and pigs could survive only as pets or as feral cows or feral pigs. Those belonging to the former group would remain parts of WH while those in the latter group would be effectively outside it since their continued existence in their new context would not depend on their fulfilment of human-relative functions.

Note also that "human-relative" does not mean "core", "authentic" or "invariant". No such essentialist commitment is implied here. A human-relative function is one that would not exist but for the existence of narrow humans (or humanoids with similar requirements and powers). These can be as artificial and as "spiritual" as you like (for example, *operatic performance, cash dispensing* and *pornography* might be human-relative functions – see §6.4). Nor does the idea of human-relativity commit us to some voluntarist account of how functions emerge. It does not require that they come to exist through the intentions of individuals or groups. It is quite compatible with the view that some human-relative functions come into being by incremental processes in which no individual intended that a particular function or activity come into being.

We can call the independence from the human-related functions of beings outside WH *negative functional autonomy* (analogously perhaps to Berlin's notion of negative liberty). If ε is a posthuman the consequence law sketched out above won't apply to it.

Arguably, however, we need a *positive* conception of posthuman autonomy to complement the claim regarding negative autonomy (henceforth "functional autonomy" will refer only to *positive* functional autonomy).

Here's why. Hulks and ruins are a) technically fashioned and b) can exist for some extended period of time after they have ceased to be useful parts of WH. However, unless they are preserved for aesthetic purposes, hulks and ruins have no functions at all (having aesthetic functions could qualify them for membership of WH). Hulks and ruins are quite unlike feral animals in that the latter seem to carry out many nonhuman-related functions: for example, mating, foraging, giving birth, etc.

A conception of disconnection that resulted in hulks and ruins having posthuman status would obviously be too broad. Hulks and ruins are existentially independent of WH but not functionally autonomous in the way feral animals are. They cannot generate functions for themselves or bestow value-status on entities through their activity. Posthumans would be able to actively *acquire functions* and *enlist* other entities in functional relations by using them or coming to depend on them (§6.4).

Rational subjects or persons, such as adult humans, get some of their functional autonomy from their capacity for practical reasoning. They can enlist things or people for their individual and collective ends and accrue functions which they serve for other people, groups or corporate entities. They can design tools like pens or arrowheads that can be adopted and reused by other rational subjects.

But suppose the posthuman in question is not a person but a powerful, self-optimizing system that lacks personal consciousness or explicit meta-cognition (§§4.1, 4.3). This being might lack the explicit beliefs or intentions of human artificers or tool users. If these were the only way in which functions could be bestowed, then nonpersonal posthumans would not be functionally autonomous.

We might try to get round this problem by adopting Dennett's stance approach to intentionality (§5.7). According to the stance approach, a system is an intentional system if we can predict it with this method and by no other (Dennett 1987: 23). The intentional stance can be applied legitimately to computers and raccoons as well as to people. Thus it entails no commitment to a specific mental architecture or phenomenology.

Thus a posthuman would be an intentional system if it could be reliably predicted by treating it as such. If imputing design intentions to it were of help in predicting its behaviour then it would have design intentions and thus the ability to impart functions to things. For example, treating it as a megalomaniac intent on controlling human minds could be a helpful predictor of its future behaviour (§8.1). In that case humans would be among the things being enlisted for new functions.

However, there are problems with this interpretationist viewpoint. As we have seen, it is an open question whether human attempts to interpret posthumans would be successful enough to justify attributing intentions to them (§§4.3, 5.7). The interpretationist could respond that certain beings whose patterns of behaviour are too weird to show up as intentional systems for beings like ourselves might be intentionally tractable from some "other" point of view. But *in principle interpretability* is ill defined unless we have some conception of *what is doing* the interpreting. For reasons that have been sufficiently explored here, transcendental philosophy cannot furnish this. We can assume every intelligent system would be interpretable by someone or something. But this assumption is numbingly unspecific about the nature of that interpreter and thus of the kind of interpretation that it applies.

A further problem is that the claim that initial design fixes subsequent function rarely applies to technologies or social structures. A designer's subjective ideas about what a thing is for need not determine its function since the function that it acquires in a culture may be different (Longy 2006: 83). Likewise, some social entities are functional kinds defined by the roles they or their members have. One explanation for the emergence of elites in complex chiefdoms or proto-states is that the relaxation of incest prohibitions on marrying close relatives would have allowed persistent concentrations of wealth, power and status (DeLanda 2011: 172). The explanation does not need the rider that incest taboos were *intended* to produce elites.

So the idea of an intentional, self-conscious designer is too narrow to capture what it is to actively enlist or acquire functions in general. We will need a more abstract conception of autonomy if we are to develop a conception of agency that fits the agentive demands of the disconnection thesis.

6.2 Aristotelian posthumans

The example of feral animals points us towards different, arguably more fundamental, conceptions of autonomy and function. In the philosophical tradition, the bodies of biological organisms have been understood as having functions fixed by their contribution to the life of the organism. This conception has its classical formulation in Aristotle's biology in which the presence of certain arrangements of parts – like teeth or eyelids – in plants or animals is explained by their contribution to the form (or integrated life activity) characteristic of a certain *type* of organism (the Aristotelian "soul").

The form or active principle of an artefact lies outside itself since it depends on its makers and users (*Met* 1070a7–8). The body of the animal, on the other hand, is an "instrument performing or making manifest its own act of living" (Moya 2000: 326). It follows that the form of an organism, unlike that of a tool, is independent of human activity.

Organic form is also an unchanging principle that explains the development of organisms (Lennox 2009). Being (actuality) is prior to becoming:

> [It] is not because each thing's coming to be is of a certain sort that it is of a certain sort; rather it came to be such a thing on account of its being of this sort; for generation follows on and is for the sake of being; being is not for the sake of generation.
>
> (*GA*: 778b2–7)

The form of an organism pre-fixes the functions of everything that contributes to it (Aristotle's metaphysics is a prime example of the "hylomorphic", form/matter ontology that DeLanda and flat ontologists reject – see §5.3). It is the determiner of the functions of anything that contributes to that activity, such as its body (enlistment). It also pre-fixes the functions of other organisms (sexual partners) that contribute to the replication of its form (Lennox 2009). Organisms thus *enlist* things for functions that contribute to their typical life activity and organisms are *enlisted* in turn for the reproduction of their type. The Aristotelian organism minimally satisfies the criteria for functional autonomy. But is this account of function-fixing a good theory of *posthuman* functional autonomy?

Well, it seems good for something. Aristotelian organisms are independent fixers of ends. So if we conceive posthumans as Aristotelian organisms, we can explain why cutting away from WH exceeds the capacities of hulks and ruins. Hulks and ruins cannot enlist or acquire functions on their own because, unlike feral pigs or cattle, they lack souls. But just as feral animals can enlist and acquire functions, so each posthuman could fix human-independent purposes so long as it possessed a "posthuman soul".

6.3 The end of the end?

However, Aristotelian posthumanism confronts standard modern objections to objective teleology: the idea that natural things have goals or purposes that do not depend on the subjective aims or purposes possessed by conscious agents. We can spell these out in terms of two "T-objections" ("T" is for "teleological"):

T1) Aristotle is committed to objective teleology pre-fixed by organic form. However, modern post-Darwinian biology provides a more satisfactory explanation of biological order. Since it rejects objective teleology, we should too (the Darwinian objection).

T2) Artefacts are soulless since they have only functions that are derived from their makers, while organisms can originate functions because they have souls. The disconnection thesis implies that posthumans could be descendants of human artefacts. But there is no technological process whereby descendants of artefacts could acquire original functions and jump ontological category by coming alive (the category objection).

T1 and T2 express a modern aversion to the idea that teleology or real functions could be a feature of the nonhuman order. Considering them will allow us to sketch a theory of functional autonomy that generalizes over biological and post-biological existence.

In my response to T1 I will argue that the problem with Aristotelian posthumanism is not its commitment to objective teleology but to *intrinsic* teleology: the claim that entities like body parts have their purposes essentially in virtue of their membership of a formal and holistic totality. In what follows I will argue that we need objective teleology if we are to describe living systems. However, this does not commit us to the claim that any entity has intrinsic functions or purposes.

Aristotle's account of organisms as independently purposeful substances is committed to a cosmos in which the natural entities of a given type have a natural state towards which they incline. Elliot Sober (1980) points out that this explanatory paradigm allows a powerful conceptual distinction between the normal function and development, on the one hand, and defects, disease and monsters on the other (p. 361). For each kind of natural object there is natural state it will assume unless subjected to perturbing influences. Variation is deviation from perturbation (p. 366).

But, Sober goes on to argue, post-Darwinian biology radically inverts this explanatory order. It is characterized by "population thinking" which explains form and functionality as an effect of variation within populations of replicators under selection constraints. Without sources of heritable difference, there could be no adaptation resulting from selection pressures upon a population of replicators. Consequently, a Darwinian kind such as a species cannot be uniform *and* evolvable. Even if there is a genetic sequence that corresponds to the current best phenotype within a population – the "wild type" – this need not be the majority and will generally be "distributed" over optimal mutants at other points in genetic sequence space (Eigen 1992: 25; Dennett 1995b: 192). The status of "wild type" is also temporary since a mutation within the population can engender a new wild type.

If the evolution of species depends on differences between particulars rather than ideal organizing principles, there is no principled limit to how much a species can alter while remaining the same *qua species* or the diversity fuelling its optimizing search. Thus population thinking implies that there cannot be an "invariant essence" or type of an evolvable population (Sterelny & Griffiths 1999: 8).

Population thinking, like assemblage theory (§§5.3, 5.4) is a flat ontology since its key explainers are differently scaled particulars – such as organisms and populations – and their differential powers, rather than formal organizing principles or Kantian subjects (DeLanda 2002: 58). However, if the universe is flat, there are no essences or forms. If there are no essences, there can be no natural states. Thus the metaphysics of modern biology seems to cut the tie between essence, form and teleology described by Aristotle.

6.4 Functions, ecological values and enlistment

Some argue that there must be a place for teleology in post-Darwinian philosophy of biology despite the failure of essentialism. It seems impossible to understand living systems without assigning functions to their parts or actions. *Heart, neuron* or *immune system* are functional kinds. They classify biological entities in terms of what they *ought to do* in living systems (see §1.3). Thus teleology appears indispensable to an understanding of the biological sphere. Kant accepted this indispensability claim but held that the natural world is exclusively governed by mechanical causation, not purposes. Nonetheless, he argued that we are entitled to treat organisms *as if* they were purposively organized where this assists our observations of their structure and behaviour (Kant 1991: 377).

While influential in the history of biological thought, Kant's reconciliation of teleology and mechanism has the drawback that it treats distinctions between biological and non-biological individuals as heuristic conveniences rather than differences in the things themselves. It implies that biology is not really a science at all. It has no distinctive subject matter and is unable to explain why even the facade of teleology arises from our encounters with nature (Zammito 2012: 122).

Darwinism might appear to save the day by positing a *real design process* (natural selection) to account for the ubiquity of teleology. Perhaps the fact of a trait being selected for a function suffices to constitute its function.

The standard selectionist account of function is the so-called etiological account. This can be expressed in terms of the consequence law schema sketched out above (see §6.1).[2] A dispositional property of a type of trait (e.g. that it assists flight) is its function if it contributes to the existence of further tokens of that type (Godfrey-Smith 1993). It explains why certain causal roles of a trait are *constitutive* of its function in terms of its selection history. Thus although wings may have lots of different causal transactions with the environment, wings were an adaptation selected for flying not for flapping (Fodor 1996).

The etiological account is intended to account for the *normativity* of function-ascription. An entity can perform its etiological-function more or less well, or fail entirely, and this is a constitutive condition of there being functions at all. It is (again) because eyes are for seeing rather than listening that loss of sight is dysfunctional.

The etiological notion of function provides an important (if contested) way of understanding the relationship between how a trait became represented in a biological population and what it is *for*. However, while widely accepted, it is ill suited for understanding the manifest functional organization that impressed Aristotle and Kant. This is because it renders a trait's current role within an organized system epiphenomenal. As Corey

Maley and Gualtiero Piccinini point out, it implies that no matter what a trait contributes to a system's operation or dealings with the world, *the trait lacks a function if it lacks a selection history*.

Thus function fails to depend on the current causal powers of a thing. If an atom for atom replica of you were to assemble randomly from a cloud of chemicals it would, according to the etiological account, lack organs whose function is to digest or expel body waste despite having parts with exactly the same inputs and outputs[3] (Maley & Piccinini 2012). Griffiths and Sterelny consider the example of a bacterium which acquires a heritable trait conferring antibiotic resistance (Sterelny & Griffiths 1999: 222). The etiological theory implies that the trait would be functionless because it lacks a selection history. Later tokens of the same type would acquire (etiological) function *only if* the trait became selected by the reproductive advantage it bestowed.

This is problematic because it seems that the trait would have added to the organization of the bacterium in a manner that could explain the later selective advantage. As Wayne Christensen and Mark Bickhard point out, the selection history of a function requires the identification of such ancestral adaptive relations (Christensen & Bickhard 2002: 12). But without an explanation of how the function of a thing depends on its current contribution to a system it is unclear what these ancestral facts consist in (see also Collier 2000).

The etiological account is also unhelpful for understanding how post-humans could (unlike hulks) acquire functions outside WH. The initial break with WH would presumably be accompanied by organizational and ecological changes in the proto-posthuman behaviour. But posthumans might not be biological systems and might not face any selection pressure at all. For example, it is conceivable that disconnection event could only ever involve one posthuman singleton.

A posthuman which breaks out of WH for the first time would need to enlist ecological resources of some kind – for example, by learning to exploit solar power as an alternative to human-provided battery or mains power. Yet such a trait would lack the function of *powering* according to the selection-based etiological account. If this behaviour is intended by the posthuman it would have an *intentional selection history* and thus would have acquired its function via a different aetiology (Longy 2013). But this model of function acquisition requires an intentional agent to get it started and we are not yet in a position to attribute florid intentionality or personhood to posthumans (see §6.1).

One of the attractions of the Aristotelian account of organism is that it provides a theory of function fixing which does not invoke explicit intentions or reasoning. The fixing occurs through the formal life activity (soul) of the organism rather than in consequence of its history.

Since we are minimally committed to posthumans being agents, we should consider whether it is possible to retain the good features of the Aristotelian account while dispensing with its essentialism and its unhelpfully categorical distinction between organisms and artefacts.

These are both features of an alternative conception of function with roots in the Aristotelian and Kantian accounts – the *autonomous systems approach* or ASA (Christensen & Bickhard 2002; Collier 2000). The version of ASA developed by Wayne Christensen and Mark Bickhard defines the functions of an entity in terms of its contribution to the persistence of a system which they conceive as a group of interdependent processes (Christensen & Bickhard 2002: 3). Functions are *process dependence relations* within *actively self-maintaining* systems.

Active self-maintenance is a specific capacity for maintaining system *cohesion*. A system is relatively cohesive if its structure causes it to exhibit unified dynamic behaviour in a wide range of contexts (Collier 1988). Systems like rocks, thunderstorms and cats are more cohesive across similar contexts than piles of sand, clouds or confraternities of cats:

> If you apply a moderate force to a rock sitting on the ground, e.g., by kicking it, the rock as a whole will move while the ground stays where it is. The rock is coupled to the ground by gravity and friction, but these forces are weaker than the molecular bonds of the rock, so the rock behaves as an integrated system when kicked, whereas the rock plus ground doesn't. Which is lucky for you. If you kick a pile of sand, on the other hand, the sand doesn't behave as an integrated system in the way that the rock does. Instead, grains of sand fly off in all directions.
>
> (Christensen & Bickhard 2002: 8)

Different systems exhibit different capacities for cohesion-making in varying degrees. A thunderstorm is a convective cell of circulating air and water vapour that depends on a temperature gradient between the surface and the air to drive it (DeLanda 2011: 10–12). A cat also needs an energy source to keep its metabolism going. But, unlike thunderstorms, cats anticipate and actively forestall some of the changes that could undermine their cohesion: for example, by fleeing danger or by initiating predatory behaviour before on-board energy stored in materials such as fats and sugars becomes too depleted (Christensen & Bickhard 2002).

Active self-maintenance is thus a capacity shared by some living things. Like all powers that belong to non-fundamental entities it is "grounded" in the specific organization of living things.[4] As Collier and Hooker note, this organization is very different to the complexity of non-living systems because it is intimately related to the vulnerability and receptivity of living systems to environmental influences:

The cohesive order of living systems must be actively maintained by processes of various kinds (cellular reproduction, structural repair, energy
supply, and so on). Their structural bonds have energies measured in electron volts, even fractions thereof, not the millions of electron volts that fix a
rock into responseless stability. This explains why systems of this kind are
adaptable, for unless they can constantly adapt to mitigate or compensate for
disturbing signals they will be disrupted and, losing their cohesion, lose
their identity as that sort of system. This same vulnerability is the basis of
their adaptability, since their internal delicacy makes them easily alterable,
allowing them both to be sensitive to signals and to respond to these signals
malleably and flexibly in order to maintain themselves. Their responses to
signals cannot be mostly passive, like those of a gas, nor largely uniform,
like those of a crystal, but must so interrelate as to preserve the organised
complexity that underwrites control of that very responsiveness and adaptability. This active independence, their characteristic organisational property,
we will call their autonomy.

(Collier & Hooker 1999: 244–5)

Autonomy is thus grounded in responsive, adaptable organization whose
resiliency depends on there being multiple, mutually supporting processes which – in complex organisms – can also generate the internal
variation on which adaptive responsiveness depends. Where a set of processes depend on one another for their continuation (e.g. respiration, fluid
transport and cellular metabolism) they produce outputs on which the
system as a whole depends (Christensen & Bickhard 2002: 19). Thus a
central process like respiration is a function for the system and its failure
induces "propagating dysfunction" (p. 20). Whereas the strong molecular
bonds holding rocks together do not depend on the processes that produced them, autonomous systems require continuous outputs from their
organizationally interdependent processes. This means that there is an
ontologically basic sense in which each of these processes *serves* the whole
that they constitute. But this also grounds the *normativity* of their functioning since each such process "can succeed or fail in supporting its
system" (p. 18).

The stipulation that functional processes be interdependent is important because it precludes identifying environmental processes outside the
system as system functions: for example, sunshine is necessary for photo-
synthesis in plants but the thermonuclear reactions in the sun do not
reciprocally depend on the plant (p. 10). The functions in question need
not only be processes that are spatially contained within the relevant
system. Social or predatory activities, for example, are similarly functional
for some creatures and similarly interdependent on other mutually
dependent processes.

This account allows us to furnish an ontologically grounded conception of value. Since functional processes can succeed or fail, their continuance is of *value* to a system because they support its autonomy. Sunshine is likewise a value for plants because their functional processes depend on it, although its propagation does not make the cut as a function (see end of section).

Does ASA furnish a positive conception of autonomy that could be extended to posthuman entities regardless of their cognitive or phenomenological structure?

As long as posthumans satisfy the minimal conditions for autonomous systemshood, I do not see a problem here. To exist and operate independently of WH posthumans would need to actively preserve the conditions for their continued existence (perhaps competing or cooperating with humans to do so). Thus they would qualify as autonomous in the ASA sense.

Second, fashioning an existence outside WH would require the posthuman to engage in activities that supported its existence and which would thus also depend on the other processes constituting the posthuman life. This would be a reciprocal dependence relation of the type that Christensen and Bickhard describe and it would be a direct outcome of the posthuman's functional autonomy. Entities or resources necessary for these reciprocally involved processes would have to be *enlisted for* these functions. Finally, there is the possibility that the posthuman could acquire further functions in wider assemblages that reciprocally sustain and depend on these new enlistments. For example, humans and posthumans might find themselves involved in a new class of political relationships. This might be something that neither party fully intended but it would be a consequence of their activity nonetheless.

Thus the ASA provides an explanation of what posthuman functional autonomy might involve which makes a minimal commitment regarding the possible natures of posthumans. The theory could apply to a unique posthuman singleton just so long as it was an agent and had the right kind of reciprocal complexity. This minimalism is wholly apt given the extreme multiple realizability of the disconnection relation noted in §5.6.

ASA is remarkably close to the Aristotelian view of the soul as the life activity that fixes the functions of contributory organs or activities (§6.2). However, it can reconcile its objective teleology with anti-essentialism because the process functions within an autonomous system depend on the system alone and upon its dealings with its world rather than on its instantiating a replicable form that necessitates a functional organization of a particular kind (it is "flat" rather than hylomorphic – see §5.3). The ground of function is a complex, organized system rather than a form that can be analytically distinguished from its matter.

However, I wish to consider two potential objections. I do not think they are fatal but they will help us integrate the model more closely into the framework of assemblage theory that I have adopted as an interpretation of SP. This in turn will help us complicate that ontology and put us on course for the remaining chapters.

The first objection is that the identification of webs of interdependent processes as the basis for function is arbitrary and depends on our pre-scientific intuition that biological systems of this kind are products of design or "natural ends" as Kant referred to them. We do not think of hulks or ruins in this way. But maybe this is an anthropocentric or bio-centric way of viewing the inorganic world. A rusting car in a scrapyard is a site of dependent processes. Rust depends upon the action of water and electrolytes upon the surface of metal. Thus why not say that the action of the water and electrolytes fulfils the function *rust-enabler*.

It is clear that this notion of function is far too wide for our purposes. If hulks can acquire the nonhuman-defined function of rusting and enlist supporting enablers for it, they can acquire functions independently of us (they were not designed to rust). But this implies functional autonomy. Since hulks are technically created but rust without our help, they would qualify as posthuman according to my proposal.

However, this objection is wide of the mark because, while rusting depends on electrolytes, the cohesion of the hulk does not (if anything, rusting is a long-term threat to its cohesion without compensatory effects). There is an ontological difference between processes dependent on other processes and systems of processes that exhibit patterns of mutual interdependence.

One might buttress the original objection by claiming that whether a system is unified or patterned is an interest- or observer-dependent fact, not an ontological one. But this anti-realism regarding structure can be rejected on the grounds that some systems just are more patterned or ordered than others. This can be expressed by comparing the minimal amount of information that would be needed to "compress" them. Compressibility is a non-observer relative measure of the computational resources required to represent the pattern (Ladyman & Ross 2007: 202; Collier & Hooker 1999). A pattern "is real" by this criterion if there is a description of it that requires less storage space than a similarly formatted "bit string" representation of its original data set (Dennett 1991: 34). For a data set consisting of random noise, there will be no instructions that can generate the pattern that would take up less space than the noise itself.

The second objection gives us occasion to explore how the explicit ontology of the ASA might relate to assemblage theory. Christensen and Bickhard's account could be taken to justify the view that organisms are non-decomposable wholes (DeLanda's idealist "totalities" – see §5.3) whose parts cannot be moved or transplanted without ceasing to be in some sense. This is because they treat autonomous systems as "webs of interdependent processes" rather than assemblages of things in which processes occur (Christensen & Bickhard 2002: 3).

Webs of processes are candidates for the kinds of entities that might be non-decomposable wholes because processes (unlike things) cannot be lifted out of context and (in Derrida's terminology) "iterated" or "grafted" onto a new one. These nascent holistic tendencies perhaps explain why Christensen and Bickhard cite Aristotle's claim that "The hand separated from the body is not a true hand" as an epigraph (*Pol* I.2.1253a20–21).[5]

To see why holism might follow from a *pure process* account of autonomous systems, consider three processes A, B and C that are organizationally interdependent – each requiring output from the other two (Christensen & Bickhard 2002: 19). Clearly A cannot be spatially transplanted elsewhere without being supplied with similar outputs by functionally equivalent processes (B' and C').

Talk of movable processes is arguably misleading in any case. Processes are not like organs. They cannot be moved from place to place or system to system because, like events, processes are everywhere their temporal parts are. An event does not happen in different locations. It *just is* its propagation through these locations. Events and processes, unlike objects, cannot be moved because they do not occupy different places at different times (Dretske 1967: 488). If processes are treated as ephemeral particulars, then they cannot be moved, only extended in space and time. So if a functioning heart is a process and is artificially kept beating outside the body of a transplant donor this would not qualify as the removal of a process but as its continuation outside the donor's body.

However, the ASA need not be committed to such an austere ontology. It is quite possible to hold that functions are process dependence relations while at the same time *basing* them in objects or systems.

A similar approach has been adopted by proponents of the *located events theory* of sound, according to which sounds are vibrational events located in resonating objects (Roden 2010b). This amendment does no violence to their process-oriented analysis of functionality but it also allows us to talk about biological entities and their chequered careers: something that seems necessary if we are to account for the historical dimension of living assemblages. For example, viruses typically lack a metabolism or any means of autonomous reproduction outside a host cell. They begin as inert lumps of RNA or DNA (or varions) prior to "docking" with a cell whose metabolism and reproductive machinery they can co-opt (Dupré & O'Malley 2009: 6). Since the processes occurring in varions and in the corresponding viruses appear very different (only the latter seem to exhibit the marks of life) it would be difficult – though perhaps not impossible – to relate this lifecycle in process terms alone. Similar considerations apply to other biological histories where entities subtend different functions or processes in different contexts (as the example of a virus – a borderline living entity – indicates, this argument should be applied to all domains in which functional indeterminacy is a factor in the history of assemblages – for example, in the history of technology or culture).

So there are good reasons to embed the process account of functionality within a richer assemblage ontology in which there are historically mobile objects as well as processes and relations (DeLanda 2006). Since assemblages are decomposable with mobile parts, the account is not committed to holism. Finally, it allows a pluralist model of composition. Objects can be composed of events and processes as well as hierarchies of objects.[6]

The reconciliation of ASA with assemblage theory allows us to respond tersely to T2 (the category objection) in short order. T2 objected that posthumans that were descended from artefacts could not be living things or organisms because this would require them to jump from the category of soulless things that cannot originate functions (such as tools) to the category of things that can (organisms).

The short answer is: *there are no souls, only variably constrained states of matter*. There are constraints on the behaviour of composite systems – such as the different form of cohesion shown by crystals or biological systems; but these depend on alterable facts about system structure rather than Aristotelian forms. Collier and Hooker give a nice example of a neural net governed by a learning rule which severs connections between neurons if the weights fall below a threshold value during learning (Collier & Hooker 1999). Such a system could undergo phase transition into a decomposed network with "modular" sub-networks buffered from changes in other parts of the system. Systems of this type can evolve in ways that less buffered systems cannot (see §6.5). If constraints on systems development are plastic in this way, then an initially passive artefact with an evolving structure might become functionally autonomous. If there are equivalents of Aristotelian souls here, then they do not belong to anything essentially.[7]

Finally, as advertised above, Christensen and Bickhard's relational teleology furnishes an ecological account of value and enlistment that furnishes a formal definition of functional autonomy. The definition has five parts, beginning with the ASA account of functions:

1) (ASA) Each autonomous system has functions belonging to it at some point in its history. Its functions are the interdependent processes it requires to exist at that point.

2) (Value) If a process, thing or state is required for a function to occur, then that thing or process is a *value* for that function. Any entity, state or resource can be a value. For example, the proper functioning of a function can be a value for the functions that require it to work.[8]

3) (Enlistment) When an autonomous system produces a function, then any value of that function is enlisted by that system.

4) (Accrual) An autonomous system actively accrues functions by producing functions that are also values for other autonomous systems.

5) (Functional autonomy) Any autonomous system that can enlist values and accrue functions is a functionally autonomous system (FAS).

People are presumably FASs on this account, but also nonhuman organisms and (perhaps) lineages of organisms. Likewise, social systems (Collier & Hooker 1999) and (conceivably) posthumans. To date, technical entities are not FASs because they are non-autonomous. Historical technologies are mechanisms of enlistment, however. For example, without mining technology, certain ores would not be values for human activities. Social entities, such as corporations, are autonomous in the relevant sense and thus can have functions (process interdependency relations) and constitute values of their own. However, while not narrowly human, current social systems are Wide Humans, not posthumans. As per the disconnection thesis: posthumans would be FASs no longer belonging to WH.

Note that this account is *psychology-free*, which is as it should be since there may be many possible posthuman psychologies and we are aware of none of them. It is an ecological account of value in the strict sense of specifying values in terms of environmental relations between functions and their prerequisites (though "environment" should be interpreted broadly to include endogenous as well as exogenous entities). It is also an objective rather than subjective account which has no truck with the spirit (meaning, culture or subjectivity, etc.). Values are just things which enter into constitutive relations with functions. (Definition 2 could, and should, be qualified by introducing degrees of dependency to prevent everything on which a system transitively depends qualifying as a value.[9]) Oxygen was an ecological value for aerobic organisms long before Lavoisier. We can be ignorant of our values and mistake non-values for values, etc. It is also arguable that some ecological values are pathological in that they support some system functions while hindering others.[10]

The theory is partial because it only provides a sufficient condition for value. Some values – opera, cigarettes and sunsets – are arguably things of the spirit, constituted as values by desires or cultural meanings. The same caveat applies to the notion of function (we might distinguish between intentionally or culturally bestowed functions and dependence functions). However, sufficiency will be sufficient in the final part of the book when we attempt to delineate posthuman value structures that are independent of parochial features of human psychology (§8.2).

6.5 Modularity and reuse

FASs of the kind that we can conceive as emerging from our technology are liable to be modular assemblages of elements that can couple opportunistically with other entities or systems, creating new, "deterritorialized", assemblages whose powers and dispositions are transformed and dynamically put into play by such couplings.

The best way of representing modularity is in terms of networks: an abstract pattern consisting of nodes and directional connections ("arcs") between nodes. A network is modular if it contains "highly interconnected clusters of nodes that are sparsely connected to nodes in other clusters" (Clune *et al.* 2013: 1). We can call a network that exhibits such bunching in its connections "network decomposable".

If processes in FASs are based in cohesive component objects – which we can refer to as *modules* – they are liable to be network decomposable since such objects need to be independent enough of their milieu to retain their pattern outside of it (as in the case of organ transplants or code reuse).

Modules may or may not be spatially localized entities. An instance of a software object class such as an "array" (an indexed list of objects of a single type) need not be instantiated on continuous regions on a computer's physical memory. It does not matter where the data representing the array's contents are physically located so long as the more complex program which it composes can locate that data when it needs it.

It is possible that all assemblages must have some spatially bounded parts – organelles in eukaryotic cells and distributors in internal combustion engines come in spatially bounded packages, for example. But not all functionally discrete parts of assemblages need be spatially discrete in the way that organelles are.

For example, cultural entities such as technologies or symbols may consist of repeatable or iterable patterns that are not spatially bound (see Roden 2004a). Where there are pattern recognizers, such entities can exert real causal influence by being repeated into varying contexts (see Chapter 7). The fact that cultural entities such as languages or ritual practices depend on the existence of beings capable of learning them does not impugn their status as particulars with causal heft. Because they are repeatable, technical entities are typically "functionally multistable" to use Don Ihde's term. For example, an Acheulian hand axe – a technology used by humans for over a million years – might have been used as a scraper, a chopper or a projectile weapon (Ihde 2012b). In Chapter 7, I will argue that repeatability in modern technical systems is a particularly striking example of their causal power.[11]

We should expect functionally autonomous assemblages to be network-decomposable because the presence of relatively independent parts confers flexibility which supports adaptation.[12] Modularity is recognized as one of the necessary conditions of *evolvability*, "an organism's capacity to generate heritable phenotypic variation" (Kirschner & Gerhart 1998: 8420). For example, some biologists argue that the transition from prokaryotic cells (whose DNA is not contained in a nucleus) to nucleated eukaryotic cells was accompanied by a decoupling of the messenger RNA *transcription* process from the subsequent *translation* of mRNA as proteins. This may have allowed noncoding (intronic) RNA to assume regulatory roles necessary for the production of more complex organisms because the separation of sites allows the intronic RNA to be spliced out of the mRNA where it might otherwise disrupt the production of proteins (Ruiz-Mirazo & Moreno 2012: 39; Mattick 2004).

The benefits of articulation apply at higher levels of organization in living beings for reasons that may hold for autonomous *proto-ex-artefacts* poised for disconnection. Nervous systems need to be "dynamically decoupled" from the environment that they map and represent because perception, learning and memory rely on establishing specialized information channels and long-term synaptic connections in the face of changing environmental stimulation (Moss 2006: 932–4; Ruiz-Mirazo & Moreno 2012: 44).

Network decomposition of internal components also seems to carry advantages within control systems, including those that might actuate relatively autonomous robots one day. Research into locomotion in insects and arthropods shows that far from using a central control system to co-ordinate all the legs in a body, each leg tends to have its own pattern generator. A coherent motion capable of supporting the body emerges from the excitatory and inhibitory interactions between the leg pattern generators rather than via signals from a central pattern generator (Cruse 1990). The evolutionary rationale for distributed control of locomotion can be painted in similar terms to that of the articulation of DNA transcription and expression considered above – a distributed system is less fragile in the face of evolutionary change than a central control architecture in which the function of each part is heavily dependent on those of other parts.

This rationale applies to human beings as well as to our immediate primate ancestors, especially in the case of sophisticated cognitive feats that require the organism to learn specific cultural patterns which would not have been stable or invariant enough to have selected for the component abilities they require (Deacon 1997: 322–34).

For example, relatively ancient areas in the human brain known to be involved in motor control are also involved in language understanding. This suggests that circuits associated with grasping the affordances and potentialities of objects may have been recruited over evolutionary time to meet the emerging cultural demands of symbolic communication (Anderson 2007: 14).[13] Peter Carruthers argues that circuits in the visual and motor areas which have been initially involved in controlling and anticipating actions have become co-opted in the production and monitoring of propositional thinking (beliefs, desires, intentions, etc.) via the production of inner speech. An explicit belief, for example, might be implemented as a globally available action-representation – an offline "rehearsal" of a verbal utterance – to which distinctive commitments to further action or inference can be undertaken (Carruthers 2009).

Andy Clark cites experimental work on *Pan troglodytes* chimpanzees which comports with Carruthers's assumption that cognitive systems adapted for pattern recognition and motor control can be opportunistically reused to bootstrap an organism's cognitive abilities. Here, an experimental group of chimps were trained to associate two different plastic tokens with pairs of identical objects and pairs of different objects respectively. They were later able to solve a difficult second-order difference categorization task that defeated the control group of chimps who had not been trained to use the tokens:

> The more abstract problem (which even we sometimes find initially difficult!) is to categorize *pairs-of-pairs* of objects in terms of *higher-order* sameness or difference. Thus the appropriate judgment for *pair-of-pairs* "shoe/shoe and banana/shoe" is "different" because the *relations* exhibited within each pair are different. In shoe/shoe the (lower order) relation is "sameness"; in banana/shoe it is "difference." Hence the higher-order relation – the relation *between* the relations – is difference.
>
> (Clark 2003: 70)

Interestingly, Clark notes that the chimps in the experimental group were able to solve the problem without repeatedly using the physical tokens, suggesting that they were able to associate the "difference" and "sameness" with inner surrogates similar to the offline speech events posited by Carruthers and Frankish (see also Wheeler 2004: this could be touted as a case of cognitive enlistment, only that it is not clear that thinking about second-order similarities and differences was central enough to the chimps' existence to constitute a function. However, were it to have become central enough to their mode of living to be a function, then it would be a case of enlistment in the strict sense).

The account of the emergence of specialized symbolic thinking and linguistic thinking via the reuse of neural circuits evolved for pattern recognition and motor control illustrate a more general moral of flat ontology. Assemblages derive a power to form new or larger assemblages both from their lower-scale components and from couplings with other assemblages.

For example, although specific neural circuits may be inherently multistable it does not follow that each can *do anything* (though estimates of neural plasticity vary – see Quartz & Sejnowski 1997). Each may have specific "biases" or computational powers that reflect its evolutionary origins (Anderson 2010: 247). Stanislas Dehaene and Laurent Cohen review some remarkable results suggesting the existence of a Visual Word Form Area (VWFA), a culturally universal cortical map situated in the fusiform gyrus of the temporal lobe, which is involved in the recognition of discrete and complex written characters. As they observe, it is not plausible to suppose that the VWFA evolved specifically to meet the demands of literate cultures since writing was invented only 5,400 years ago, and only a fraction of humans have been able to read for most of this period (Dehaene & Cohen 2007: 384). Thus it appears that the cortical maps in the VWFA have structural properties rendering them apt for reuse in script recognition despite not being selected for the representation of written characters (among the factors suggested is that the VWFA is located in a part of the fusiform area receptive to highly discriminate visual input from the fovea – p. 389).

The coupling of a biological assemblage with a cultural assemblage such as a language may increase the functional autonomy of the first assemblage, allowing it to respond fluidly and adaptively to the demands of its environment. For example, there is evidence that having a language for precise numerical quantities enhances the pre-linguistic human number sense by allowing speakers to remember and recognize quantities across time, space and sensory modality (Frank *et al.* 2008; Clark 2003).

These studies suggest that language is a "cognitive technology" which has significantly enhanced human capacities; giving us a "virtual wire" between cognitive subsystems and sense modalities as well as qualitatively new capacities for self-monitoring and abstraction. Yet, it also appears to have turned humans, as Deacon argues, into "symbolic animals" which see themselves as persistent biographical subjects, or measure their conduct against socially ambient norms (Dennett 1991; Deacon 1997).

These examples illustrate how enlisting entities for functions and actively accruing functions fundamentally alter FASs by generating new dispositions or capacities. If Deacon is right, humans enlisted symbols because of their role in emergent forms of social life that required understanding symbolic relationships. But these symbolic functions were enlisted in turn. As symbolic abilities evolved they became values for the forms of social life that reciprocally depended on them (§6.4). For this reason, assemblage ontology, as John Johnston argues, provides an important corrective to instrumentalist conceptions of technologies as tools for the realization of pre-existent human values: "What is human and not human within the assemblage is never given in advance. The human never transcends the assemblages within which it is always to be found" (Johnston 2008: 116).

6.6 Assemblages, time and becoming

The expression "line of flight" – like "deterritorialization" – is among the ramifying coinages introduced by Deleuze and Guattari in the two volumes of *Capitalism and Schizophrenia*: *Anti-Oedipus* and *A Thousand Plateaus*. Like Derrida's conceptions of differential temporality, they provide an important conceptual tool for thinking about the temporal complexity of change on the cusp of becoming where no stable state of being has yet been formed. Both models, then, can be justified in terms of their capacity to understand change where there is no essence underlying change of the kind that was once thought to repose in a subject or substance. In what follows, I will argue that they provide us with an indispensable insight into the ontological structure of disconnection events that would elude us if we think of disconnections as mere juxtapositions of entities whose natures are defined independently of their historical encounter.

Because assemblages are decomposable, with mobile components that can play elsewhere, their unity is always provisional and susceptible to derangements that alter their nature or that of their components. Deterritorialization occurs where material or formal elements of an ordered assemblage (a territory) rupture their associations with a settled context generating new assemblages with new capacities, new rules or modes of functioning. As such, deterritorialization is not a process peculiar to the non-living or living, the social or technological domains. It is the ineluctable activity of nature operating "against itself"; threatening stable assemblages with anomalous relationships (Deleuze & Guattari 1988: 242–4). In any modular system there will be components with the potential to be coupled in another assemblage or iterated into a new context "to play elsewhere".

This capacity is "virtual" insofar as it is a tendency or power which needs to be unlocked by a *difference maker* in order to be manifested. Deleuze refers to such difference makers as "intensities". An intensity is a difference between states of entities that make a difference to the world and thus unlock new possibilities for existence (Deleuze 1994: 222). A particular intensity might be a gradient of fitness within a population of biological organisms or a temperature gradient in a vat of liquid that is on the point of producing convection cells. DeLanda understands this virtual potential in mathematical terms as the singular points or "singularities" (e.g. attractors, chaotic regimes) which represent the tendencies of physical systems to follow certain families of paths through a space of possible states rather than others (DeLanda 2002: 80–81). The distribution of intensities in the state space of a system can then be understood as a vector field or "flow" which represents the momentary gradient or tendency to evolve along a certain path at each point in the system's state space (pp. 30–31).

While mathematical tools like vector fields are invaluable for modelling change, they do not ontologically commit us to the existence of entities such as the temperature differential at a point in a liquid or gas, although both point and differential are assigned definite real number values in mathematical analysis. As Adrian Moore reminds us, many intensive differences involve statistical features of lower-scale properties which lack discrete values: "What are fundamentally given as differing in heat are sections of the poker, not points on it, albeit sections that may themselves have sub-sections of variable heat, in which case their own heat is some kind of mean" (Moore 2012: 559). The same point applies to intensities in a biological population. The absolute fitness of a given replicator in a biological population under selection pressures is not definable. Only its differential fitness is: the selective advantage it has over its competitors in a specified population and environment.

Thus according to this ontological model, intensities such as fitness, temperature and chemical gradients are the engines that drive the emergence of form in natural and social systems (the effect of lax incest provisions on the emergence of state forms mentioned above could be a further example of the way intensities manifest form). However, although intensities result from combinations of mobile components in assemblages, they are irreducibly relational and non-mobile: they are event-like rather than thing-like. This is why the reality and mind-independence of events and intensities squares with a rejection of Putnam's claim that metaphysical realism entails the correspondence thesis (§3.6). Incompatible theories may describe reality without fully corresponding to it if it contains entities whose location, boundaries or sorting are metaphysically indeterminate (Roden 2010b: 155).

I have argued that FASs are liable to be modular because the model provided by biological systems suggests that modularity shields such systems from the adverse effects of experimentation while allowing greater opportunities for couplings with other assemblages. Since humans and their technologies are also modular and highly adaptable, a disconnection event would offer extensive scope for anomalous couplings between the relevant assemblages at all scales. Some of the evidence cited in this and the previous chapter suggests that couplings between biological and non-biological assemblages (in particular, humans and symbol-systems) have enabled the emergence of sapient human persons, as we know them. While we need not be committed to strong ontological emergence (§5.6), the generation of sapients is arguably the production of a new kind of thing whose capacities for existing in new ways are not the capacities of its biological and non-biological components.

A disconnection would be the relationship between assemblages with high orders of functional autonomy (WH, posthumans, technologies, individual humans) but very different powers. Since these differences would be sources of intensity themselves, a disconnection is best thought of as a singular event produced by an encounter between assemblages. It could present possibilities for becoming-other that should not be conceived as incidental modifications of the natures of the components since their virtual tendencies would be unlocked by an utterly new environment. It follows that a disconnection would not be a bare conjunction of a) the Wide Human with its constituent technologies and human individuals and b) posthumans. Rather, it would be a difference-making event from which stable behaviours or natures might emerge only over time. Thus the disconnection thesis does not only leave the nature of our posthuman successors undetermined, it leaves the nature of all the *human participants* in a disconnection undetermined ahead of the real thing.

If a disconnection is an intensity, it is an event not a thing. Since the natures of its components remain undetermined through its development, it is a clear case of a becoming that lacks a *subject* of becoming. It is formally akin, then, to the ecstatic temporality described in §4.2. However, unlike Heidegger's *Dasein*, a disconnection is not an agent and does not resemble anything like a transcendental subject. Thus if we were to import any ontological models for understanding disconnection from this tradition, the work of Derrida, along with Deleuze, would be among the more appropriate. Both thinkers, as we have seen, relocate temporality outside the phenomenological sphere. What I have referred to as decomposability or modularity is formally similar to what Derrida variously describes as "generalized writing" and "articulation". The existence of independent but mutually interacting mobile components lends assemblages an open-textured capacity for anomalous couplings.[14] This, in turns, allows a becoming that need not be the becoming of something whose essence is already given in nature's repertoire.

Looking forward

If disconnections are intense becomings, becomings without a subject, then this is something we will need to take into account in our ethical and political assessment of the implications of SP. Becoming human may not be best understood as a transition from one identifiable nature to another despite the fact that the conditions of posthumanity can be analysed in terms of the functional roles of entities within and without the Wide Human. Before we can consider the ethics of becoming posthuman more fully, however, we need to think about whether technology can be considered an independent agent of disconnection or whether it is merely an expression of human interests and powers. What is a technology, exactly, and to what extent does technology leave us in a position to prevent, control or modify the way in which a disconnection might occur?

Notes

1 Though see §8.2 for a further discussion of the meanings of "life" in the context of philosophical vitalism.

2 Though note that I used the consequence law to express the form of functional explanation; not to explicate the notion of function.

3 This conception of function thus comes apart from the causal role notion of function introduced in Chapter 1.

4 In his posthumously published *Powers*, George Molnar argues that the powers of fundamental particles such as electrons are ungrounded in non-dispositional properties (Molnar 2006). Such entities, he claims, can be thought of as having ungrounded powers.

5 They could have cited Heidegger's claim that an "eye taken independently is not an eye at all" (Heidegger 1995: 220).

6 Assuming the persuasiveness of Dretske's argument, it seems appropriate to reserve the category of event for "one-off" ephemera that propagate through space and time. Within the analytic tradition this brings us closer to Davidson's metaphysics of ephemeral events (Davidson 2001a). Within the continental tradition, arguably, it brings us closer to the theory of the radically singular event that Jean-François Lyotard sets out in *The Inhuman* (Lyotard 1991: 155).

   In earlier work I had assumed that singular events were incompatible with the Derridean account of textual temporality (characterized by the structures of iterability, trace and *différance* – see Roden 2004a). So conceding them is a significant revision but not fatal to my use of Derridean ideas in this book. Singular events that occur in a particular location or context seem to be indispensable whereas repeatable ones are not. Including both seems irreparably confusing. Moreover, we can reconcile the singularity of the event with Derrida's claims about the iterability of text and the ecstatic temporality of the trace (§4.2) by treating texts as *repeatable particulars* whose instances are ephemeral events. (In Chapter 7 this model will be extended to deal with the abstract condition of technologies.) Just as an object can be composed of events or processes occurring concurrently in a given volume of space, so an object can be composed of events occurring successively in disparate contexts.

7 Some contemporary metaphysicians have argued that there is an equivalent to Aristotelian form to be found in mechanism-independent constraints on variation and development in dynamic systems (Walsh 2006). However, as DeLanda points out, these constraints or ideal singularities are not logical entities that can be iterated from individual to individual and are, as the Collier–Hooker example shows, acutely contingent on lower scale material organization (DeLanda 2006: 29; Collier & Hooker 1999).

8 An issue I do not have time to consider is that ecological dependency is transitive. If a function depends on a thing whose existence depends on another thing, then it depends on that other thing. Ecological dependencies thus overlap.

9 I am grateful to R. Scott Bakker for pointing this out (see previous note).

10 Addictive substances may fall into this class.
11 My use of the term "module" to refer to the mobile parts of an assemblage should not be confused with its standard usage in philosophy of mind and cognitive science. The classical modularity thesis holds that human and animal minds contain encapsulated, fast, automatic (mandatory) domain-specific cognitive systems dedicated to specialized tasks such as kinship-evaluation, sentence-parsing or classifying life forms (Fodor 1983; Frankish 2011; Barkow *et al.* 1995).
12 One of the benefits of so-called "objected oriented" programming languages (OO) like Java over "procedural" programming languages such as COBOL is that OO programs organize software objects in *encapsulated* modules. When a client object in the program has to access an object (e.g. a data structure such as a list) it sends a message to the object that activates one of the object's "public" methods (e.g. the client might "tell" the object to return an element stored in it, add a new element or carry out an operation on existing elements). However, the client's message does not specify how the operation is to be performed. This is specified in the code for the object. From the perspective of the client, the object is a black box that can be activated by public messages yielding a consumable output. This means that changes in how the proprietary methods of the object are implemented does not force developers to change the code in other parts of the program since these do not "matter" to the other objects. Maintenance and development of software systems become simpler.
13 In a recent target article on neural reuse in *Behavioural and Brain Sciences*, Michael Anderson cites research suggesting that older brain areas tend to be less domain-specific and more multistable – that is, that they tend to get re-deployed in a wider variety of cognitive domains (Anderson 2010: 247).
14 Readers who are philosophical naturalists might feel queasy about extending the trace structure to the most basic levels of matter, as in Hägglund (2008). Derrida's argumentation still hinges on a conception of time as passage; one derived, arguably, from our conscious experience of succession, even if applied in a topic-neutral way (Roden 2005). Perhaps, at some level, time will resolve into a series of discrete events, like the operations of a cellular automaton. If that were the case, both trace and virtuality would have to have emerged from a physical micro-dynamic in which they are not present. However, it is less clear whether either could be compatible with a physics of metaphysics that denies the reality of time.

7 New substantivism
A theory of technology

Introduction

Chapter 5 used the principle of accounting to argue that we have a moral interest in making or becoming posthumans since the dated nonexistence of posthumans is the primary source of uncertainty about the value of posthuman life (§§5.1, 5.8).

I have argued that accounting is not objectionable if we apply a sensibly etiolated version of the precautionary principle (§5.8). But might there be other moral objections to the policy? I will consider these in Chapter 8 where I urge major revisions to the politics and ethics of accounting. The diachronic side of disconnection explored in Chapter 6 will assume an ethical valence there. However, before considering the pros and cons of accounting, we need to consider whether having an ethics of becoming or avoiding the posthuman makes any difference in a complex technological society such as ours.

At first sight, the answer to this seems obvious. A disconnection would result from decisions taken by human agents. Following a disconnection, posthuman agents would be independent of our designs and perhaps largely beyond our control. But until then, each step of the process of making posthumans could be attributed to humans.

So we may conclude that humans will determine whether a disconnection event occurs or not. After all, if a final outcome of a process depends on humans doing a, b and c in that order, it will not occur if someone fails to do c. So even if disconnections are hard to predict, they are not hard to control. If humans do not want to make posthumans, posthumans will not be made. Until disconnection, humans will be in charge and responsible for the effects (good or bad) that ensue from their technical activity.

This claim assumes a position that is called "instrumentalism" by philosophers of technology (e.g. Verbeek 2005: 11). For instrumentalists, there is a clear tripartite distinction between 1) a technique, 2) the agent who employs it and 3) the purpose for which it is used. Since tools have no agency of their own, the agent (not the tool) is causally and morally responsible for what it is and what it does. Aristotle's conception of the tool as a "pure means" whose animating principle lies outside of it, in humans, is a clear example of instrumentalism (Galston 1993: 238; §6.2).

Most significant philosophy of technology has been critical of instrumentalism. Critics of modernity from Rousseau to Adorno and Heidegger have argued that technique does not merely extend our capacities – making it easier to hunt, kill or cook – but radically alters our self-understanding, our aims and our relationship to the world. The claim that technology, rather than a neutral means, exerts a "determining and controlling influence on society and culture" is often referred to as *substantivism* (Verbeek 2005: 11).

For example, in "The Question Concerning Technology", Heidegger claims that modern technology is a historically specific way in which reality is disclosed or "unconcealed", one that reveals it as a "standing reserve" convertible to human uses (Heidegger 1978). As Peter-Paul Verbeek summarizes it: for Heidegger, "Reality acquires its identity from what can be done with it" (Verbeek 2005: 55). Technology is not a neutral instrument but a structure of disclosure that determines how humans are related to things and to one another. If Heidegger is right, we may control individual devices, but our technological mode of being exerts a decisive grip on us: "man does not have control over unconcealment itself, in which at any given time the real shows itself or withdraws" (Heidegger 1978: 299). If this is right, the assumption that humans will determine whether our future is posthuman or not is premature.

So substantivism needs to be addressed before we can consider the scope of any ethics of becoming posthuman. To this end I will address certain conceptual issues in the substantivist theory of technology developed by Jacques Ellul in his book *The Technological Society* (1964).

Unlike Heidegger, Ellul does not use a transcendentalist methodology to formulate his substantivist account. If anything, his approach is partially naturalistic, treating the agency of technology as a function of socio-technical complexity. This makes it a more promising approach for the present work since Heidegger's formulation of substantivism presupposes a transcendental methodology we have independent grounds for rejecting (Chapter 4, §4.2). In addition, the "transcendentalist" style of analysis is incapable of addressing the concrete input of technologies and actions to the disposition of technological systems. Ellul thus avoids the charge of deducing the character of modern techniques from their transcendental conditions of possibility (Verbeek 2005: 64–6).

Ellul's substantivism claims that technique in the modern era develops according to its own logic of efficiency and, in so doing, marginalizes non-technical norms and values:

> Technical progress today is no longer conditioned by anything other than its own calculus of efficiency. The search is no longer personal, experimental,

workmanlike; it is abstract, mathematical, and industrial. This does not mean that the individual no longer participates. On the contrary, progress is made only after innumerable individual experiments. But the individual participates only to the degree that resists all the currents today considered secondary, such as aesthetics, ethics, fantasy. Insofar as the individual represents this abstract tendency, he is permitted to participate in technical creation, which is increasingly independent of him and increasingly linked to its own mathematical law.

(Ellul 1964: 74)

Ellul's *technique* is thus similar to Heidegger's technological mode of framing the world. It is not a collection of devices or methods which serve narrow human ends, but a nonhuman system that adapts narrow humans to its ends. As we see from this passage, Ellul does not deny human technical agency but claims that the norms according to which agency is assessed are fixed by the system rather than by human agents. Modern technique, for Ellul, is thus "autonomous" because it determines its own principles of action (Winner 1977: 16). The content of this pre-scription can be expressed as the injunction to maximize efficiency, a principle overriding conceptions of the good adopted by human users of technical means.

Ellul has been criticized by theorists of a more social constructionist bent for divorcing the notion of efficiency from social or cultural contexts of technology use. I think this criticism can be rebutted from within Ellul's theory. But seeing how Ellul obviates the efficiency criticism helps us to see where the real conceptual tensions of the theory of autonomous technique lie. This will allow us to reconfigure some of Ellul's core ideas for a kind of "substantivism without substance": a philosophy of technology that accounts for the distinctiveness of technical modernity without misreading it as an all-controlling power.

In what follows, I will argue that a condition of technical autonomy – which Ellul calls "self-augmentation" – is in fact incompatible with autonomy. This refers to the propensity of modern technique to catalyse the development of further techniques. Thus while *technical autonomy* is a normative concept, *self-augmentation* is a dynamical one.

I claim that technical self-augmentation presupposes the independence of techniques from culture, use and place (a property I call "technical abstraction"). Technical abstraction is incompatible with technical autonomy, I argue, because where techniques are relatively abstract they cannot be *functionally individuated*. Self-augmentation can only operate where techniques do not determine how they are used. Thus sub-stantivists like Ellul and Heidegger are wrong to treat technology as a system that subjects humans to its strictures.

Although self-augmenting technique is not *in* control because it is not a subject or stand-in for a subject, I argue that there are grounds for claiming that it may be beyond our capacity to control. So there is something right about the substantivist picture (which earns this chapter its title). But while technology exerts a powerful influence on individuals, society and culture, this cannot be an "autonomous" influence because there are no ends or purposes proper to it. Technology is *counter-final*.

7.1 Ellul, essentialism and the efficiency criticism

Ellul's theory of autonomous technique has two main components: 1) a theory of the essence of technique, which sets out necessary and sufficient conditions for something being a technique; and 2) an account of the historical conditions for the emergence of autonomous technique.

All particular techniques, according to Ellul, are goal-directed operations (Ellul 1964: 19). The technical operation is distinguished from other processes by being the result of an intelligent search for greater efficiency. This tendency – which Ellul terms the "technical phenomenon" – is not the exclusive preserve of modernity. It characterizes Zulu military technology and Roman law as much as object-oriented programming or nuclear fission (p. 77). As we shall see, however, in contrast to autonomous technique, pre-modern technical development is characterized by a slow rate of diffusion and by its subordination to goals other than efficiency.

Now, a technique is never just efficient. It is efficient *in certain respects, measured against certain implicit or explicit goals*. A process may be energy-efficient but environmentally wasteful (Tiles & Oberdeik 1995: 27). A program may be computationally efficient in terms of the number of statement executions required in "worst-case" situations, yet less easy to maintain than one requiring more statement executions for worst-case inputs.

There are different efficiency criteria reflecting the cultural or social contexts in which techniques are used rather than any overall technical phenomenon. Thus, it is arguable that "efficiency" is not an invariant property. It is naïve to claim that modern societies are dominated by the imperative of efficiency-optimization since the extension of the concept of efficiency is fixed by contexts of use and, in particular, the values by which we judge some process to be an efficient one.

However, according to Ellul, a particular technology "*is* a use" (emphasis added) not just a means to some end. Automobile technology is not just cars, their components and their material infrastructure; it is also constituted by publicly sanctioned functions:

> The use of an automobile as a murder weapon does not represent the technical use, that is, the one best way of doing something. Technique is a means

> with a set of rules for the game. It is a "method of being used" which is unique and not open to arbitrary choice; we gain no advantage from the machine or from organization if it is not used as it ought to be.
>
> (Ellul 1964: 97)

This idea should be familiar from our discussion of Heidegger's claim that we primarily experience objects as functions and affordances (§3.7). If each technical thing has its proprietary ways of being used, its efficiency relations will also be intrinsic to it. Techniques are not found in a state of nature, waiting to be choreographed by humans but are always already "purposed" (Arthur 2009: 54). To program computers, I must have learned the syntax and semantics of a relevant language, but also understand the point of writing effective software. To play the piano, I must understand that a piano is a device for musical performance.

There are many conceptions of efficiency but only *some* efficiency relations will be pertinent to any technical thing if understood in this way.

The prescriptive force that Ellul ascribes to efficiency considerations comes from this tacit contract: "If you desire X and if you have chosen the appropriate means to X, then you must supply all the conditions for the means to operate" (Winner 1977: 198, 101). In adopting a given means, for Ellul, we buy into the appropriate ways of using it.

This claim seems plausible if we consider the way artefacts like jet engines or computers are organized into hierarchies of modular components, each contributing uniquely and vitally to the operation of the whole. A technology seems to be nothing other than a set of phenomena "programmed to some purpose", as Brian Arthur puts it (Arthur 2009: 51–2).

Thus, in Ellul's defence, it can be argued that the notion of efficiency employed in his essentialist account is *a second-order property exemplified by diverse but functionally determinate particular techniques*. Each particular technique exemplifies the higher-order efficiency property because for each means there is a contextually determined function specifying the goal that it can achieve more or less effectively.

7.2 Self-augmentation and technical complexity

Nonetheless, the fixation of purposes through technical use is patently insufficient for technical autonomy. Even if each means has its context-determined ends, we might not want to make a covenant with it because it is incompatible with our plan of life. Becoming a competent driver may result in me internalizing the norms that distinguish effective car use, as Ellul claims. But I may still prefer to walk to work rather than drive because I want to decrease my carbon footprint or keep fit.

So wherever the covenant with technique is optional at either an individual or a political level, it is hyperbolic to claim that technical demands can override human conceptions of the good.

As Langdon Winner emphasizes, however, Ellul does not subscribe to a global technological determinism. He does not claim that technical needs trump non-technical ones under all historical conditions. He thinks that technical means had a tacit opt-out clause in the pre-modern era (Ellul 1964: 77; Winner 1977: 118–19). Technical autonomy is predicated on technological culture expanding its hold on everyday life to the point at which the covenant with technique is mandatory. This stage is reached when the pace and scope of technique is determined exclusively by technical requirements. According to Ellul this happens when technique becomes *self-augmenting*.

"Self-augmentation" refers to the tendency for techniques to have a multiplicative effect on the development of other techniques in adjoining or separate domains.

Technique is self-augmenting, according to Ellul, where it "tends to act, not according to arithmetic, but according to a geometric progression" (Ellul 1964: 89). We should not take this mathematical representation too literally – for one thing, it seems unlikely that all the relevant variables by which we might measure the development of a technical system will grow indefinitely. Particular technologies – like particular biological populations or sales of commodities – tend to be characterized by logistic growth functions or "S-curves" whose middle parts approximate to the endlessly accelerating growth that Ellul describes but whose later parts flatten out as the process hits resource limits (Kurzweil 2005: 44). For example, Theodore Modis notes that US oil production followed an accelerating growth pattern between 1859 and 1951 only to decelerate in the 1960s and 1970s. The same considerations will probably apply to Moore's Law – which states that the number of silicon transistors in microprocessors approximately doubles every two years – since physical limits on the size of microcircuitry will tell eventually (Modis 2012: 316–17).

The important property about *self-augmenting technical systems* (SATS), for our purposes, is not whether a cascade of S-curves within a "broad area of technology" can transcend the resource limits of any single technological "paradigm" (pp. 346–7). Rather, it is the qualitative dynamics whereby technical developments in a complex and extended technological system or assemblage – including the actions of its sapient human components – tend to catalyse one another. The more techniques have the capacity to combine, converge or prompt further technical development, the more interrelations become possible (Ellul 1964: 92). Self-augmenting technique thus has an independent reality and causal power:

> [In self-augmenting technical systems] it is possible to speak of the 'reality'
> of technique – with its own substance, its own particular mode of being,
> and a life independent of our power and decision. The evolution of techniques
> then becomes exclusively causal; *it loses all finality.*
>
> (Ellul 1964: 93, emphasis added)

It is vital to re-emphasize Ellul's point that autonomy and self-augmentation
do not preclude a role for human agency in technical change. Were they
to come into existence, posthuman technologies would presumably replicate
without human intervention. But this is not a necessary condition for self-
augmentation. Self-augmentation can take place, Ellul claims, where the
development of a technique results from thousands of efforts and decisions so
that an action in one technical domain incrementally influences developments
and decisions in other areas.

Self-augmenting technique does not remove human agency but mediates it through networks where no single agent or collective is able to
exercise decisive control over the technical system. Ellul thinks that this
situation justifies the claim that the ensemble of techniques or technical
system can constitute an effective reality in its own right.

Self-augmentation can occur when a technique generates a problem
which can only be fixed through a series of supplementary fixes, some of
which initiate a cascade of problems and fixes. Arguably, *this will happen
more as techniques become more complex, interconnected and multiply applicable.* In
the 1980s Tim Berners-Lee developed hypertext protocols in response to
file-sharing problems experienced by scientists at the European Particle
Physics Lab (CERN). The problem confronted by Berners-Lee was that
work at CERN required a very large quantity of information to be made
available to computers using different viewing software, for example, with
incompatible fonts or formats. His solution was to create a way of
encoding metadata about the relevant files that could be interpreted by any
other computer running his browser software. The invention of freely available browser software and HTML in response to these highly specific and
local problems contributed to the development of the World Wide Web
and influenced the development of other languages, particularly interpreted platform-independent languages such as Java. Java is particularly
significant because a Java program is initially compiled in a platform-
independent format on a Java Virtual Machine, which effectively simulates
the operation of a real computer. On runtime the "intermediate code"
created by the virtual machine is interpreted by the host computer and
executed. The interpreted character of Java allows a single program to be
ported to a variety of different devices allowing a protocol for communicating between them. It has thus contributed to the development of so-called
"ubiquitous computation" and the "internet-of-things", the diffusion of

information processing capacity throughout an ever-diversifying range of human artefacts (Open University 2006).

Ellul cites John Kay's invention of the flying shuttle in 1733. This greatly increased the amount of cloth producible by a single weaver but necessitated increases in the production of yarn, later addressed with the invention of the spinning jenny. However, this initially caused an *over-production* of yarn – a problem resolved by the invention of Cartwright's power loom (Ellul 1964: 112). This in turn allowed the introduction of "adjunct" techniques such as steam power and the development of mechanized textile production, with all its concomitant demands on transportation, raw materials and the organization of factory life (Winner 1977: 102).

Both processes are instances of technical self-augmentation insofar as both innovations addressed problems that could not have existed without an earlier technique, whether computer-mediated communications or factory based textile production.

7.3 Self-augmentation and autonomy

So does the self-augmenting character of a particular state of technology – modern planetary technique – constitute a basis for technical autonomy? Well, the range and power of a SATS, such as the current global system, makes technology hard to avoid for all but the excluded or the extremely privileged (who can presumably pay others to drive their cars, surf the internet or answer their phone calls). In a twenty-first-century economy, one is notionally free to relinquish computer technology, for example, but not if one wants to pursue almost any non-manual occupation. I managed to live without a mobile phone until around 2007, when it became increasingly clear that I would be expected to maintain communications with colleagues and students while travelling to Open University meetings and tutorials. My covenant with the mobile phone was necessitated by the new social norms of the twenty-first-century media landscape.

Since these norms apparently exemplify an overarching efficiency relation, then Ellul's inference from technical self-augmentation to technical autonomy might appear secure. Our lives will be increasingly governed by efficiency considerations as our SATS becomes ever more complex and encompassing.

Ellul is unspecific about the causes of self-augmentation, but he emphasizes that additional "stage setting" is required for technology to become self-augmenting. Prior to the eighteenth century, according to Ellul, technique was *local, and tended to diffuse relatively slowly* (Ellul 1964: 68). As long as technical dissemination is spatially and temporally constrained, an invention like Hero of Alexandria's simple steam engine (the aeolipile) in the first century AD can be "forgotten" and is unlikely to be subject to further innovation or deployment.

It seems plausible to suppose that a number of key developments at the threshold of modernity – including de-skilled factory production, the development of patent law and the development of technologies for the rapid transfer of information and materials – contributed to this independence of culture and place. This new transmissibility – "technical abstraction" – increases the likelihood of a given technological development propagating from one node to lots of others, and thus for each subsequent node: for example, well beyond a cabal of nuclear physicists in Switzerland.

Technical abstraction is thus a precondition of *technical nonlocality*, and thus of self-augmentation.

Techniques are more abstract the more they are available for reapplication or reconfiguration in disparate contexts. Relatively abstract techniques are (relatively) functionally indeterminate, or "multistable" to use Ihde's terminology (§6.5). The internal combustion engine, for example, can be used for "producing electricity, or pumping air in order to drive a sledge hammer, or moving a car or an airplane" (Dumouchel 1992: 420, n7). A cell phone also makes a serviceable detonator. A module of code which extracts the elements of a list from computer memory can be used to faithfully print a series of library borrowers with overdue books or could be modified to randomize note values for an algorithmic music composition. Even simple artefacts are characterized by multistability. Ihde cites the example of sardine cans left in New Guinea by Australian gold prospectors and later appropriated by the indigenous inhabitants as ornaments for headgear (cited in Verbeek 2005: 136).

In line with their shared phenomenological methodology, Ihde and Verbeek argue that the phenomenon of multistability shows that technologies are just their roles in human practice (as in the case of Heidegger's equipment). As Verbeek puts it:

> Just as perception can be understood intentionally only as perception-of, and consciousness only as consciousness-of, so technology can only be understood as technology-in-order-to. The "in order to" indicates that technologies always and only function in concrete, practical contexts and cannot be technologies apart from such contexts.
>
> (Verbeek 2005: 117)

However, if phenomenology has a dark side, even appearances are not exhausted by how they appear (§4.2). It is precipitate to reduce technologies to phenomenology when phenomenology itself eludes reduction to phenomenology. It is also plain wrong – as a brief consideration of the property of multistability shows.

Multistability is only possible if technical entities such as code-modules or transistors are not restricted to any given context of use or "in-order-to". Parts of technical assemblages, as we have noted already, are always susceptible to reuse and re-grafting elsewhere (§6.5). This capacity to transcend any given context or design phase is also intrinsic to the power of technical systems of all kinds (§7.4). A technical object like Java is obviously designed to be multifunctional.

If technologies transcend their uses in particular contexts, it follows that they are *ontologically independent of the rules or practices that fix their function*. A technical entity such as an Acheulian hand axe can be used *as* a scraper, a chopper or a projectile weapon because its potential for use extends beyond any single use (§6.5). Functional indeterminacy is even more evident in technical modernity, as Brian Arthur points out:

> Global positioning technology provides direct location, but it rarely stands alone. It is used as an element in combination with other elements to navigate aircraft and ships, to help survey territory, to manage agriculture. It is like a highly reactive building block in chemistry – the hydroxyl ion say – doing little on its own, but appearing in a host of different combinations. The same can be said for other elements of the digital revolution: algorithms, switches, routers, repeaters, web services. And we can say the same for the elements that comprise modern genetic engineering or nanotechnology.
>
> (Arthur 2009: 25)

No less than signs, then, technologies are intrinsically functionally indeterminate and multistable. Their transformative power derives from this and not from the contextual uses humans or cultures affix to them.

This abstraction is also a matter of degree. GPS or the For Loop are far more transferable than the "cracking process for crude oil" (Arthur 2009: 24). The more functions that a technique can undertake, the less its use is constrained by existing usage in "concrete contexts". The more abstract it is, the more configurations it can adopt, and the more susceptible it is to "creative abuse" (greater abstraction implies greater functional indeterminacy). Modern technology is characterized by high transmissibility, global reach and promiscuous couplings with other techniques.

We have seen that Ellulian technical autonomy presupposes self-augmentation, while self-augmentation clearly presupposes high transmissibility and promiscuous reuse. So self-augmentation presupposes a high degree of abstraction.

However, highly abstract technology is also extremely functionally indeterminate. It is easy to see, then, that this blocks Ellul's argument for technical autonomy. As we saw, each particular technique, for Ellul, exemplifies the higher-order efficiency property because for each there is a contextually determined function specifying the goal that it can achieve more or less effectively.

If each particular technique is functionally indeterminate to a high degree, then there cannot be a fixed function satisfying higher-order efficiency.

It follows that technique cannot be prescriptive in the way that Ellul's autonomy thesis requires, and be abstract. A second-order efficiency concept can only dictate technical activity if it somehow works its influence on situated rules of use, which, in turn, determine the natures of technical entities (§7.1).

Ellul the substantivist, like Aristotle the instrumentalist, assumes that the governing principle of the technical thing lies outside of it. But if technology is not reducible to our access to it, there is no conceivable channel of influence by which the technical ensemble, as Ellul sees it, can communicate with its parts.

From the purview of assemblage theory, the claim that technological systems are governed by second-order conceptions of efficiency gets things back to front. The behaviour of technical assemblage – like any assemblage – supervenes on interactions between human and nonhuman parts. Efficiency maximization, where it occurs, emerges from these manifold knots of influence. Despite the fact that the dynamic principle of self-augmentation acknowledges the role of complexity in technical modernity, the idea of technical autonomy mixes this with a view of technique as a top-down transcendental organizing principle; a kind of quasi-subject (§5.4).

This is not to deny that we internalize values when we use technologies. We do, but these habits and sensitivities are embodied states, which can be modified in our technological dealings. Abstraction exposes habits and values to a manifold of sensory affects and encounters (§8.2). It entails that the evolution of particular technologies depends on hugely complex and counter-final interactions, catalysed by transmissibility and promiscuous reusability (Ellul 1964: 93).

Thus we need not attribute agency or purposiveness to technology to explain why the evolution of technical systems eludes our control. If technology is "out of control", it does not follow that it is "in control" of us or under its own control. If planetary technique is a SATS, then, it cannot be autonomous.

Note that this denial of technical autonomy is compatible with a looser dependence claim about values and technique. Even if techniques are not uses, the way resources are distributed within technical systems constrains the kinds of lives that can be adopted within them.

For example, the absence of writing or other physically persistent forms of expression is often held incompatible with the existence of laws or state institutions. If this is true, then understanding oneself as a citizen of a state has technical conditions of possibility. But there are many possible expressions and forms of citizenship within modern societies. Again, it is possible that our conception of the author was made possible by the modern copyright law developed to control the dissemination of print technology. The special rights of the author over reproductions and translations of her text, according to this view, make the experience of the unique "work" possible (Derrida 1992). Nonetheless, there are many different ways of responding to this predicament, from literary naturalism to the modernism of Kafka and Joyce, through twenty-first-century Flarf composition and beyond.

Thus while increasing abstraction increases the opportunities for variations in technical entities to elicit yet more variations in other contexts, it undermines the normative hegemony of particular uses and higher-order efficiency concepts. Ellulian technical autonomy is contradicted by its own conditions of possibility.

7.4 Technique and repetition

To pursue the implications of this argument further we need an adequate theory of abstraction for technical entities. Faced with this demand, some may be tempted to adopt an ontology of techniques as abstract procedures (algorithms) which diagram the internal operations of each technical entity. This is problematic, however, because algorithm is distinct from its implementations while a technique is not distinguishable from its instances in the same way. A given technique can be instanced in different ways; but this does not entail a Platonic technique transcending these instances. The petrol engine and diesel engine instance the internal combustion engine but implement different algorithms. The first compresses air and fuel, then ignites it with an induction coil. The second involves a compression ignition system.

Just as the same technique can be realized in different algorithms, so the same algorithm can be "concretized" by technical objects which exhibit greater or lesser synergy between their functional components. According to Gilbert Simondon, technical progress does not occur *fonction par fonction, mais synergie par synergie* as disparate functions are successively integrated or "concretized" in physical structures (Simondon 1969: 34). Simondon's account is illustrated in his analysis of the successive improvement of the vacuum tube – a device in which free electrons are focused into a beam onto a positive electrode (the anode). The earliest vacuum tube – the Crookes tube – was instrumental in the discovery of high energy X-rays (created when electrons, accelerated by the potential difference between cathode and anode, strike the anode).

Simondon notes that these functions were better integrated in the improved Coolidge tube. For example, the Crookes tube produces electrons by ionizing a gas which occupies the tube, then focuses these onto the anode using the same potential difference that causes the ionization. The Coolidge tube separates these functions using a "hot" (thermionic) cathode to produce the electrons. This allows the tube to contain a more perfect vacuum which impedes the electrons less in their path to the anode. Moreover, the hot cathode in the Coolridge tube produces a thinner beam which can be more effectively focused (Simondon 1969: 34–5).

As Stiegler observes, the moral of this analysis is that the essence of a technology is not simply to be found in an analysis of its internal functioning but in the concrete ways in which these functions are integrated in matter. The invention of a new device is neither the instantiation of an abstract Platonic diagram nor the invention of an isolated thing, but the production of a mutable pattern open to dynamic alteration (Stiegler 1998: 77–8). As Arthur writes: "In the real world, technologies are highly reconfigurable; they are fluid things, never static, never finished, never perfect" (2009: 42).

This reaffirms my claim that a phenomenological ontology which reduces abstract technical entities to their uses is inadequate. Technical entities are more than bundles of internal or external functions. They are materialized potentialities for generating new functions as well as modifiable strategies for integrating and reintegrating functions (as in the transition from Crookes to Coolidge).

As such, any technical entity must transcend any of its possible uses or realizations. It is not reducible to them.

Furthermore, while the algorithm/implementation distinction is "brute" metaphysics, modern technique involves *distinctive mechanisms of abstraction*. There is a massive difference in capital outlay between reproducing car engines and re-compiling Java code on one's PC or Mac. This is not related to a difference of complexity – software objects can be multiplied with greater ease than engine parts – but to the singular replications involved. Different mechanisms of abstraction entail different speeds of change, different scope for local modification, democratic legitimation, etc. and thus different possibilities for multiple causal influences to operate in technical change.

These mechanisms are in a process of flux even as I write. In the 1980s the open-sourced software movement made the source code of computer applications freely available to developers across the Web. Open source applications like the visual programming environment Pure Data (Pd) have dedicated communities of developers who add functionality to the original software package and make their work available without charge. However, cheap internet-based DNA writing and the extension of the software technique of "code reuse" to the biological domain may herald an age of open-source synthetic biology based around large libraries of functionally specified, reusable genetic sequences (Smolke 2009; Ledford 2010).

Likewise the era of downloading things is upon us. In April 2013, a libertarian group calling themselves "Defence Distributed" announced that they would distribute files that program the assembly of a usable plastic gun in a 3D printer (currently priced at around US$8,000). The group's spokesman, Cody Wilson, anticipates an era in which search engines will provide components "for everything from prosthetic limbs to drugs and birth-control devices" (Rayner 2013).

A metaphysics of technical repetition needs, then, to be sensitive both to the abstract, repeatable nature of the technical individual – emphasized by Simondon – and the historical particularity of modes of repetition. The technical thing must be able to exist independently of human praxis so that humans can find different ways of understanding and appropriating it. The conditions for the phenomenology of technology thus show that the existence of technological items exceeds their phenomenological manifestation. Technologies can withdraw from particular human practices (Verbeek 2005: 117). If SP is correct, they may even withdraw from *all* human practices.

Thus we should embrace a realist metaphysics of technique in opposition to the phenomenologies of Verbeek and Ihde. Technologies according to this model are abstract, repeatable particulars realized (though never finalized) in ephemeral events (§6.5).

Despite being associated with postmodernist forms of textualism and antirealism, Derrida's account of "generalised writing" and iterability (§2.1) in the area of language and representation provides a model that addresses the "abstract particularity" of technique while leaving room for a more detailed metaphysical treatment of technicity (Derrida 1988: 10–12; Roden 2004a). Iterability exhibits the incompleteness of semantic or functional taxonomies faced with the world's inherent variability (Roden 2005: 84). *Iterabilia* are neither eternal nor ephemeral (see Roden 2004a: 204). They are repeatable particulars without transcendent criteria of reinstantiation. There is no essential beginning to an iterative series.

If this structure of repetition carries over to techniques, then, to the extent that techniques are iterable, there are no hard rules fixing in advance what counts as a token of a given abstract technical type. The distinction between the technical and the non-technical is porous. Is a theory of pure mathematics, like Boolean algebra, technical? However we arbitrate between technics and theory, nineteenth-century Boolean logic appears to have *acquired* technicity during the twentieth century through iterative transformations. No computer program could make a decision or control statement repetition without evaluating to Boolean values ("true" or "false"). Iterative repetition crosses categorical distinctions between technical and non-technical entities. Thus as well as accounting for technical abstraction, the iterability of technique entails anti-essentialism regarding technicity as such.

7.5 In or out of control?

If planetary technology is a self-augmenting system, it cannot be the system described in Ellul's theory of normative technological determinism. A theory of self-augmenting technique is thus incompatible with the substantivist picture of an all-controlling technology (§7.3). However, the claim that modern planetary technique is self-augmenting throws up questions for the politics of technology comparable to those incited by the Molochs of Heidegger and Ellul.

To control a system we also need some way of anticipating what it will do as a result of our attempts to modify it. But given the accounts of SATSs developed above, it is likely that planetary technique is, as Ellul argues, a distinctive causal factor which ineluctably alters the technical fabric of our societies and lives without being controllable in its turn.[1]

This hypothesis is, admittedly, quite speculative but there are some *prima facie* grounds for at least entertaining it:

- In a planetary SATS local sites can exert a disproportionate influence on the organization of the whole but may not "show up" for those lacking "local knowledge". Thus even encyclopaedic knowledge of current "technical trends" will not be sufficient to identify all future causes of technical change.
- The categorical porousness of technique as a category adds to this difficulty. As the case of Boolean algebra demonstrates, the line between technical and non-technical is systematically fuzzy. If technical abstraction amplifies the potential for "crossings" between technical and extra-technical domains, it must further ramp up uncertainty regarding the sources of future technical change.
- Given SP, technical change could engender posthuman life forms that are functionally autonomous and thus withdraw from any form of human control.
- Any computationally tractable simulation of a SATS would be part of the system it is designed to model. It would, moreover, be a disseminable, highly abstract part. So multiple variations of the same simulations could be replicated across the SATS, generating a system that could be qualitatively different from the one that it was originally designed to simulate.

This is a problematic conclusion for those who predicate social emancipation on technological democracy. Andrew Feenberg believes that technology should be more democratic and argues that the democratic control and legitimation of technology is possible where design choice is underdetermined relative to individual techniques. For this allows the instantiation of techniques to be shaped by diverse social constituencies. Thus MS DOS lost out to Windows not because it was a less efficient interface (as Ellul might attest) but because it failed to reflect the new social context of computation and the novel uses and needs it entailed: "A system that was more efficient for programming and accounting tasks proved less than ideal for secretaries and hobbyists interested in ease of use" (Feenberg 1999: 79).

The process of design fixing is likely to be mediated in a democratic fashion where multiple shapes for a particular technique can be actively considered within a population of deciders. In Feenberg's example, this resulted in a choice between a graphical user interface and a command-line interface. But it is arguable that this is only likely to happen where techniques are *abstract enough* to be simultaneously available in a variety of forms to a critical mass of users. Thus democratizing technique with 3D printing or open-source biotech is liable to turn the control knob up on self-augmentation, disseminating the very abstract technical resources that are the source of its unpredictability.

Thus if our planetary technical system is a SATS, there are grounds for believing that it is:

- Uncontrollable
- A decisive mediator of social actions and cultural values, but
- Not a controlling influence.

On the foregoing hypothesis, the human population is now part of a complex technical system whose long-run qualitative development is out of the hands of the humans within it. This system is, of course, a significant part of WH (§5.3). The fact that the global SATS is out of control doesn't mean that it, or anything, is in control. *There is no finality to the system at all* because it is not the kind of thing that can have purposes. So the claim that we belong to a self-augmenting technical system (SATS) should not be confused with the normative technological determinism that we find in Heidegger and Ellul. There is nothing technology wants.

Note

1 Though this is not to say that it controls us, since, *pace* Ellul, it prescribes nothing.

8   The ethics of becoming posthuman

Nothing human makes it out of the near future.

("Meltdown", Land 2012: 443)

Introduction

In *On the Human Condition* Dominique Janicaud argues that the thought of passing from a human state to that of some inhuman successor can have no moral content for us. The meaning of the inhuman is either contaminated by our understanding of human subjectivity or it is utterly inconceivable and, thus, ethically irrelevant:

> Even though we speak of a "totally inhuman" reality, the adverb "totally" does not manage to erase the reference to the human. That does not mean that there neither is nor ever could be a reality that is totally other (what do we know of what "takes place" on the fringes of the universe?), but it always testifies to the specificity of human consciousness: human consciousness poses in opposing, and asserts itself in overcoming itself; in this sense, it cannot entirely extricate itself from itself, it cannot cut itself off completely from the remarkable relation that binds it to things and to itself – this irreplaceable bond is called "subjectivity" or "openness to Being". That is to say that if the disappearance of the human is not impossible, the content of this disappearance remains as inconceivable to man as that which awaits him (or does not await him) beyond his physical disappearance: if I decide to commit suicide (*me donner la mort*), I do not really know what I "give" ("*donne*") myself: I know only what I reject.
>
> (Janicaud 2005: 29–30)

Janicaud is correct to point out that our current understanding of the posthuman must be specified by its relation to humanity. The satisfaction conditions for posthumanity in the disconnection thesis are a case in point. A Wide Human Descendent (WHD) is a posthuman (recall) if and only if:

It has ceased to belong to WH (the Wide Human) as a result of technical alteration.
Or is a wide descendant of such a being (outside WH).

However, he is wrong to claim that the posthuman can have no other content than an overcoming or "transcendence" of human consciousness. The very idea of transcendence implies an apophatic structure in which there is some *a priori* invariance (of subjectivity, worldhood or meaning) that is transcended and can be known only in terms of its transcendence (§5.4). But there are no good grounds for assuming such invariants: our parochial grasp of the phenomenology of "subjectivity" or "being" has no epistemological privileges (see Chapter 4).

Moreover, the disconnection thesis does not describe the posthuman apophatically but functionally: in terms of its capacity to cut free from WH. Disconnections can be realized by technologies and states with no more in common than that disconnection is among their effects. Some of these may involve strange states of being with which we are presently unacquainted, but this is not a prerequisite for disconnection.

While the disconnection thesis makes no detailed claims about posthuman lives, it has implications for the complexity and power of posthumans and thus the significance of the differences they could generate. Posthuman entities would need to be powerful relative to WH to become existentially independent of it (§6.1). The disconnection relation is thus multiply realizable by entities with, conceivably, very disparate natures. But since all these would be powerful enough to become "feral", the majority of these would be hot cores of influence of a kind humans have not encountered before.

We can thus think about disconnections and their human implications without knowing whether and how they might occur and without having to understand posthumans in terms of transcendence. Given the likely magnitude of the changes that would result from a disconnection, we also have an interest in understanding what the eventual realizers of disconnection might be.

But it remains to be seen how strong this interest is and what we should do about it. The principle of accounting implies that we should explore potential posthuman-makers by cultivating the associated technologies. However, I conceded at the end of Chapter 5 that this conclusion must be bracketed pending fuller ethical discussion. The fact that accounting is consistent with a weak form of precautionary principle is not decisive, since there may be opposing principles that are also compatible (§5.8).

Thus we need to consider likely candidates for principles that oppose or restrict the posthuman-making prescribed by accounting. But we also need to reconsider the *content of the principle itself.* Is it an expression of our responsibility to future generations – as suggested in §5.1 – or did the categorical form in which it was introduced there obscure the real ethical basis for cultivating posthuman lives? In §8.2 I argue that our interest in exploring posthuman possibility space (PPS) could be traced to a late modern understanding of our physical and ecological contingency. This forms part of a qualified reconciliation between SP and critical post-humanist claims that we are currently living through the cultural and technological erosion of human subjectivity as a norm or foundation (§§1.4, 2.1).

The discussion will fall into two main parts. First, I will consider some arguments for blocking or limiting disconnection-potent technology which thus tell against accounting. These are all *anthropocentric* arguments (§1.1). They assume the moral priority of the human understood in a biological, phenomenological or moral sense. I will argue that none of these tell decisively against accounting; though I will concede the force of appealing to our solidarity as a species. Having rejected anthropocentric constraints on posthuman ethics, I will conclude by considering the possibility of an affirmative, post-anthropocentric approach to deciding our posthuman prospects.

8.1 Anthropocentrism and speculative posthumanism

Let us consider, first, whether naturalistic anthropocentrism can inform or constrain the exploration of posthuman possibility required by accounting.

The most common arguments for limiting experimentation with post-human-makers are based on the assumption that the integrity of the human species is a paramount good or a condition for paramount goods. For example, Francis Fukuyama argues that the existence of a shared human nature is a condition for the applicability of the ideas of political equality and rights (Fukuyama 2003; see also Annas *et al.* 2002).

SP gives precise expression to this concern (Meacham forthcoming). A disconnection could threaten human species integrity, first, by "exporting" individuals outside the human species or by producing new synthetic beings whose nature or relationship to humans is liable to undermine or corrupt human moral nature in some way.

Both positions can be expressed in a traditional "antimodernist" way by claiming that disconnection would result in humans or posthumans that failed to realize the ends determined by their species nature or by God (Habermas 2005: 24–5). We have reviewed the grounds for rejecting notions of species based on essences or natural states, so I will assume that the antimodernist objections are unfounded (§§6.3, 6.4). For our purposes, the significant objections to posthuman-making come from modernists who accept that there are no intrinsic purposes in nature but argue that the integrity of the human species *is a good* or a *condition for the good* nonetheless.

In *Humanity's End*, Agar is mainly concerned with the first type of threat from radical technical alteration.[1] His argument against radical alteration rests on a position he calls *species relativism* (SR). SR states that only certain values are compatible with membership of a given biological species:

> According to species-relativism, certain experiences and ways of existing properly valued by members of one species may lack value for the members of another species.
>
> (Agar 2010: 12)

Agar's position is modernist. He rejects Aristotelian or theistic views which assign species intrinsic purposes. Instead, he uses Mayr's biological species concept according to which species are reproductively isolated populations lacking essential properties or purposes (§5.4). He does not claim that disconnection would violate natural purposes but that it would constitute a kind of "biological exile" making it impossible for the disconnected to act and feel in valuable ways only members of the human reproductive population can act and feel (p. 27). For example, acquiring effective immortality (negligible senescence) might export certain former humans out of the human species by making them psychologically ill-disposed to raise families. Negligibly senescent posthumans might also become morbidly risk-averse, according to Agar, because death would deprive them of a potential eternity of life rather than our three score years and twenty (pp. 115–21). To take another example, digital uploading would fail to preserve the capacity for conscious thought if functional re-instantiation is not sufficient for phenomenal awareness (§1.3). Thus digital uploadees would not have any experiences at all, valuable or otherwise.

Even if SR is correct, it does not follow that individual humans should only promote human values. In a disconnection any human may be in a position to weigh up posthuman experiences and values.

Thus, as John Danaher argues, we need to add an additional premise to give SR bite. Disconnection or radical enhancement would, according to this proposal, violate the principle that humans should promote and cultivate *their values* rather than undermining them (Danaher 2011). If governments were to implement this principle along with SR, disconnection-potent technologies would be policed in the interests of human species values.

Thus posthuman-accountants would fall foul of the human preservation police.

I think we can ask two questions of Agar's critique:

Is an SR philosophy of policing viable?
Is the anthropocentrism of SR coherent?

Clearly, if anthropocentrism is unsupportable on independent grounds, so is the dogged humanist response. However, even if anthropocentrism is defensible, its policy may still be unimplementable within modern, self-catalysing technical systems (Chapter 7). In this case, our attachment to human values might be internally consistent but ultimately irrelevant to conditions of technical modernity. Incoherence and irrelevance would both be reasons for giving up humanist or anthropocentric morality and thinking through alternatives that are relevant and coherent.

Let us consider the issue of viability first with the help of a case study from the ethics of artificial intelligence.

Is an SR policy towards evaluation and policing implementable?

There are grounds for believing that certain paths to *artificial general intelligence* (AGI) are more liable to produce AIs that are antagonistic to humans than other paths. Itamar Arel (2012) has argued that the use of recurrent neural architecture with a dynamically alterable structure combined with reward-driven learning (*reinforcement learning* – RL) is a promising path to the development of autonomous systems capable of reasoning across many problem domains; but liable to produce malevolent AIs who view humans as an impediment to their well-being (see §§1.2, 1.4).

The problem, according to Arel, is that a plausible learning algorithm places no bounds on the estimate of future rewards based on past rates of return (Arel 2012: 49–50). Suppose that we succeed in creating an RL-driven machine intelligence that happens to be a far faster and more fluent general intelligence than any existing human. If it has some means of acting in the world, it may, he writes, "reach the inevitable conclusion that human beings are too often hurdles in its path of self-improvement, and thus constitute an adversary". Reasoning along these lines, humans would reach the same conclusion and the machine intelligence would factor this into its estimate of human malevolence (Arel 2012: 56). If all these conditions are in place, then it is quite likely that a conflict between humans and superhumans would ensue, with only one realistic winner.

William Rapaport suggests one kind of strategy for dealing with diffi-cult AGIs in his commentary on Arel, "Can't We Just Talk?" (Rapaport

2012: 59–60). He argues that we should expect AGIs to have language understanding (this being, he claims, a condition for domain-general cognition) and to be capable of conscious, explicit reasoning, as opposed to the tacit knowledge that resides in the inter-neural weights of neural networks. Thus any AGI would be a reasonable, speaking subject with which we could negotiate and reason rather than the implacable monomaniac Arel describes (p. 60; see §4.1).

Rapaport *may* be right in his claim about language but we have no *a priori* assurance that the phenomenology of a successful AGI will correspond to human phenomenology. For example, it may not need to co-opt language for metacognition (§§4.1, 4.2, 4.3). In the absence of future-proof knowledge, the best way of testing Rapaport's proposal is to pursue our research into RL-based intelligence to an advanced stage. Naturally, this might also be disconnection-potent.

Other solutions might involve not giving the AGI a real body but only a simulated one locked in a virtual environment. This is the "leak-proof singularity" option touted in Chalmers (2010). Alternatively, we might equip the AGI with a fragile body and an accessible "off" button.

However, Chalmers points out that no singularity could be leak-proof unless it was causally isolated from its human creators. A simulated AGI of any interest would have to be observable by the humans who control its virtual environment and thus would be capable of interacting with them. A *very* smart AGI that wished us ill might find it easy to circumvent these limitations (Chalmers 2010: 38). Similar reservations apply to the strategy of making the AGI physically frail: a frail superintelligence might have highly effective ways of emulating human armourers and mitigating its vulnerability.

At this point, conservative opponents of disconnection-technology might be expected to wield the precautionary mallet against such research. However, as argued in §5.8, an overly stringent precautionary principle implies paralysis while a more realistic approach to flagging research for disconnection-potency requires that research to be pursued.

A moderate policing approach might be sensible, then, but its implementation is parasitic on the sources of disruptive influence it aims to police. Moreover, in a planetary SATS with fast transmission and multiple production nodes, a disconnection-potent technology is liable to become available. Even if we had a global enforcement organization of *Neuromancer*-style "Turing Cops" charged with ensuring that AIs do not become *too intelligent*, the prospects of noncompliance by governments, individuals or corporations would be significant (Arel 2012: 57; Gibson 2000).

It seems, then, that we can have only qualified confidence that the human-first approach to policing disconnection technology would be implemented successfully.

Is the anthropocentrism of SR coherent?

Apart from the implementation issues, it is not clear that an ethic that identifies deep human values with states accessible to members of a particular biological species will be helpful in understanding the ethical issues surrounding singularities or other posthuman difference-makers.

The key problem is that the values accessible to members of any biological species must be technology-contingent. Otherwise, species relativism would not be pertinent to the present debate because the range of accessible forms of life open to humans would be fixed by their biology.

Agar wants to distinguish his position from those of cultural relativists who argue that ethical claims such as "Slavery is evil" may be true relative to the standards of one culture such as cosmopolitan liberalism but false relative to the standards of a slave-owning aristocracy like that of ancient Sparta (Agar 2010: 13). Agar does not provide a detailed refutation of cultural relativism. But he suggests that intra-species disagreements between members of different cultures do not reflect deep constraints on the values accessible to their members. Thus, "if the Spartans were to find that they were under no threat of invasion and that sporting rivalries with Australia were their only outlet for collective aggression, then they too might abhor slavery" (p. 13).

The implication of this passage is that cultural relativism (CR) is false for humans because, for any human, there are accessible forms of cultural life other than the ones she occupies.[2] Cosmopolitan liberalism is not inaccessible for a typical Spartan. Under favourable circumstances they could engage with it and compare its virtues with Spartan *arête* without altering their biological substrate. Understanding or acquiring a new culture is not easy but it is well within the biological scope of most humans.

Culture, then, is too soft a constraint on the possibilities accessible to individual humans to settle moral disputes about the desirability of forms of life. The set of truth-makers (values, phenomenologies) for moral claims made within any culture *C* is fixed by the range of accessible forms of life for its members. CR would be true only if the forms of life accessible to members of *C* were limited to those compatible with *C*. But they are not so limited. Thus CR is false.

Species relativism states that there is a set of human values that should constrain our technology options (we may have some list of these to hand, but the content of the selection doesn't matter for the purpose of our argument – just call these *H-values*). Given that SR must have some technology-invariant content, SR implies commitment to *H-values*.

Now, why should we believe that species membership is not analogously pliant?

We have noted that Agar wisely eschews species essentialism. He does not think that species membership is conferred by satisfying historically invariant conditions. Nor (on pain of irrelevance) can he claim that any member of a species is necessarily a member of it (p. 19; §5.4).

So what is the difficulty about jumping species that justifies SR and thus commitment to *H-values*? Well, if a key isolation mechanism is reproductive compatibility, then you could jump species by undergoing a biological change that allows you to mate with members of a nonhuman species. Agar imagines genetic engineers travelling back 45,000 years and conducting this procedure on a human, turning him into a Neanderthal. Following the procedure, the subject "can no longer produce offspring with humans. He is, in compensation, attracted to Neanderthals and can reproduce with them" (p. 24). But jumping species barriers is currently impossible while jumping cultures is not; so Neanderphilia is not in our current repertoire of *H-values*. Does this suffice to protect SR from the objections levelled at CR?

If species-jumping were metaphysically possible but technically impossible, this would also render Agar's principle moot. Let us assume, then, that species-jumping is technically feasible.

The Neanderphilia example shows that the range of forms of life accessible to representative humans is contingent on culturally available technology. In a posthuman dispensation characterized by great morpho-logical variability, species membership might become as pliant as cultural membership has been to date. It would have no more constraining power on accessible values than culture membership currently has (see Sterling 1996). So if the accessibility of culturally variable forms of life furnishes an argument against CR, the dated accessibility of morphologically variable forms of life could support an argument against SR.

The truth of the SR objection to disconnection or radical enhancement is dated. It holds, if at all, while posthuman-making is unfeasible and our accessible forms of life remain species-constrained. If posthuman-making were to become feasible, species relativism would decline in relevance and truth.

But the species relativist can insist that it is relevant *now* and *this* is why we should insist that technology options be governed by *H-values*. This is well put by Agar in a response to a post of mine on this topic:

> However strong you find the arguments for cultural relativism, the argu-
> ments for species relativism are likely to be stronger. It's possible for cultural
> relativism to be false and species relativism to be true. The boundaries
> between species are (likely to be) more substantial/robust than those separating
> different human cultures. You're right that evolutionary and technological
> pressures might make these boundaries more pliable. But I wonder about

the relevance of this to members of the human species here and now. There are possible evolutionary pressures/applications of technology that could turn all humans into ruthless psychopaths. This doesn't have direct implications for what we should value now – we aren't required to evaluatively anticipate these changes.

(Agar, in Roden 2012a: np)

I think this response is consistent but problematic. First, it concedes the original point that constraints on species membership are technology contingent. Under disconnection conditions, SR could become irrelevant to the *present debate* because the forms of life it would support would include the then-accessible posthuman forms of life that Agar sees as outside the charmed circle of human values that we must promote and cultivate.

Admittedly, Agar can insist that the term "H-values" designates some *accessible set of values* associated with some or other technological phase of human development and is not a descriptive term that applies to any possible set of values that past or future members of the human species might adopt.

But this invites the accusation of moral vacuity. For sure, most of us have good reasons not to become psychopaths. But we do not reject psychopathy because of a general commitment to humanity. We just find the lifestyle wanting. The consideration that should discourage us from turning every human into a psychopath does not militate against options that are not *H-values*. The fact that certain forms of life are currently accessible for humans is relevant to whether *we can* pursue them, not to whether we should pursue them. Aberrant ways of life like fascism and aggressive religious fundamentalism are also accessible and valued by their adherents. This is not a warrant for fascism and fundamentalism, so it is an inadequate basis for supporting *H-values* (whatever they are) over nonhuman values or life-form options.

Disconnecting from the human community

I conclude that there are no *biological* species-relative values that could provide a basis for objecting to accounting or the pursuit of posthuman-making technology more generally. This is a not altogether unsurprising consequence of working within the modernist view of nature. Biological species unity is not based on a common essence or purpose, so it is an unpromising basis from which to support anthropocentric constraints on technological change.

Nonetheless, some writers in the phenomenological and post-Kantian tradition have argued that human moral capacities presuppose a prereflective[3] understanding of a shared human identity because this is a basis for our capacity to recognize and reflect on communal norms (see, for example, Wennemann 2013: 78–90; Habermas 2005).

This version of anthropocentrism has a response to the objection from technological contingency that I levelled against Agar. Although the unity of the species may depend on the state of our technology, its character *as unity* remains. Either the human species has a unity that supports paramount values or it does not. If we can show that certain values which depend on the unity of the species are ones that we should cherish and cultivate, then we should not risk that unity even if doing so might allow us to access other values or experiences. What is important about human species membership, according to this view, is that it provides a shared horizon for our moral experience. So this position is consistent with the denial that species members must have an unchanging core of essential properties and with the claim that the many accessible experiences and values for their members are technology contingent.

However, for human species membership to furnish a context for moral norms, it must be possible for each morally competent human agent to recognize humanity when they see it. So, again, it is implausible to look to evolutionary biology to reveal the underlying nature of human species membership. The nature of biological species is a matter of open philosophical and scientific controversy and liable to theoretically motivated conceptual change. Yet species identity, according to this version of anthropocentrism, must be a persistent background of our moral thinking that is implicit in our ordinary pre-scientific understanding of the human. For this reason, Darian Meacham's notion of a phenomenological species concept (PSC) seems to furnish a more "ethically salient" basis for ethical recognition and practice that we should preserve against disconnection.

A PSC is based on our preflective experience of others' experiential and affective relation to the phenomenological worlds that they share with us – for example, as having a susceptibility to pain, suffering or joy (§3.7). It is thus independent of species concepts issuing from natural science while obviously reflecting ordinary practices by which we identify others as potential members of the moral community. Meacham's account of species recognition is based on Husserl's claim that our experience of others involves an empathic awareness that they could be having experiences like our own:

> Empathy for Husserl entails an immediate apperception (the perceptual presentation of something not immediately present) of another being as having a structure of experience that is analogous to my own; or, empathy is the pre-reflective experience of another being as having experiences that could potentially be my own – this need not entail that I actually imagine the experiences

of the other as my own. The shared structure of experience is apperceived rather than directly perceived as it is mediated by the expressivity of the body.

(Meacham forthcoming)

Meacham argues that a disconnection event might generate posthumans – "most radically, android or cyborg life forms" – whose bodily activity would fail to prompt an empathic response in humans.

Thus a disconnection could be a "phenomenological speciation event" which weakens the bonds that tie sentient creatures together on this world:

> This refers us back to a weakened version of Roden's description of post-human disconnection: differently altered groups, especially when those alterations concern our vulnerability to injury and disease, might have experiences sufficiently different from ours that we cannot envisage what significant aspects of their lives would be like. This inability to empathize will at the very least dampen the possibility for the type of empathic species solidarity that I have argued is the ground of ethics.
>
> (*Ibid.*)

Meacham's position suggests that human species recognition has an "ethical pull" that should be taken seriously by any posthuman ethics.

However, it remains uncertain whether we should regard this pull as a decisive constraint on experimentation with posthuman possibility. To consider this further, I shall approach phenomenological speciation as a problem of radical interpretation in Davidson's sense since this provides an ideal model of interpretation in situations where the interpreter and interpreted do not readily or naturally agree in the way they view the world.

A radical interpreter, recall, constructs a theory of meaning for an alien language which she tests by observing whether its speakers tend to utter alien sentences when the truth conditions assigned to them in the theory hold. Radical interpretation can be thought of as a kind of semantic modelling where an interpreter creates an artificial idiom that means something for her – the interpreting "theory" – and considers the degree to which an interpreted being shares that idiom (Roden 2004a: 200–01).[4] If speakers do not say what the theory predicts them to say (and we assume them not to be massively mistaken) then the theory will need to be revised until interpreters and interpretees converge.

Errors of interpretation are recoverable so long as meaning does not have an irreducibly "inner" component. As Bjørn Ramberg puts it:

> [Even] the most bizarre discourse is in principle accessible to [the radical interpreter]. If she hangs around long enough, is sufficiently observant, and combines a remarkable memory with an equally remarkable flexibility of

mind, there is no reason, in principle, why she should not come to understand even a group of speakers who on any given day are concerned solely,
say, with what happened two days earlier.

(Ramberg 1989: 120)

Ramberg's example of the temporally displaced speakers nicely illustrates
the relationship between coming to understand a language and coming to
understand speakers' values.

We might not be able to appreciate what it is like to be entirely pre-
occupied with two-day-old events, but this does not mean that we cannot
detect this temporal fixation and interpret those who have it. For example, we might succeed in developing a theory that says of a two-day displacee that any sentence in the displacee's language that reports an event
at time t is true if and only if p (where p reports some event two days
prior to t in our home idiom – see Chapter 3, §3.6).

Such a theory would provide an empirically adequate theory of meaning for the displacees since it would state the truth conditions of every
displaced utterance in terms accessible to non-displaced speakers. To be
pragmatically warranted, though, the theory or simulation will have to
yield a method for communicating with the displacees. Mere empirical
adequacy is not enough. Overcoming the semantic obstruction generated
by their displacement and becoming fluent in their language would
require the interpreter to develop similar temporal sensitivities. To
achieve this, she might need to use a few transhuman fixes: for example,
smart mnemonics, phone apps or neural implants to supplement her
working memory. *Encountering* the displacees would thus force these two-
day-old events into the shared context of her day-to-day communication;
they would become part of her passing scene.

Thus radical interpretation gives us traction on what might count as
success in the more exotic cases we might encounter during disconnection.
In the case of most human–human interpretation, our phenomenologies
converge enough to make such derangements unnecessary.[5]

Under disconnection, derangements of awareness or conceptual structure may be necessary for communication with posthumans. These may
force significant differences in saliences and values. In the toy case of the
two-day-displacees, facts that were not integrated into the interpreter's
original present become integrated into a new, more capacious "now"
transforming her personal phenomenology. By the same token, the
narrow human "window of presence" of around three seconds would have
to become less salient while the interpreter becomes habituated to her
displacement (Metzinger 2004: 127).

The moral of this tale is that differences in phenomenology can be
significant obstructions to our understanding without being impassable

barriers. It follows that the situation following phenomenological speciation might not preclude interpretation where it is technically possible to
adapt human phenomenology to cope with posthuman phenomenology
(see §§5.5, 5.7). In extreme cases, no available technology may suffice to
overcome the phenomenological obstruction confronting human interpreters so long as they remain empathically attuned to the human life-
world. It may be that all idioms are interpretable in principle, but it is
always an open question whether they are interpretable for some variable "we". But these phenomenological fixes might necessitate derangements that modify or extinguish the values brought to encounter by
interpreters.

A further thought experiment will concretize the ethical problems this
would present within a technical system that has become disconnection-
potent. Suppose your world is poised for disconnection, following which a
proportion of formerly human individuals will acquire some disruptive
cognitive capacity caused by a new intelligence amplification (IA) technology. The IA technology has been tested on rats and consenting human
subjects in deregulated corporate interzones. There is, consequently, some
fragmentary information about its functioning and its effects on human
and nonhuman cognition and subjectivity. Perhaps it assimilates users
into a Churchlandish centipede or eliminates their folk-understanding of
human psychology by patching them into non-symbolic workspaces (see
Introduction; §4.1).

The IA technique turns out to be incompatible with human social
relations for reasons we can fill in, giving rise to a phenomenological
speciation event. It might be because its users are cognitively far more
adept than unaugmented humans, cease to think in propositions, or have
a phenomenology that makes no sense to us.

However it works its derangements, the technology irreversibly dis-
connects its users from the human life-world, giving rise to deep social
divisions between users and non-users. As a result, the users devise their
own social arrangements and proprietary infrastructure. Increasingly
autonomous posthuman enclaves flower across the globe.

As the IA technology disseminates over the planetary network (§7.4)
you would have no choice about whether to deal with the personal and
social consequences of disconnection. You would have to decide whether
to become posthuman or to remain human. Suppose some of your friends
have adopted the IA. Their wayward and cryptic emails imply they are
exploring "caverns measureless to man"; but they seem indifferent to
Italian food, sex with other humans, REM or landscape painting.
You cannot yet understand their idiosyncratic joys, but risk losing much
that made existence meaningful to the human you will have been if you
adopt the IA.

The IA example illustrates Meacham's claim that the phenomenological unity of the human species has an ethical pull. For although dialogue with posthumans is not precluded, it might require partially abandoning the human phenomenological purview for an altogether different one. This process might be incremental and reversible, as in Ramberg's example of radical interpretation, or it might involve a transformative and irreversible change in embodiment or phenomenology, as in the IA thought experiment, where any benefits of posthumanity would only be apparent on leaving humanity.

The relative abruptness and irreversibility of its effects would presumably discourage less risk-averse humans from adopting the IA technology and leaving their phenomenological moorings.

Most importantly, for our purposes, there would be no milieu in which shared moral norms could be easily discussed or adjudicated by members of both groups, even if radical interpretation of posthumans is always possible *in principle*. Neither group can enter into a unitary moral community without extirpating the other. Transitional models – like the vestigially propositional cognizers discussed in §5.5 – might facilitate communication between the two groups, but, given the derangements involved, interpretation could remain patchy and unsatisfactory. Both groups might be composed of beings worthy of moral consideration. But this might never be expressible in a shared moral experience or democratic dialogue (Habermas 2005: 40).

It could be objected that modern political thought has eschewed grounding in metaphysical ideas such as human nature. Rousseau and successors like Rawls argued that there can be no metaphysical justification for a given political order outside that order (for example, in the Will of God). A political structure is legitimate if its governing principles could enlist the consent of its members.

If this "postmetaphysical" view of legitimacy is applicable to human societies, perhaps it is applicable in some hybrid human–posthuman dispensation in which not all the prospective members of the polity are human. There are many different models of justification which fit with this approach. However, the model is inherently democratic. As Michael Walzer puts this, a political structure must be acceptable to those who live under it because of "who they are" not because of what they know or what they can do (Walzer 2003: 365).

However, purging political language of metaphysical elements is tenable only where the nature of the participants is not at odds with the communicative demands of democracy and shared governance. This implies, as Meacham (forthcoming) writes: "[That] species recognition and disconnection are relevant to the understanding of intersubjectivity in general." Establishing and arbitrating intersubjective norms require a community of beings sufficiently alike that dialogue among them is not significantly burdensome or risky. Thus a disconnection could undermine the inter-subjective unity of the human community if the burdens of interpretation or radical interpretation became significant.

This has serious consequences for a *democratic* conception of accounting. We can envisage a select band of intrepid posthuman accountants who act like technological food tasters. Their role would be to test the effects of disconnection-potent technologies and summarize the results for the public, allowing them to make informed decisions about potentially disruptive technologies.

Given the principled difficulties involved in leak-proof testing and the limitations on control implied by new substantivism, the democratic model of accounting sketched here is self-undermining. Any posthuman experimentation that could contribute to an understanding of emergent behaviours or modes of life post-disconnection would also increase the disconnection-potential of the technological system as the associated technologies iterated across its communication networks (§§5.6, 7.4).

Democratic accounting would override the democratic process it is intended to inform. Even allowing for interpretability in principle, the results might fail the publicity test since only posthumans or near-posthumans might be in positions to understand them. Thus the composition of the community that deliberates on the posthuman would be put in doubt by the very attempt to deliberate upon it. There can be posthuman accounting only if, *pace* Walzer, we do not know who can participate in it.

We appear to have found a strong principle with which to oppose experimentation with incipient posthuman-makers, even where this is undertaken to evaluate different options for posthuman life. The back-ground stability of the pan-species ethical community is a condition for appraising one's experiences or actions, or for debating collective action (§3.5). A threat to phenomenological species integrity threatens *the con-ditions for ethical and political agency itself* rather than specific or putatively "human" norms, values or practices.

For Wennemann in *Posthuman Personhood*, the overriding requirement of posthuman ethics is to preserve agency and the communal identity that supports it – regardless of whether it is subsequently extended to tech-nologically engendered beings such as androids, cyborgs or human-equivalent AIs: "If there is an historical movement to supersede [moral personhood] I must set myself against that movement" (2013: 133).

Of course, the considerations that cast doubt on the implementability of Agar's proposals (see above) also apply to any policing policies aimed at preventing phenomenological speciation. The postmetaphysical modern-ism which bases political legitimacy on democratic acceptance may be at odds with a technological modernity whose systems elude democratic control (Chapter 7). But the proponent of limits on posthuman experimentation could reasonably argue that we should seek to control what we can since technological fatalism would undermine our capacity to prevent baneful threats to human species integrity in any case.

But does the argument from species integrity provide a decisive objection to exploring disconnection-potent technology?

The proposed veto on superseding personhood presupposes that the moral person bound by communal norms stands at the tip of a dualist moral hierarchy in which there are just two possible positions: Kantian persons answerable to communally expressible reasons and merely sentient beings incapable of moral agency (§§1.1, 3.5). Once at its apex, the only direction is down! From the dualist perspective, it makes sense to attach paramount importance to retaining the powers of moral agency and democratic deliberation.

This agentive dualism requires future-proof, *a priori* knowledge of a notionally vast domain of possible psychologies and phenomenologies, not merely actual ones. But if our phenomenology is striated with darkness, we are not in a position to survey kinds of minds that could occur in posthuman possibility space (PPS) *a priori*. Consequentially there are no current grounds for assuming that there is such a hierarchy of agents (§4.3).

As emphasized in earlier sections, I am not denying either that humans have agentive capacities that most known biological entities lack – the existence and integrity of the WH depend on these – or that these might confer a moral status that these nonhuman others lack (§2.1). However, the claim that human moral agency confers paramount status is based on a very partial acquaintance with local phenomenological space.

The domain with which SP is concerned might be vastly greater, given that it is anthropologically unbounded. Thus the claim that we should attach paramount value to the preservation of human moral agency is specious if applied to the totality of PPS *ex ante*. We cannot exclude the possibility of agents lacking the *I–Thou* structure of human intersubjectivity whose existences have an integrity or meaning we cannot imagine or yet conceive (§4.3).

In conclusion, the phenomenological species integrity argument for policing disconnection-potent technologies presupposes an unwarrantable transcendental privilege for Kantian personhood. Since the privilege is unwarrantable this side of disconnection, the phenomenological argument for an anthropocentric attitude towards disconnection fails along with naturalistic versions of the species integrity argument such as Agar's. Thus even if we accept that our relationships to fellow humans compose an ethical pull, as Meacham puts it, its force cannot be decisive as long we do not know enough about the contents of PPS to support the anthropocentrist's position. What appears to be a moral danger on our side of a disconnection could be an opportunity to explore morally considerable states of being of which we are currently unaware.

8.2 Vital posthumanism: a speculative-critical convergence

It follows that only a post-anthropocentric ethics of becoming posthuman is compatible with the metaphysical and epistemological position developed here; one that does not require posthumans to exhibit human intersubjectivity or moral autonomy. Such an ethics would need to be articulated in terms of ethical attributes that we could reasonably expect to be shared with posthuman WHDs whose phenomenologies or psychologies might diverge significantly from those of current humans.

In Chapter 6 we were able to define a psychology-free moral prerequisite for all posthuman entities: functional autonomy. A functionally autonomous system (FAS) can enlist values for and accrue functions (§6.4). Functional autonomy is related to power. A being's power is its capacity to enlist other things and be reciprocally enlisted (Patton 2000: 74). With great power comes great articulation (§6.5).

The FAS account is derived from biological rather than moral theory. It is based on a minimal conception of a living agent able to constitute functions and values. This might suggest that a body of ethical ideas framed in terms of the ontology of living systems – a "vitalism" – would have the generality that we require for a posthuman ethics. However, the sense of "vitalism" will need to be qualified to forestall potential misunderstandings. The term is generally reserved for the metaphysical claim that reality contains a life essence (*élan vital*) which cannot be explained in terms of non-living or non-subjective entities. As Levi Bryant observes, philosophers influential on the posthumanist scene like Nietzsche, Bergson, Husserl and Deleuze have all made claims of this kind. For example, in his more cosmic moments Nietzsche characterizes will to power as a universal striving in organic and inorganic matter (Nietzsche 1968: 332–3; Richardson 2004: 46–52).

But posthumanists have good reason not to emulate *metaphysical* vitalism (Bryant 2013). Understanding fundamental physical dispositions in mentalistic terms betrays a confusion about the metaphysical basis of the intentionality of living systems. Biological agents are distinctive because they respond "malleably and flexibly" to environmental changes in virtue of the complexity of the interlacing processes that form them (§6.4). This capacity is compatible with an ontological materialism that denies that the basic constituents of reality have an irreducibly mental character.

For example, the capacity of an ant colony superorganism to locate food sources does not depend on individual ants striving to secure the food nearest the nest but on their robotic responses to pheromone signals that furnish information about the most promising trails (§2.1). Thus malleable quasi-striving can emerge from interactions between non-strivers (a point amply illustrated by the use of ant-colony optimization algorithms in telecommunication routers).

A second precaution applies to the status of the concept of life itself.

I characterize posthumans as living because they must exhibit functional autonomy. This is a sufficient functional condition of life *at best* (Cleland 2012: 130). As Carol Cleland reminds us, it is conceivable that there are *no defining features (functional or otherwise) common to all living things*. Even if there are, it is possible that we are as ignorant of the constitutive conditions for life as pre-molecular alchemists were of the features common to all forms of water (Cleland 2012: 129).[6]

Fortunately, SP does not require a grasp of life's hidden essence (assuming it has one). The characteristics that qualify posthumans as living in SP need not correspond to any real properties to possess descriptive content. It is in the spirit of the assemblage ontology that I have adopted here to be dubious about properties that make no difference to anything – our rejection of essentialism, for example, assumes that formal entities play no role in forming anything (§§5.4, 6.3).[7] This does not entail that the differences it picks out are unimportant.[8] The metaphysical bearing of the disconnection thesis does not depend on it denoting a unitary difference-maker but on the disconnection conditions being satisfiable by a disparate class of difference makers that would all be of great significance for human and nonhuman lives.

Given these precautions, are there fruitful ethical consequences which can be inferred from our tentative conception of posthuman vitality?

Our metaphysical hypothesis regarding posthuman life employed a Deleuze-inspired assemblage ontology (Chapters 5 and 6). The unity and function of an assemblage is always provisional and susceptible to derangements which alter its nature and affiliations (§6.6). Our ontology assumes that posthumans would have network-independent components like the human fusiform gyrus, allowing flexible and adaptive couplings with other assemblages (§6.5). Posthumans would need a flexibility in their use of environmental resources and in their "aleatory" affiliations with other human or nonhuman systems sufficient to break with the purposes bestowed on entities within the Wide Human.

None of these external relationships would be essential to posthuman assemblages since no function is essential to *any* assemblage (§§5.4, 6.5). For a materialist vitalism "there can be no pre-established boundaries and no fixed determination of what constitutes the parameters and identities of individuated entities, such as organisms and machines" (Pearson 2002: 143). However, the lack of *fixed or essential* identities does not imply that living beings lack contingent identities. For example, if humans can become disconnected from WH, they cannot be necessarily human, and significant ethical consequences flow from remaining connected, or becoming disconnected, as we saw in the previous section.

Some may have spotted that the argument ranged against Omohundro's claim that hyperplastic posthumans would want to clamp their own values is derived from Derrida's iterability argument for irreducible semantic indeterminacy (§4.3). Iterability and the differential possibilities of meaning are constrained because our embodiment is not *currently* subject to extensive technological intervention (§§2.1, 4.3). However, it also implies that iterability may be constrained very differently in other physically possible entities. Hyperplastic posthumans could be more like the unstable SATSs discussed in Chapter 7 than the selves to which we are accustomed (§3.3). Any part of such a system would be highly replicable and modifiable in much the ways that technologies are within contemporary socio-technical systems. For such a distributed, iterable system, self-modification might be a precipitate venture resembling a polyphonic, open-ended improvisation rather than the practical realization of abstractly conceived norms or goals.

This serves to reinforce the generality of the concepts of "life" and "agency" used here.

This ontologically minimalist, epistemologically fallabilist vitalism has certain affinities with the post-anthropocentric theory of agency recently set out in Braidotti's 2013 book *The Posthuman*, but also some important differences that will help us to indicate how it might be applicable to the ethics of disconnection. Braidotti is at one with other critical posthumanists in rejecting a human-centred basis for ethics and politics. However, she is impatient with a disabling political neutrality that can follow from junking human moral subjectivity as the arbiter of the right and the good (Roden 2002). She argues that a critical posthumanist ethics should retain the posit of political subjectivity capable of ethical experimentation with new modes of community and being, while rejecting the Kantian model of an agent subject to universal norms (Braidotti 2013: 38–9).

For Braidotti, this vital subject reflects a disposition for self-assembly immanent in all living matter rather than a parochial feature of human agency such as moral autonomy. She designates this power with the ancient Greek term for nonhuman/non-political life (*zoe*) – as opposed to the cultivated life (*bios*) of the human citizen. *Zoe* includes the tendency of living matter to affiliate and form new functional assemblages:

> "Life", far from being codified as the exclusive property or the unalienable right of one species, the human, over all others or of being sacralised as a pre-established given, is posited as process, interactive and open-ended. This

vitalist approach to living matter displaces the boundary between the portion of life – both organic and discursive – that has traditionally been reserved for *anthropos*, that is to say *bios*, and the wider scope of animal and nonhuman life.

(Braidotti 2013: 60)

Although little philosophical support for this ontology is provided in *The Posthuman*, it converges with the assemblage-based position defended here. However, Braidotti's account appears more vulnerable where she positions vital posthumanism in relation to conventional identity politics or anti-capitalism. For example, she thinks that it motivates an egalitarianism opposed to the "trans-species commodification of Life" effected by advanced capitalism (§1.4). A disconnect between ontology and ethics is apparent at this point, since Braidotti concedes that capitalism produces a form of posthuman subjectivity by erasing boundaries between humans, animals, species and technique:

> Advanced capitalism and its biogenetic technologies engender a perverse form of the posthuman. At its core there is a radical disruption of the human–animal interaction, but all living species are caught in the spinning machine of the global economy.
>
> (p. 7; see also pp. 61, 74)

A perversion is a diversion of a thing from its proper or natural state. It can thus be ascribed only to a nature with intrinsic or God-given ends. This anti-modern view is at odds with the materialist thinking that informs Braidotti's vitalism and my own version of assemblage ontology. "The perverse materiality of advanced capitalism" (p. 88) is an oxymoron. Where there are no essences or boundaries there can be no intrinsic teleology and no deviations from natural purposes (§6.4). Consider Monsanto's transgenic cotton Bollgard II. Bollgard II contains genes from a soil bacterium *Bacillus thuringiensis* that produce a toxin deadly to pests such as bollworm. Unless we believe that there is some purpose immanent to *B. thuringiensis* or to cotton that renders gene-engineered crossings aberrant, there appears to be no *zoe*-centred perspective that could warrant her objection to this form of use (Ronald 2013).

As Claire Colebrook points out, materialist vitalism cannot tell us what kind of creatures we should become because *zoe* enacts "lines of life beyond organic or living purposiveness" (Colebrook 2012b: 200; §6.5). However, since it provides a language for understanding the contingency of identity or subjectivity, it can help us think about the possibilities and problems forced by a modernity that ceaselessly deracinates settled norms or identities:

We have perhaps always lived in a time of divergent, disrupted and diffuse
systems of forces, in which the role of human decisions and perceptions is a
contributing factor at best. Far from being resolved by returning to the
figure of the bounded globe or subject of *bios* rather than *zoe*, all those features that one might wish to criticize in the bio-political global era can only
be confronted by a non-global temporality and counter-ethics.

(Colebrook 2012a: 38)

The self-augmenting/counter-final nature of modern technological systems implies that the conditions under which human ethical judgements
are adapted can be overwritten by systems over which we have no ultimate
control. A disconnection would be only the most extreme consequence of
this "divergent, disrupted and diffuse systems of forces". An ethics
anthropologically bounded by the human world thus ignores its monstrously
exorbitant character (p. 32).

In §2.1 I pointed out that many critical posthumanists make an invalid
inference from the claim that human subjectivity is contingent upon
complex systems within and beyond the body to the claim that (since we
are complex systems) we are not the rational subjects we thought we
were. The fact that subjectivity and agency depend on complex, distributed networks that (for example) level differences between organisms
and machines is still important because self-augmenting changes in these
networks may alter our agency or lead to entirely new kinds of agent. So
while it is hyperbolic to claim that we are already posthuman, it is not
exaggerated to claim that we are in a "posthuman predicament" in which
the manifest nature of life has come to depend on counter-final technical
change (Wennemann 2013: 126). Hayles is right to say that this condition does not signify the end of humanity. However, like the Silver
Surfer, it may herald the beginning of its excision.

The ethics of vital posthumanism is thus not prescriptive but a tool for
problem defining. The problem is simple and is posed by our current
predicament. Disconnection just presents it in its starkest terms. The
problem is that of agency: how to stay functionally autonomous (or
deterritorialized). For technology-dependent beings, functional autonomy
can only be maintained following a disconnection by exploring regions of
PPS conducive to it and avoiding those that are not.

As we have seen, accounting pre-empts democratic deliberation and
cannot make decisive appeal to pre-existent ethical norms. Realistically, it
requires a peculiar ethical variant of what Kant calls "reflective judgement".
Whereas determinate judgements subsume particulars under existing
concepts, reflective judgement "arrives at its judgment, its way of making
sense, in the very process of exploring the manifold given it" (Protevi
2009: 75; Kant 1991). Accounting would not evaluate posthuman states

according to human values but according to values generated in the process of constructing and encountering them.

Kantian reflective judgement implies its universal necessity for the community of all human subjects (Kant 1991: 18; §6.4). However, a reflective judgement of value in the context of disconnection cannot enlist universal assent because it would be made by a being exiting one community for no community, or for one that is not yet. Thus judgement under disconnection might be more like shaping an artwork than the act of disinterested contemplation described in Kant's account of judgements of beauty. Such mid-air appraisals frequently employ communal standards or recipes (the fourteen-line sonnet or the twelve-bar blues, say) but these do not program the development of individual works. In a successful jazz improvisation, the player builds evolving figures or patterns on the fly. Time-worn blues or "bop" clichés are transformed in response to idiomatic patterns of sound and gesture in a specific performance situation.

This open-textured assessment requires an ability to register potentials for transformation rather than static facts. It is clearly a generalization of our experience of ordinary objects which, as Kant also saw, must register the complex and uncertain unfolding of events in time (Churchland 2012: 140–41; Clark 2013; §§3.3, 4.1).

However, art escalates the indeterminacy of these processes. Art assemblages form sensation-machines that modify the cultural meanings that we apply to them. Anna Hicky-Moody describes a dance theatre-piece of her devising in which the concept of a "birthday wish" is enacted by a male dancer lighting twenty-seven cupcake candles in succession, each time drawing "the small flame nestled in each cake to his chest" then extinguishing it. The performance event uniquely realized "a cumulative sense of a somewhat forlorn and difficult wish" transforming the received concept (Hicky-Moody 2009: 278).

In the limit cases of radical art, these sensations may potentiate future shifts in collective understanding. Wagner's famous "Tristan chord" segues between classical harmony, late romanticism and twentieth-century atonality due to its ambiguous relationship to its tonal context. The aesthetic value of Xenakis's *Concret Ph* lies partly in the technological and creative possibilities for the refined control of sonic masses it implies – potentials realized subsequently in *granular synthesis* techniques that employ global statistical parameters to control flocks of auditory events.

Such sensations are, in Brian Massumi's words, "in excess over experience", suspending practices and meanings in ways that catalyse "deterritorializing" movement towards non-actual futures (Massumi 2005: 136). The aesthetics of excess provides a limit case of the reflective creation of value that occurs when we modify existing modes of sense-making or embodiment, whether in art or accounting. It also provides a window upon the *posthuman as potentiality* which defines the posthuman predicament anatomized in the work of Haraway, Hayles, Braidotti and other critical posthumanists. This is the insight into human morphological and phenomenological potentiality implied in our increasingly intimate couplings with diffuse, counter-final technological systems.

This contingency is aesthetically heightened in radical works of art like J. G. Ballard's novel *Crash*, which represents automobile technology as the adjunct to a violent sexuality. *Crash* employs a system of linked metaphors to construct an entirely self-referential system of desire and symbolic acts oriented around sites, surfaces and interstices of a late twentieth-century technological landscape of motorways and airport annexes (Roden 2002). The auto-destructive desires of its characters refer always to a singular and impossible event encoded by auto-collisions. For example, the hoodlum scientist Vaughan remarks of his longed-for death in an auto-collision with Elizabeth Taylor that it would be "a unique vehicle collision, one that would transform all our dreams and fantasies" (Ballard 1995: 130).

The actual collision with which Ballard opens the novel is, by contrast, Vaughan's "one true accident" (p. 7). Instead of hitting Taylor's chauffeured limousine, Vaughan's car careens into an airline bus below the London Airport Flyover.

The bathetic divergence between accident and crash keeps the novel's machinery of representation and desire functioning. The absent referent indicated by the imaginary auto-disaster can articulate Vaughan's desires because he is there purely to express the novel's substitutive symbolic structure. Vaughan is that Ballardian stock-in-trade, a totemic figure of authority (characteristically a scientist) who valorizes senseless concatenations of bodies and technique. Modern technological systems furnish rich material for fantasies of apocalypse or transcendence. But these are rarely, if ever, reasons for acting.

Despite its contemporary setting, *Crash* does not describe the world of late twentieth-century capitalism: it potentiates it. It affords a way of thinking about the contingency of human subjectivity and social relationships in the light of our irrevocably technological condition. Whereas *Schismatrix* and *Accelerando* are *about* posthumans, *Crash* formalizes the iterative structure of modernity in which our posthuman predicament arises.

A similar claim is made about the work of the Australian performance artist Stelarc in Massumi's essay "The Evolutionary Alchemy of Reason". Massumi points out that the content of Stelarc's performances – such as his series of body suspensions or his hook-ups with industrial robots, prosthetic hands and compound-eye goggles – is nothing to do with the functional utility of these systems or events. They have no use. Rather their effect is to place bodies and technologies in settings where their incorporation as use-values (within WH, as I would qualify it) is interrupted. Of the compound-eye goggles that Stelarc created for his work *Helmet no. 3: put on and walk 1970* he writes: "They extended no-need into no-utility. And they extended no-utility into 'art'" (Massumi 2005: 131).

Stelarc's stated rationale is to "extend intelligence beyond the Earth". These performances decouple the body from its ecology and from the empathic responses of observers – even when dangling from skin hooks over a city street, Stelarc never appears as suffering or abject. They register the body's potential for "off world" environments rather than its actual functional involvements with our technological landscape. Space colonization is not a current use-value or industrial application, but a project for our planned obsolescence:

> The terrestrial body will be obsolete from the moment a certain sub-population feels compelled to launch itself into an impossible, unthinkable future of space colonization. To say that the obsolescence of the body is produced is to say that it is compelled. To say that it is compelled is to say that it is "driven by *desire*" rather than by need or utility.
>
> (pp. 151–2)

These performances embody a potential that is "unthinkable" because aesthetically disjoined from our phenomenological species and world. But, as Colebrook suggests, we have been incipiently "off world" since the dawn of the industrial era (2012a: 37–8). The "desire" that Massumi refers to is not something that we can own up to as willing, active subjects. This is not because it is too horrible to be expressed, but because it has no expression beyond a speculative engagement with technical systems whose long-run evolution eludes us. Thus despite telling us little or nothing about potential realizers of the disconnection relation, the work of Stelarc and Ballard shines through the cracks in the human life-world implied in the dependence of subjectivity on its iterating technical infrastructure.[9] The passive dynamisms that make disconnection a liability of the near or further future extend from our present and constitute our relationship to it.

The basis of our interest in becoming posthuman is not our formal responsibility to current or future members of our species; any attempt to account for the posthuman is a necessarily irresponsible risk to the integrity of the species (§8.1). However, if the analysis of the posthuman predicament offered here is correct, our entanglement with counter-final planetary technique presents difficult ethical choices for us, or any functionally autonomous agent that belongs to these assemblages. Given SP, some narrow or wide humans could become posthumans or encounter posthumans. As we saw, even encountering posthumans could transform humans in unpredictable ways, whether as a consequence of the "burdens of interpretation" discussed in the previous section, or of ramifying technological or environmental changes in the composition of WH. As a consequence, humans would be liable to enlist new values (new resources, new forms of association with humans/nonhumans/posthumans) and, of course, the existence of posthumans would also generate new ecological values as a consequence of posthuman enlistments (§6.4).

Although problematic, this need not be viewed as a "negative" consequence of the posthuman predicament, or disconnection. From a vital posthumanist perspective, life is equivalent to the agentive power to enter into intense, functional couplings that can fundamentally alter the powers of living systems (§6.6). Disconnection is simply a further expression of the capacity of living systems to enact "lines of life beyond organic or living purposiveness" (Colebrook 2012b: 200).

However, we can distinguish alterations of values from alterations that affect the power of a system to undergo change and thus exercise functional autonomy. This latter is a kind of second-order function. For any sufficiently complex and delicate system, the capacity to acquire new functional couplings with the world determines its adaptability and power. By the same token, a drastic diminution of functional autonomy is a reduction in power. For humans this is usually experienced as damage or harm. Arthritis of the back or limbs painfully reduces freedom of movement and thus the ability to cultivate agency in many other ways. By contrast, new skills or techniques like bicycle riding or coding "increase one's capacities to affect and be affected, or to put it differently, increase one's capacities to enter into novel assemblages" (DeLanda 2006: 50).

It would be presumptive to generalize from this by assuming that all diminutions of functional autonomy are morally equivalent. Nor can we assume with Nietzsche and other vitalists that it is written into the nature of life that any FAS will experience an increase in its power as "joyful" (Braidotti 2006). However, potential posthumans capable of passing through disconnection would need high levels of functional autonomy to escape the technological pull of WH and maintain their existential independence of it (§6.1). This is the basis for assuming that disconnections would be the intense difference-makers described above.

Any FAS that exists in a disconnection-potent system will thus be faced with an uncertain future. If it is a proto-posthuman, it has the option of attempting a feral existence outside WH. If not, it is liable to confront a radically transformed world in which some of its former functions and values may no longer apply. Thus the problem posed by a disconnection to all FASs is the same: how does one sustain functional autonomy at a level at which its exercise is also self-sustaining? Likewise, the same ethical problem is posed for humans and nonhumans within current self-catalysing technical networks. In political (though not ontological) terms, disconnection is just the posthuman predicament distilled.[10]

Highly functionally autonomous entities – human or posthuman – would be more likely to flourish or even survive in the new dispensation than those less able to acquire new values and functional affiliations. If functional autonomy were very unevenly distributed between powerful groups and much less powerful groups existentially challenged by the new world, it could be disastrous for the latter since skills and practices that had sustained them prior to disconnection might be inadequate in the new dispensation.

It follows that any functionally autonomous being confronted with the prospect of disconnection will have an interest in maximizing its power, and thus structural flexibility, to the fullest possible extent. The possibility of disconnection implies that an ontological hypermodernity is an *ecological value* for humans and any prospective posthumans. Possessing a highly adaptive, structurally complex and plastic nature is not, as I have conceded, an intrinsic value. However, given SP and given that the evolution of our technical systems is largely out of our control, *it is a local ecological value* (since it is necessary for the fullest exercise of functional autonomy under technical modernity, or disconnection). Any technology liable to increase our ability to enlist and accrue new values and couplings in anomalous environments is a local ecological value: for example, space technology, nanotechnology, or the use of brain–computer interfaces mentioned in the opening of the book. This is not because such technologies make us better or happier, but because the only viable response to the deracinative effects of our modernity is even more of the same.[11] To exploit Braidotti's useful coinage, ramping up their functional autonomy would help to *sustain* agents – allowing them to endure change without falling apart (Braidotti 2006).

I have argued that making space for agency through a disconnection would require the active sensing and discrimination of sustainable paths through it, whether on the human or the posthuman side. This would also require the cultivation of technical means for forming or forcing these paths. Like any revolutionary politics, then, posthuman politics would have to be a politics of invention, of "experimenting with new subject formations" (Braidotti 2013: 60–61).

Although I do not know what kinds of associations or structures would be best equipped to pursue such experiments, I will end by proposing a hypothesis that can be put to the test by others working in science and technology, the arts, and in what we presumptively call "humanities" subjects. This is that interdisciplinary practices that combine technoscientific expertise with ethical and aesthetic experimentation will be better placed to sculpt disconnections than narrow coalitions of experts. There may be existing models for networks or associations that could aid their members in navigating untimely lines of flight from pre- to post-disconnected states (Roden 2010a). "Body hackers" who self-administer extreme new technologies like the IA technique discussed above might be one archetype for creative posthuman accounting. Others might be descendants of current bio- and cyber-artists who are no longer concerned with representing bodies but, as Monika Bakke notes, work "on the level of actual intervention into living systems" (Bakke 2008: 21).

Perhaps Stelarc defines the problem of a post-anthropocentric posthuman politics best when describing the role of technical expertise in his art works: "This is not about utopian blueprints for perfect bodies but rather speculations on operational systems with alternate functions and forms" (in Smith 2005: 228–9). I think this spirit of speculative engineering best exemplifies an ethical posthuman becoming – not the comic or dreadful arrest in the face of something that cannot be grasped.

Notes

1 I use this term in preference to the more usual "enhancement" for reasons set out in our discussion of value neutrality in §5.2.
2 By "accessible" I take it we should mean something like "biologically accessible".
3 Awareness is preflective if it does not involve explicit judgement, thought or belief.
4 Success in interpretation need not depend on exactly replicating the form of the alien state she wishes to understand (for example, the state by virtue of which the raccoon is able to represent the fact that a box is a trap is unlikely to involve sentences). However, if the modelling procedure helps us to shape and cope with raccoon behaviour, the interpretation can be warranted on pragmatic grounds.
5 For example, having a language for colour may help its users remember colours and deal with distractors but does not appear to alter their discriminatory prowess (Frank *et al.* 2008: 823). Consequently, anthropologists interested in alien colour vocabulary do not need to have their visual systems altered to discriminate between different colours.
6 As with alien life elsewhere in the universe, the possibility of posthuman lives which do not depend on organic substrates provides further grounds for uncertainty about whether we have grasped something like an essence of life.
7 It is arguable that not all predicates (sentence components that modify subjects) actually designate properties. For example, a contradictory predicate such as "is a property to which no predicate corresponds" corresponds to a property only if it does not. Another argument against predicate–property isomorphism is that predicates, being parts of language, must form a countable set, whereas there could be a nondenumerable infinity of properties – e.g. corresponding to each position on a continuum of spatial positions. If this is true, then the infinity of properties is greater than the merely countable infinity of predicates and there can be no univocal predicate–property isomorphism (Molnar 2006: 26). So there are strong grounds for claiming that the disconnection predicate *describes* the world without corresponding to a unitary property (Heil 2003). One might also view posthumanness as a second-order "determinable" property whose particular instances are its determinations (Molnar 2006: 31–2).
8 For a given entity, becoming posthuman could (not unkindly) be compared with a "Cambridge change" – a change that occurs merely by virtue of a statement ceasing to be true or false of that entity.

9 To reiterate, critical posthumanism works best as a statement about the dependence of our agency, subjectivity, cognition, etc. on technical infrastructures that are *nothing like* agents or subjects (§2.1).

10 This is why Stross's *Accelerando* can double as post-singularity space opera and anti-corporatist satire.

11 There are some obvious affinities between posthuman politics, as conceived here, and the ultra-modernizing Marxist movement known as "Accelerationism" (see e.g. Williams 2013). However, accelerationists propose a globalizing and Universalist politics whose subject is the working class. For reasons that should be apparent by now, a posthuman politics cannot presuppose any individual or collective subject as a given. It does not follow that it precludes collective activity *per se*.

Bibliography

Agar, N. 2010. *Humanity's End: Why We Should Reject Radical Enhancement.* Cambridge, MA: MIT Press.

Anderson, M. L. 2007. "Massive Redeployment, Exaptation, and the Functional Integration of Cognitive Operations". *Synthese* 3: 329–45.

——2010. "Neural Reuse: A Fundamental Organizational Principle of the Brain". *Behavioural and Brain Sciences* 33(4): 245–66.

Annas, G. J., L. B. Andrews & R. M. Isasi 2002. "Protecting the Endangered Human: Toward an International Treaty Prohibiting Cloning and Inheritable Alterations". *American Journal of Law & Medicine* 28(2/3): 151–78.

Arel, I. 2012. "The Threat of a Reward-driven Adversarial Artificial General Intelligence". In *The Singularity Hypothesis: A Scientific and Philosophical Assessment,* A. Eden, J. Søraker, J. Moor & E. Steinhart (eds), 43–60. London: Springer.

Aristotle 1982. *Complete Works of Aristotle,* J. Barnes (ed.). Princeton, NJ: Princeton University Press.

Armstrong, S. & K. Sotala 2012. "How We're Predicting AI—or Failing To". In *Beyond AI: Artificial Dreams,* J. Romportl, I. Pavel, E. Zackova, M. Polak & R. Schuster (eds), 52–74. Pilsen: University of West Bohemia.

Arthur, W. B. 2009. *The Nature of Technology: What It Is and How It Evolves.* New York: Free Press.

Badmington, N. 2000. *Posthumanism.* Basingstoke: Palgrave Macmillan.

——2001. "Pod Almighty!; or, Humanism, Posthumanism, and the Strange Case of Invasion of the Body Snatchers". *Textual Practice* 15(1): 5–22.

——2003. "Theorizing Posthumanism". *Cultural Critique* 53(1): 10–27.

Bakke, M. 2008. "Zoe-philic Desires: Wet Media Art and Beyond". *Parallax* 14(3): 21–34.

Bakker, R. S. 2010. *Neuropath.* New York: Tor.

Ballard, J. G. 1995. *Crash.* London: Vintage.

Barkow, J. H., L. Cosmides & J. Tooby 1995. *The Adapted Mind: Evolutionary Psychology and the Generation of Culture.* New York: Oxford University Press.

Bedau, M. A. 1997. "Weak Emergence". *Noûs* 31(11): 375–99.

Berlin, I. 2000. "The Originality of Machiavelli". In *Reading Political Philosophy: Machiavelli to Mill*, N. Warburton, J. Pike & D. Matravers (eds), 43–58. London: Routledge.

Bermudez, J. L. 2002. "Domain Generality and the Relative Pronoun". *Behavioural and Brain Sciences* 25: 676–7.

Biermann, A. W. 1997. *Great Ideas in Computer Science: A Gentle Introduction*. Cambridge, MA: MIT Press.

Block, N. 1978. "Troubles with Functionalism". *Minnesota Studies in the Philosophy of Science* 9: 261–325.

——2007. "Consciousness, Accessibility, and the Mesh between Psychology and Neuroscience". *Behavioral and Brain Sciences* 30: 481–548.

Bostrom, N. 2005a. "A History of Transhumanist Thought". *Journal of Evolution and Technology* 14(1): 1–25.

——2005b. "In Defence of Posthuman Dignity". *Bioethics* 19(3): 202–14.

——2008. "Why I Want to Be a Posthuman When I Grow Up". In *Medical Enhancement and Posthumanity*, B. Gordijn & R. Chadwick (eds), 107–36. New York: Springer.

Bostrom, N. & M. Cirkovic 2011. "Introduction". In *Global Catastrophic Risks*, N. Bostrom & M. Cirkovic (eds), 1–30. Oxford: Oxford University Press.

Bostrom, N. & A. Sandberg 2008. "Whole Brain Emulation: A Roadmap". Future of Humanity Institute Technical Report, Future of Humanity Institute, University of Oxford, http://www.fhi.ox.ac.uk/brain-emulation-roadmap-report.pdf (accessed 13 June 2013).

Braidotti, R. 2006. "The Ethics of Becoming Imperceptible". In *Deleuze and Philosophy*, C. Boundas (ed.), 133–59. Edinburgh: Edinburgh University Press.

——2013. *The Posthuman*. Cambridge: Polity.

Brandom, R. 2001. *Articulating Reasons: An Introduction to Inferentialism*. Cambridge, MA: Harvard University Press.

——2002. *Tales of the Mighty Dead: Historical Essays in the Metaphysics of Intentionality*. Cambridge: Cambridge University Press.

——2006. "Kantian Lessons about Mind, Meaning, and Rationality". *Southern Journal of Philosophy* 44: 49–71.

——2007. "Inferentialism and Some of Its Challenges". *Philosophy and Phenomenological Research* 74(3): 651–76.

Brassier, R. 2011. "The View from Nowhere". *Identities: Journal for Politics, Gender and Culture* 17: 7–23.

Braver, L. 2007. *A Thing of This World: A History of Continental Anti-realism*. Evanston, IL: Northwestern University Press.

Briscoe, R. E. 2007. "Communication and Rational Responsiveness to the World". *Pacific Philosophical Quarterly* 88(2): 135–59.

Brooks, R. A. 1991. "Intelligence without Representation". *Artificial Intelligence* 47(1): 139–59.

Bryant, L. 2013. "Vitalism? No Thanks!", https://larvalsubjects.wordpress.com/
2013/02/26/vitalism-no-thanks/ (accessed 11 November 2013).

Buchanan, A. 2009. "Moral Status and Human Enhancement". *Philosophy and Public Affairs* 37(4): 346–81.

——2011. *Beyond Humanity? The Ethics of Biomedical Enhancement*. Oxford: Oxford University Press.

Button, T. 2013. *The Limits of Realism*. Oxford: Oxford University Press.

Caputo, J. D. 1984. "Husserl, Heidegger and the Question of a 'Hermeneutic' Phenomenology". *Husserl Studies* 1(1): 157–78.

Carruthers, G. 2008. "Types of Body Representation and the Sense of Embodiment". *Consciousness and Cognition: An International Journal* 17(4): 1302–16.

Carruthers, P. 2009. "An Architecture for Dual Reasoning". In his *In Two Minds: Dual Processes and Beyond*, 109–27. Oxford: Oxford University Press.

Chalmers, D. J. 1995. "Absent Qualia, Fading Qualia, Dancing Qualia". In *Conscious Experience*, Thomas Metzinger (ed.), 309–28. Paderborn: Ferdinand Schöningh.

——2010. "The Singularity: A Philosophical Analysis". *Journal of Consciousness Studies* 17(9–10): 9–10.

Christensen, W. D. & M. H. Bickhard 2002. "The Process Dynamics of Normative Function". *The Monist* 85(1): 3–28.

Churchland, P. M. 1981. "Eliminative Materialism and the Propositional Attitudes". *The Journal of Philosophy* 78(2): 67–90.

——1998. "Conceptual Similarity across Sensory and Neural Diversity: The Fodor/Lepore Challenge Answered". *The Journal of Philosophy* 95: 5–32.

——2012. *Plato's Camera: How the Physical Brain Captures a Landscape of Abstract Universals*. Cambridge, MA: MIT Press.

Cilliers, P. 2002. *Complexity and Postmodernism: Understanding Complex Systems*. Abingdon: Routledge.

Clark, A. 1989. *Microcognition: Philosophy, Cognitive Science, and Parallel Distributed Processing*. Cambridge, MA: MIT Press.

——1994. "Beliefs and Desires Incorporated". *The Journal of Philosophy* 91(8): 404–25.

——2003. *Natural-born Cyborgs: Minds, Technologies, and the Future of Human Intelligence*. New York: Oxford University Press.

——2008. *Supersizing the Mind: Embodiment, Action, and Cognitive Extension*. New York: Oxford University Press.

——2013. "Whatever Next? Predictive Brains, Situated Agents, and the Future of Cognitive Science". *Behavioural and Brain Sciences* 36(3): 181–204.

Clark, A. & D. Chalmers 1998. "The Extended Mind". *Analysis* 58: 7–19.

Cleeremans, A., B. Timmermans & A. Pasquali 2007. "Consciousness and Metarepresentation: A Computational Sketch". *Neural Networks* 20(9): 1032–9.

Cleland, C. E. 2012. "Life without Definitions". *Synthese* 185(1): 125–44.

Clune, J., J-B. Mouret & H. Lipson 2013. "The Evolutionary Origins of Modularity". *Proceedings of the Royal Society B – Biological Sciences* 280(1755).

Cohen, G. A. 1982. "Reply to Elster on Marxism, Functionalism and Game Theory". *Theory & Society* 11(4): 483–95.

Cohen, M. A. & D. C. Dennett 2011. "Consciousness Cannot Be Separated from Function". *Trends in Cognitive Sciences* 15(8): 358–64.

Colebrook, C. 2012a. "A Globe of One's Own: In Praise of the Flat Earth". *Substance: A Review of Theory & Literary Criticism* 41(1): 30–9.

——2012b. "Not Symbiosis, Not Now: Why Anthropogenic Change Is Not Really Human". *Oxford Literary Review* 34(2): 185–209.

Collier, J. D. 1988. "Supervenience and Reduction in Biological Hierarchies". *Philosophy and Biology: Canadian Journal of Philosophy Supplementary* 14: 209–34.

——1999. "Causation Is the Transfer of Information", H. Sankey (ed.). *Australasian Studies in History and Philosophy of Science* 14: 215–46.

——2000. "Autonomy and Process Closure as the Basis for Functionality". *Annals of the New York Academy of Sciences* 901(1): 280–90.

Collier, J. D. & C. A. Hooker 1999. "Complexly Organised Dynamical Systems". *Open Systems & Information Dynamics* 6(3): 241–302.

Copeland, B. J. 2000. "Narrow versus Wide Mechanism: Including a Re-examination of Turing's Views on the Mind-Machine Issue." *The Journal of Philosophy* 97(1): 5–32.

Cranor, C. F. 2004. "Toward Understanding Aspects of the Precautionary Principle". *Journal of Medicine and Philosophy* 29(3): 259–79.

Critchley, S., R. Schürmann & S. Levine 2008. *On Heidegger's Being and Time*. London: Routledge.

Cruse, H. 1990. "What Mechanisms Coordinate Leg Movement in Walking Arthropods?" *Trends in Neurosciences* 13(1): 15–21.

Danaher, J. 2011. "The Species-Relativist Argument: An Introduction", http://philosophicaldisquisitions.blogspot.co.uk/2011/05/species-relativist-argument.html (accessed 3 November 2013).

Davidson, D. 1984. *Inquiries into Truth and Interpretation*. Oxford: Clarendon Press.

——1986. "A Nice Derangement of Epitaphs". In *Truth and Interpretation*, E. LePore (ed.), 433–46. Oxford: Blackwell.

——2001a. *Essays on Actions and Events*, Vol. 1. Oxford: Oxford University Press.

——2001b. *Subjective, Intersubjective, Objective*, Vol. 3. Oxford: Oxford University Press.

Deacon, T. W. 1997. *The Symbolic Species: The Co-evolution of Language and the Brain*. London: Penguin.

Dehaene, S. & L. Cohen 2007. "Cultural Recycling of Cortical Maps". *Neuron* 56(2): 384–98.

Dehaene, S. & L. Naccache 2001. "Towards a Cognitive Neuroscience of Consciousness: Basic Evidence and a Workspace Framework". *Cognition* 79(1–2): 1–37.

DeLanda, M. 1997. "Immanence and Transcendence in the Genesis of Form (Gilles Deleuze, Philosophy of Physics)". *South Atlantic Quarterly* 96(3): 499–514.

——2002. *Intensive Science and Virtual Philosophy*. London: Continuum.

——2006. *A New Philosophy of Society: Assemblage Theory and Social Complexity*. London: Continuum.

——2010. *Deleuze: History and Science*. New York: Atropos.

——2011. *Philosophy and Simulation: The Emergence of Synthetic Reason*. London: Continuum.

Deleuze, G. 1994. *Difference and Repetition*, P. Patton (trans.). London: Athlone Press.

Deleuze, G. & F. Guattari 1988. *A Thousand Plateaus: Capitalism and Schizophrenia*. London: Athlone Press.

Della Mirandola, P. 1948. *On the Dignity of Man*. Chicago, IL: University of Chicago Press.

Deneubourg, J. L., S. Aron, S. Goss & J. M. Pasteels 1990. "The Self-Organizing Exploratory Pattern of the Argentine Ant". *Journal of Insect Behavior* 3(2): 159–68.

Dennett, D. C. 1987. *The Intentional Stance*. Cambridge, MA: MIT Press.

——1991. *Consciousness Explained*. London: Penguin.

——1995a. "Do Animals Have Beliefs?" In *Comparative Approaches to Cognitive Science*, H. L. Roitblat & J.-A. Meyer (eds), 111. Cambridge, MA: MIT Press.

——1995b. *Darwin's Dangerous Idea: Evolution and the Meanings of Life*. London: Penguin.

Derrida, J. 1978. *Writing and Difference*, A. Bass (trans.). Chicago, IL: University of Chicago Press.

——1979. *Speech and Phenomena: And Other Essays on Husserl's Theory of Signs*, D. Allison (trans.). Evanston, IL: Northwestern University Press.

——1984. *Margins of Philosophy*, A. Bass (trans.). Chicago, IL: University of Chicago Press.

——1988. *Limited Inc*, S. Weber (trans.). Evanston, IL: Northwestern University Press.

——1992. *Acts of Literature*, D. Attridge (ed.). London: Routledge.

——1998. *Of Grammatology*, G. Chakravorty Spivak (trans.). Baltimore, MD: Johns Hopkins University Press.

——2002. *Acts of Religion*, G. Anidjar (ed.). London: Routledge.

Descartes, R. 1986. *A Discourse on Method: Meditations on the First Philosophy Principles of Philosophy*, J. Veitch (trans.). London: Everyman Library.

Devitt, M. 1984. *Realism and Truth*. Princeton, NJ: Princeton University Press.

——1991. "Aberrations of the Realism Debate". *Philosophical Studies* 61(1): 43–63.

Dostal, R. J. 1993. "Time and Phenomenology in Husserl and Heidegger". In *Cambridge Companion to Heidegger*, C. B. Guignon (ed.), 141–69. Cambridge: Cambridge University Press.

Dretske, F. 1967. "Can Events Move?" *Mind* 76: 479–92.

Drexler, K. E. 1992. *Nanosystems: Molecular Machinery, Manufacturing, and Computation.* New York: John Wiley & Sons.

Dreyfus, H. L. 1990. *Being-in-the-world: A Commentary on Heidegger's Being and Time, Division I.* Cambridge, MA: MIT Press.

Dries, M. 2010. "On the Logic of Values". *The Journal of Nietzsche Studies* 39(1): 30–50.

Dumouchel, P. 1992. "Gilbert Simondon's Plea for a Philosophy of Technology". *Inquiry* 35(3–4): 407–21.

Dupré, J. & M. A. O'Malley 2009. "Varieties of Living Things: Life at the Intersection of Lineage and Metabolism". *Philosophy and Theory in Biology* 1, http://quod.lib.umich.edu/cgi/t/text/idx/p/ptb/6959004.0001.003?rgn=main; view=fulltext;q1=Livin (accessed January 2013).

Eigen, M. 1992. *Steps Towards Life: A Perspective on Evolution.* Oxford: Oxford University Press.

Ekbia, H. R. 2008. *Artificial Dreams: The Quest for Non-biological Intelligence.* Cambridge: Cambridge University Press.

Eliasmith, C. 2002. "The Myth of the Turing Machine: The Failings of Functionalism and Related Theses". *Journal of Experimental & Theoretical Artificial Intelligence* 14: 1–8.

Ellison, H. 2012. *I Have No Mouth and I Must Scream.* London: Hachette.

Ellul, J. 1964. *The Technological Society*, J. Wilkinson (trans.). New York: Vintage Books.

Elman, J. L. 1995. "Language as a Dynamical System". In *Mind as Motion: Explorations in the Dynamics of Cognition*, R. F. Port and T. Van Gelder (eds), 195–225. Cambridge, MA: MIT Press.

Evnine, S. 1991. *Donald Davidson.* Cambridge: Polity.

Farrell, F. B. 1996. *Subjectivity, Realism, and Postmodernism: The Recovery of the World in Recent Philosophy.* Cambridge: Cambridge University Press.

Feenberg, A. 1999. *Questioning Technology.* London: Routledge.

Fine, K. 2002. "Varieties of Necessity". In *Conceivability and Possibility*, T. Szabo Gendler & J. Hawthorne (eds). Oxford: Oxford University Press.

Fodor, J. A. 1980. "Methodological Solipsism Considered as a Research Strategy in Cognitive Psychology". *Behavioural and Brain Sciences* 3(1): 63–73.

——1983. *The Modularity of Mind.* Cambridge, MA: MIT Press.

——1990. *A Theory of Content and Other Essays.* Cambridge, MA: MIT Press.

——1996. "Deconstructing Dennett's Darwin". *Mind & Language* 11(3): 246–62.

Fodor, J. A. & E. LePore 1992. *Holism: A Shopper's Guide.* Oxford: Blackwell.

Foucault, M. 1970. *The Order of Things: An Archaeology of the Human Sciences.* London: Tavistock Publications.

Frank, M. C., D. L. Everett, E. Fedorenko & E. Gibson 2008. "Number as a Cognitive Technology: Evidence from Piraha Language and Cognition". *Cognition* 108(3): 819–24.

Frankfurt, H. G. 1971. "Freedom of the Will and the Concept of a Person". *Journal of Philosophy* 68(1): 5–20.

Frankish, K. 2011. "Cognitive Capacities, Mental Modules, and Neural Regions". *Philosophy, Psychiatry, & Psychology* 18(4): 279–82.

Fukuyama, F. 2003. *Our Posthuman Future: Consequences of the Biotechnology Revolution.* New York: Farrar, Straus & Giroux.

Galston, W. 1993. "Liberal Democracy and the Problem of Technology". In *Technology in the Western Political Tradition*, A. Melzer, J. Weinberger & R. Zinman (eds), 229–52. London: Cornell University Press.

Gasché, R. 1986. *The Tain of the Mirror: Derrida and the Philosophy of Reflection.* London: Harvard University Press.

Gibson, W. 2000. *Neuromancer.* London: Penguin.

Godfrey-Smith, P. 1993. "Functions: Consensus without Unity". *Pacific Philosophical Quarterly* 74(3): 196–208.

Goertzel, B. 2006. "Patterns, Hypergraphs and Embodied General Intelligence". In *Proceedings IJCNN'06. International Joint Conference Neural Networks, 2006*, 451–8.

Good, I. J. 1965. "Speculations Concerning the First Ultraintelligent Machine". *Advances in Computers* 6: 31–88.

Goodman, N. 1968. *Languages of Art: An Approach to a Theory of Symbols.* Indianapolis, IN: Hackett Publishing Company.

Graham, E. L. 2002. *Representations of the Post Human: Monsters, Aliens, and Others in Popular Culture.* Manchester: Manchester University Press.

Griffiths, P. E. & K. Stotz 2006. "Genes in the Postgenomic Era". *Theoretical Medicine and Bioethics* 27(6): 499–521.

Guggenmos, D. J., M. Azin, S. Barbay, J. D. Mahnken, C. Dunham, P. Mohseni & R. J. Nudo 2013. "Restoration of Function after Brain Damage Using a Neural Prosthesis". *Proceedings of the National Academy of Sciences* 110(52): 21177–82.

Guyer, P. 2006. *Kant.* Abingdon: Routledge.

Habermas, J. 2005. *The Future of Human Nature*, W. Rehg, M. Penksy & H. Beister (trans.). London: Polity.

Hägglund, M. 2008. *Radical Atheism: Derrida and the Time of Life.* Stanford, CA: Stanford University Press.

——2011. "The Trace of Time and the Death of Life: Bergson, Heidegger, Derrida", https://www.youtube.com/watch?v=9qqaHGUiew4 (accessed November 2011).

Hale, B. & C. Wright 1999. "Putnam's Model-theoretic Argument against Metaphysical Realism". In *A Companion to the Philosophy of Language*, B. Hale & C. Wright (eds). Oxford: Blackwell Publishing. Blackwell Reference Online: http://www.blackwellreference.com/subscriber/tocnode.html?id=g97806 31213260_chunk_g978063121326019 (accessed 14 December 2013).

Han-Pile, B. 2010. "The 'Death of Man': Foucault and Anti-Humanism". In *Foucault and Philosophy*, T. O'Leary & C. Falzon (eds), 118–42. Oxford: Blackwell.

Haraway, D. 1991. *Simians, Cyborgs, and Women: The Reinvention of Nature.* New York: Routledge.

Hardcastle, V. 2001. "The Nature of Pain". In *Philosophy and the Neurosciences. A Reader*, 295–311. Malden, MA: Blackwell.

Harman, G. 2008. "DeLanda's Ontology: Assemblage and Realism". *Continental Philosophy Review* 41(3): 367–83.

——2011. *Quentin Meillassoux: Philosophy in the Making*. Edinburgh: Edinburgh University Press.

Hauskeller, M. 2012. "My Brain, My Mind, and I: Some Philosophical Assumptions of Mind-Uploading". *International Journal of Machine Consciousness* 4(1): 187–200.

Hayles, N. K. 1999. *How We Became Posthuman: Virtual Bodies in Cybernetics, Literature, and Informatics*. Chicago, IL: University of Chicago Press.

——2011. "Wrestling with Transhumanism", http://www.metanexus.net/essay/h-wrestling-transhumanism (accessed December 2013).

Heidegger, M. 1962. *Being and Time*, J. Macquarrie & E. Robinson (trans). New York: Harper & Row.

——1978. "The Question Concerning Technology". In his *Basic Writings*, D. Farrell Krell (ed.), 283–317. London: Routledge & Kegan Paul.

——1995. *The Fundamental Concepts of Metaphysics: World, Finitude, Solitude*, W. McNeill & N. Walker (eds). Bloomington: Indiana University Press.

Heil, J. 2003. *From an Ontological Point of View*. Oxford: Clarendon Press.

——2011. "Powers and the Realization Relation". *The Monist* 94(1): 34–53.

Hickey-Moody, A. 2009. "Little War Machines: Posthuman Pedagogy and Its Media". *Journal of Literary & Cultural Disability Studies* 3(3): 273–80.

Hirstein, W. 2012. *Mindmelding: Consciousness, Neuroscience, and the Mind's Privacy*. Oxford: Oxford University Press.

Hochberg, L. R., M. Serruya, D. Friehs, *et al.* 2006. "Neuronal Ensemble Control of Prosthetic Devices by a Human with Tetraplegia". *Nature* 442(7099): 164–71.

Hohwy, J., A. Roepstorff & K. Friston 2008. "Predictive Coding Explains Binocular Rivalry: An Epistemological Review". *Cognition* 108(3): 687–701.

Hollinger, V. 2009. "Posthumanism and Cyborg Theory". In *The Routledge Companion to Science Fiction*, M. Bould, A. Butler, A. Roberts & S. Vint (eds), 267–87. Oxford: Routledge.

Horgan, T. & J. Tienson 1994. "A Nonclassical Framework for Cognitive Science". *Synthese* 101(3): 305–45.

Hughes, J. 2010. "Contradictions from the Enlightenment Roots of Transhumanism". *Journal of Medicine and Philosophy* 35(6): 622–40.

Hull, D. L. 1986. "On Human Nature". In *PSA: Proceedings of the Biennial Meeting of the Philosophy of Science Association*, Vol. 2, 3–13.

Humphreys, P. 2008. "Computational and Conceptual Emergence". *Philosophy of Science* 75(5): 584–94.

Husserl, E. 1931. *Ideas: General Introduction to Pure Phenomenology*, W. R. B. Gibson (trans.). London: George Allen & Unwin.

——1960. *Cartesian Meditations*, D. Cairns (trans.). The Hague: Martinus Nijhoff.

——1964. *The Phenomenology of Internal Time-Consciousness*, J. Churchill (trans.). The Hague: Martinus Nijhoff.

——1970. *Crisis of European Sciences and Transcendental Phenomenology*, D. Carr (trans.). Evanston, IL: Northwestern University Press.

Ihde, D. 2012a. "Can Continental Philosophy Deal with the New Technologies?" *The Journal of Speculative Philosophy* 26(2): 321–32.

——2012b. "Embodiment and Multistability", http://vimeo.com/49101825 (accessed February 2013).

Janicaud, D. 2005. *On the Human Condition*, Eileen Brennan (trans.). Oxford: Routledge.

Johnston, J. 2008. *The Allure of Machinic Life: Cybernetics, Artificial Life, and the New AI*. Cambridge, MA: The MIT Press.

Jones, R. 2009. "Brain Interfacing with Kurzweil", http://www.softmachines. org/wordpress/?p=450 (accessed September 2009).

Kant, I. 1978. *Critique of Pure Reason*, N. K. Smith (trans.). New York: St. Martin's Press. (Originally published in German as *Kritik der reinen Vernunft* [Johann Hartknoch, 1787].)

——1991. *The Critique of Judgement*, J. C. Meredith (trans.). Oxford: Oxford University Press.

——2002. *Groundwork for the Metaphysics of Morals*, Allen W. Wood (trans.). London: Yale University Press. (Originally published in German as *Grundlegung zur metaphysik der sitten* [J. F. Hartknoch, 1785].)

Keijzer, F. & M. Schouten 2007. "Embedded Cognition and Mental Causation: Setting Empirical Bounds on Metaphysics". *Synthese* 1: 109–25.

Kirov, R., C. Weiss, H. Siebner, J. Born & L. Marshall 2009. "Slow Oscillation Electrical Brain Stimulation During Waking Promotes EEG Theta Activity and Memory Encoding". *Proceedings of the National Academy of Sciences* 106(36): 15460–5.

Kirschner, M. & J. Gerhart 1998. "Evolvability". *Proceedings of the National Academy of Sciences* 95(15): 8420–7.

Kitcher, P. 1984. "1953 and All That. A Tale of Two Sciences". *The Philosophical Review* 93(3): 335–73.

Kornblith, H. 2002. *Knowledge and Its Place in Nature*. Oxford: Clarendon Press.

Kurzweil, R. 2005. *The Singularity is Near*. New York: Viking.

Ladyman, J. & D. Ross 2007. *Every Thing Must Go: Metaphysics Naturalized*. Oxford: Oxford University Press.

Laland, K. N., J. Odling-Smee & M. W. Feldman 2000. "Niche Construction, Biological Evolution, and Cultural Change". *Behavioral and Brain Sciences* 23(1): 131–46.

Land, N. 2012. *Fanged Noumena: Collected Writings 1987–2007*, R. Mackay & R. Brassier (eds). Falmouth: Urbanomic Publications.

LaPorte, J. 2004. *Natural Kinds and Conceptual Change*. Cambridge: Cambridge University Press.

Ledford, H. 2010. "Garage Biotech: Life Hackers". *Nature* 467(7316): 650–2.

Lee, K. 2003. *Philosophy and Revolutions in Genetics: Deep Science and Deep Technology.* New York: Palgrave Macmillan.

Legg, S. & M. Hutter 2007. "Universal Intelligence: A Definition of Machine Intelligence". *Minds and Machines* 17(4): 391–444.

Lennox, J. G. 2009. "Form, Essence, and Explanation in Aristotle's Biology". In *A Companion to Aristotle*, G. Anagnostopoulos (ed.). Oxford: Blackwell Publishing, Blackwell Reference Online: http://www.blackwellreference.com/subscriber/tocnode.html?id=g9781405122238_chunk_g978140512223825 (accessed March 2013).

Levine, S. 2010. "Rehabilitating Objectivity: Rorty, Brandom, and the New Pragmatism". *Canadian Journal of Philosophy* 40(4): 567–90.

Lewis, D. 1989. "Dispositional Theories of Value". *The Proceedings of the Aristotelian Society, Supplementary Volume* 63: 113–37.

Locke, J. 1990. *An Essay Concerning Human Understanding*, P. H. Nidditch & G. A. J. Rogers (eds). Oxford: Oxford University Press.

Longuenesse, B. 2005. *Kant on the Human Standpoint.* Cambridge: Cambridge University Press.

Longy, F. 2006. "Function and Probability". *Technè* 10(1): 81–97.

——2013. "Artifacts and Organisms: A Case for a New Etiological Theory of Functions". *Synthese Library* 363: 185–212.

Lovecraft, H. P. 1999. *The Call of Cthulhu and Other Weird Stories*, S. T. Joshi (ed.). New York: Penguin Books.

Lyotard, J.-F. 1991. *The Inhuman: Reflections on Time*, G. Bennington & R. Bowlby (trans.). Cambridge: Polity Press.

Maley, C. & G. Piccinini 2012. "The Ontology of Functional Mechanisms", http://philosophyofbrains.com/2012/12/22/the-ontology-of-functional-mechanisms.aspx (accessed March 2013).

Malpas, J. E. 1992. *Donald Davidson and the Mirror of Meaning: Holism, Truth, Interpretation.* Cambridge: Cambridge University Press.

——1999. "Constituting the Mind: Kant, Davidson, and the Unity of Consciousness". *International Journal of Philosophical Studies* 7(1): 1–30.

Mandik, P. 2012. "Colour-Consciousness Conceptualism". *Consciousness and Cognition* 21(2): 617–31.

Massumi, B. 2005. "The Evolutionary Alchemy of Reason: Stelarc". In *Stelarc: The Monograph*, M. Smith (ed.), 125–92. Cambridge, MA: MIT Press.

Mattick, J. S. 2004. "The Hidden Genetic Program of Complex Organisms". *Scientific American* 291(4): 60–7.

Meacham, D. Forthcoming. "Empathy and Alteration: The Ethical Relevance of a Phenomenological Species Concept". *Journal of Medicine and Philosophy.*

Meillassoux, Q. 2010. *After Finitude: An Essay on the Necessity of Contingency*, R. Brassier (trans.). London: Continuum.

Metzinger, T. 2004. *Being No One: The Self-Model Theory of Subjectivity.* Cambridge, MA: MIT Press.

Modis, T. 2012. "Why the Singularity Cannot Happen". In *The Singularity Hypothesis: A Scientific and Philosophical Assessment*, A. Eden, J. Søraker, J. Moor & E. Steinhart (eds), 311–46. London: Springer.

Mohanty, J. N. 1989. *Transcendental Phenomenology: An Analytic Account*. Oxford: Basil Blackwell.

Molnar, G. 2006. *Powers: A Study in Metaphysics*, S. Mumford (ed.). Oxford: Oxford University Press.

Mooney, T. 1999. "Derrida's Empirical Realism". *Philosophy & Social Criticism* 25(5): 33–56.

Moore, A. W. 2012. *The Evolution of Modern Metaphysics: Making Sense of Things*. Cambridge: Cambridge University Press.

Moran, D. 2000. "Hilary Putnam and Immanuel Kant: Two 'Internal Realists'?" *Synthese* 123: 65–104.

Moran, K. A. 2009. "Can Kant Have an Account of Moral Education?" *Journal of Philosophy of Education* 43(4): 471–84.

Moss, L. 2006. "Redundancy, Plasticity, and Detachment: The Implications of Comparative Genomics for Evolutionary Thinking". *Philosophy of Science* 73(5): 930–46.

Moya, F. 2000. "Epistemology of Living Organisms in Aristotle's Philosophy". *Theory in Biosciences* 119(3–4): 318–33.

Newell, A. & H. A. Simon 1976. "Computer Science as Empirical Inquiry: Symbols and Search". *Communications of the ACM* 19(3): 113–26.

Nietzsche, F. 1968. *The Will to Power*, W. Kaufmann & R. J. Hollingdale (trans.). New York: Vintage.

Okasha, S. 2002. "Darwinian Metaphysics: Species and the Question of Essentialism". *Synthese* 131(2): 191–213.

Okrent, M. 2006. "On Layer Cakes", http://www.bates.edu/philosophy/files/2010/07/onlayer.pdf (accessed June 2013).

Omohundro, S. M. 2008. "The Basic AI Drives". *Frontiers in Artificial Intelligence and Applications* 171: 483.

Open University 2006. *M255, Object-oriented Programming with Java, Unit 1*. Milton Keynes: The Open University.

Pais-Vieira, M., M. Lebedev, C. Kunicki, J. Wang & M. Nicolelis 2013. "A Brain-to-brain Interface for Real-time Sharing of Sensorimotor Information". *Scientific Reports* 3.

Parvizi, J. & A. Damasio 2001. "Consciousness and the Brainstem". *Cognition* 79(1–2): 135–60.

Patton, P. 2000. *Deleuze and the Political*. London: Routledge.

Pearson, K. A. 2002. *Viroid Life: Perspectives on Nietzsche and the Transhuman Condition*. London: Routledge.

Persson, I. & J. Savulescu 2008. "The Perils of Cognitive Enhancement and the Urgent Imperative to Enhance the Moral Character of Humanity". *Journal of Applied Philosophy* 25(3): 162–77.

Petzold, C. 2008. *The Annotated Turing: A Guided Tour through Alan Turing's Historic Paper on Computability and the Turing Machine*. Indianapolis: Wiley Publishing.

Philippou, A. 2013. "You Should Obliterate Your Self: A Defence of Mind Uploading", Master's thesis, Department of Philosophy, The Open University.

Piccinini, G. 2010. "The Mind as Neural Software? Understanding Functionalism, Computationalism, and Computational Functionalism". *Philosophy and Phenomenological Research* 81(2): 269–311.

Protevi, J. 2009. *Political Affect: Connecting the Social and the Somatic*. Minneapolis: University of Minnesota Press.

Punzo, V. C. 1969. *Reflective Naturalism: An Introduction to Moral Philosophy*. New York: Macmillan.

Putnam, H. 1978. *Meaning and the Moral Sciences*. Oxford: Routledge & Kegan Paul.

——1981. *Reason, Truth and History*. Cambridge: Cambridge University Press.

——1983. *Realism and Reason. Philosophical Papers*, Vol. 3. Cambridge: Cambridge University Press.

——1988. *Representation and Reality*. Cambridge, MA: MIT Press.

Quartz, S. R. & T. J. Sejnowski 1997. "The Neural Basis of Cognitive Development: A Constructivist Manifesto". *Behavioral and Brain Sciences* 20(4): 537–56.

Quine, W. V. 1968. "Ontological Relativity". *The Journal of Philosophy* 65(7): 185–212.

Raffman, D. 1995. "On the Persistence of Phenomenology". In *Conscious Experience*, T. Metzinger (ed.), 293–308. Thorverton: Imprint Academic.

Ramberg, B. T. 1989. *Donald Davidson's Philosophy of Language: An Introduction*. Oxford: Basil Blackwell.

Ramsey, W., S. Stich & J. Garon 1990. "Connectionism, Eliminativism and the Future of Folk Psychology". *Philosophical Perspectives* 4: 499–533.

Rapaport, W. J. 2012. "Can't We Just Talk? Commentary on Arel's 'Threat'". In *The Singularity Hypothesis: A Scientific and Philosophical Assessment*, A. Eden, J. Søraker, J. Moor & E. Steinhart (eds), 59–60. London: Springer.

Rawls, J. 1980. "Kantian Constructivism in Moral Theory". *Journal of Philosophy* 77(9): 515–72.

——1999. *A Theory of Justice*. Oxford: Oxford University Press

——2005. *Political Liberalism*. New York: Columbia University Press.

Rayner, A. G. 2013. "3D-printable Guns are Just the Start, Says Cody Wilson". *Guardian* (6 May). http://www.theguardian.com/world/shortcuts/2013/may/06/3d-printable-guns-cody-wilson (accessed June 2013).

Richardson, J. 2004. *Nietzsche's New Darwinism*. Oxford: Oxford University Press.

Ricoeur, P. 1990. *Time and Narrative*, Vol. 3. Chicago, IL: University of Chicago Press.

Roden, D. 2002. "Cyborgian Subjects and the Auto-destruction of Metaphor". In *Crash Cultures: Modernity, Mediation and the Material*, J. Arthurs & I. Grant (eds), 89–100. Bristol: Intellect Books.

——2004a. "Radical Quotation and Real Repetition". *Ratio* 17(2): 191–206.

——2004b. "The Subject". In *Understanding Derrida: An Invitation to Philosophy*, J. Reynolds & J. Roffe (eds), 93–102. New York: Continuum Press.

——2005. "Naturalising Deconstruction". *Continental Philosophy Review* 38(1): 71–88.

——2008. "Cylons in the Original Position: Limits of Posthuman Justice". In *Battlestar Galactica and Philosophy: Knowledge Here Begins Out There*, J. Eberl (ed.), 141–51. New York: Wiley Blackwell.

——2010a. "Deconstruction and Excision in Philosophical Posthumanism". *The Journal of Evolution & Technology* 21(1): 27–36.

——2010b. "Sonic Art and the Nature of Sonic Events". *Review of Philosophy and Psychology* 1(1): 141–56.

——2012a. "Agar on Species Relativism and Cultural Relativism", http://enemyindustry.net/blog/?p=3400 (accessed June 2012).

——2012b. "The Disconnection Thesis". In *The Singularity Hypothesis: A Scientific and Philosophical Assessment*, A. Eden, J. Søraker, J. Moor & E. Steinhart (eds), 281–98. London: Springer.

——2013. "Nature's Dark Domain: An Argument for a Naturalised Phenomenology". *Royal Institute of Philosophy Supplements* 72: 169–88.

Rollin, B. 2003. "Ethics and Species Integrity". *The American Journal of Bioethics* 3(3): 15–17.

Ronald, P. 2013. "The Truth about GMOs". *Boston Review*, http://www.bostonreview.net/forum/pamela-ronald-gmo-food (accessed September 2013).

Rorty, R. 1980. *Philosophy and the Mirror of Nature*. Cambridge: Cambridge University Press.

——1985. "Texts and Lumps". *New Literary History* 17(1): 1–16.

——1989. *Contingency, Irony, and Solidarity*. Cambridge: Cambridge University Press.

Ruiz-Mirazo, K. & A. Moreno 2012. "Autonomy in Evolution: From Minimal to Complex Life". *Synthese* 185(1): 21–52.

Rupert, R. D. 2009. *Cognitive Systems and the Extended Mind*. Oxford: Oxford University Press.

Russell, B. 2009. *Autobiography*. Oxford: Routledge.

Samuels, R. 2010. "Classical Computationalism and the Many Problems of Cognitive Relevance". *Studies in History and Philosophy of Science Part A* 41(3): 280–93.

Sandberg, A. 1999. "The Physics of Information Processing Superobjects: Daily Life among the Jupiter Brains". *Journal of Evolution and Technology* 5(1).

Sandberg, A. & S. Armstrong 2012. "Indefinite Survival through Backup Copies". Future of Humanity Institute Technical Report, Future of Humanity Institute, University of Oxford, http://www.fhi.ox.ac.uk/indefinite-survival-backup.pdf (accessed 5 March 2013).

Sandberg, A. & N. Bostrom 2006. "Converging Cognitive Enhancements". *Annals of the New York Academy of Sciences* 1093(1): 201–27.

Sandel, M. J. 1998. *Liberalism and the Limits of Justice*. Cambridge: Cambridge University Press.

Sartre, J.-P. 1948. *Existentialism and Humanism*, P. Mairet (trans.). London: Methuen.

Sellars, W. 1963. *Science, Perception, and Reality*. London: Routledge & Kegan Paul.

Simondon, G. 1969. *Du mode d'existence des objets techniques*, Vol. 1. Paris: Aubier-Montaigne.

Smith, M. 2005. *Stelarc: The Monograph*. Cambridge, MA: MIT Press.

Smolke, C. D. 2009. "Building Outside of the Box: iGEM and the BioBricks Foundation". *Nature Biotechnology* 27(12): 1099–102.

Sober, E. 1980. "Evolution, Population Thinking, and Essentialism". *Philosophy of Science* 47(3): 350–83.

Sorgner, S.L. 2009. "Nietzsche, The Overhuman, and Transhumanism". *Journal of Evolution and Technology* 20(1): 29–42.

——2013. "Perfecting Human Beings: From Kant and Nietzsche to Trans- and Posthumanism". Paper presented at the 5th International Conference on Kant and Nietzsche, Università del Salento, 18–19 April, Lecce, Italy.

Sterelny, K. & P. E. Griffiths 1999. *Sex and Death: An Introduction to Philosophy of Biology*. Chicago, IL: University of Chicago Press.

Sterling, B. 1996. *Schismatrix Plus*. New York: Ace Books.

Stiegler, B. 1998. *Technics and Time, 1: The Fault of Epimetheus*, Vol. 1. Stanford, CA: Stanford University Press.

Stross, C. 2006. *Accelerando*. New York: Ace.

Taylor, C. 1985. *Philosophical Papers: Volume 2, Philosophy and the Human Sciences*, Vol. 2. Cambridge: Cambridge University Press.

Tieszen, R. 2002. "Gödel and the Intuition of Concepts". *Synthese* 133(3): 363–91.

Tiles, M. & H. Oberdeik 1995. *Living in a Technological Culture: Human Tools and Human Values*. New York: Routledge.

Tomasello, M. 2008. *Origins of Human Communication*. Cambridge, MA: MIT Press.

Tuggy, D. 2010. "Trinity". In *Stanford Encyclopaedia of Philosophy*, Edward N. Zalta (ed.), http:// plato.stanford.edu/archives/fall2009/entries/trinity (accessed September 2011).

Tye, M. 2002. *Consciousness, Colour and Content*. Cambridge, MA: MIT Press.

Van Gelder, T. 1999. "Wooden Iron? Husserlian Phenomenology Meets Cognitive Science". In *Naturalizing Phenomenology*, J. Petito, F. Varela, B. Pachoud & J.-M. Roy (eds), 245–65. Stanford, CA: Stanford University Press.

Verbeek, P.-P. 2005. *What Things Do: Philosophical Reflections on Technology, Agency, and Design*. University Park, PA: Penn State Press.

Vinge, V. 1993. "The Coming Technological Singularity", http://www-rohan.sdsu.edu/faculty/vinge/misc/WER2.html (accessed June 2011).

Walsh, D. 2006. "Evolutionary Essentialism". *British Journal for the Philosophy of Science* 57(2): 425–48.

Walter, C. 2005. "Kryder's Law". *Scientific American* 293(2): 32–3.

Walzer, M. 2003. "Philosophy and Democracy". In *Debates in Contemporary Political Philosophy*, D. Matravers & J. Pike (eds), 361–80. New York: Routledge.

Warren, M. A. 1973. "On the Moral and Legal Status of Abortion". *The Monist* 57(1): 43–61.

Wennemann, D. J. 2013. *Posthuman Personhood*. New York: University Press of America.

Wheeler, M. 2004. "Is language the ultimate artefact?". *Language Sciences*, 26(6): 693–715.

——2005. *Reconstructing the Cognitive World: The Next Step*. Cambridge, MA: MIT Press.

——2011. "Martin Heidegger". In *The Stanford Encyclopedia of Philosophy* (summer 2009 edn), http://plato.stanford.edu/entries/heidegger (accessed February 2012).

Wheeler, S. C. 2000. *Deconstruction as Analytic Philosophy*. Stanford, CA: Stanford University Press.

Wiedermann, J. 2012. "Is There Something Beyond AI? Frequently Emerging, but Seldom Answered Questions About Artificial Super-Intelligence". In *Beyond AI: Artificial Dreams*, J. Romportl, I. Pavel, E. Zackova, M. Polak & R. Schuster (eds), 76–86. Pilsen: University of West Bohemia.

Williams, A. 2013. "Escape Velocities". *E-flux* 46, http://worker01.e-flux.com/pdf/article_8969785.pdf (accessed July 2013).

Williams, G. P. 1997. *Chaos Theory Tamed*. Washington, DC: Joseph Henry Press.

Wilson, E. A. 1999. "Introduction: Somatic Compliance-Feminism, Biology and Science". *Australian Feminist Studies* 14(29): 7–18.

Winner, L. 1977. *Autonomous Technology: Technics-out-of-control as a Theme in Political Thought*. Cambridge, MA: MIT Press.

Wolfe, C. 2010. *What Is Posthumanism?* London: University of Minnesota Press.

Wood, D. 2001. *The Deconstruction of Time*. Evanston, IL: Northwestern University Press.

World Transhumanist Association and others 1998. "The Transhumanist Declaration", http://humanityplus.org/philosophy/transhumanist-declaration/ (accessed March 2013).

Zammito, J. H. 2012. "The Lenoir Thesis Revisited: Blumenbach and Kant". *Studies in History and Philosophy of Science Part C: Studies in History and Philosophy of Biological and Biomedical Sciences* 43(1): 120–32.

Index